D0620852

THE FLESH AND THE WORD

THE FLESH AND THE WORD

Eliot, Hemingway, Faulkner

FLOYD C. WATKINS

VANDERBILT UNIVERSITY PRESS

Nashville 1971

International Standard Book Number
0–8265–1169–4
Library of Congress
Catalogue Card Number 75–157740

Printed in the United States of America
by The TJM Corporation
Baton Rouge, Louisiana

For Kirk, Rose, Kay, Jan

PREFACE and Confessions of the Author

THE embodiment or incarnation of meaning in image has been a chief element in style, in the struggle of literatures to come to terms with life, and in the ultimate questions of religion. This book is the result of years of labor to understand the phenomenon in modern literature. I have selected three authors—T. S. Eliot, Ernest Hemingway, and William Faulkner—in whom the struggle is especially apparent, and in many ways the choice is somewhat arbitrary. No writer of merit can fail to consider image and meaning. To save space and time I have treated some works of these writers briefly or not at all—Eliot's "The Hollow Men" and his plays, Faulkner's *Pylon* and *Snopes,* and Hemingway's short stories.

I am much indebted to the John Simon Guggenheim Memorial Foundation and Emory University for years of support and free time. The Yale University Library has been especially kind to me. Albert E. Stone, William B. Dillingham, and James M. Cox were unusually helpful with different versions of the manuscript. From many friends and my family I derived emotional support during years when the end of a long study seemed to fade beyond the western stars.

CONTENTS

THE FLESH AND THE WORD

1

Introduction— The Season of Flesh

MOST great writers of the early twentieth century wrote about object, fact, and person and rejected abstractions of all kinds. This is often true of a good writer, but in no other age have men of letters been more devoted to the empirical fact and more wary of statements of meanings. Men of letters were not alone in their emphasis on the world which could be observed by the five senses. Especially from about World War I until the end of the 1920s, historian, semanticist, psychologist, philosopher, and scientist distrusted general statements and trusted the facts. Few doubted that data had meaning which transcended the factual ways of representation; most had little faith in the ability of the mind and language to describe transcendence. Many writers did not deny the possibility of the existence of mind and spirit, but they refused to contemplate the meanings in words. Many authors and the characters they created believed that words might destroy meanings for a person of sensibility. Abstract words were a shallow pose. William Faulkner described the death of language: "now what we hear is a cacophony of terror and conciliation and compromise babbling only the mouth-sounds, the loud and empty words which we have emasculated of all meaning whatever—freedom, democracy, and patriotism."[1]

Writers in later decades turned from the hardness of fact and flesh in the early century toward abstract, moralistic, didactic discursiveness. Authors and their characters more and more discussed patriotism, morals, and religion. The change was greater in language and technique than in belief. Indeed, Hemingway in some ways possibly believed less and less as he preached more and more. To know what in the writer and what in the times caused this trend would be to understand much of the history of our age and to comprehend what old age does to many artists. But we cannot know the exact roles of all the causes. The point is that the trend did occur with remarkable similarities in the works of these three writers and others.

The general movement from objectiveness to abstraction, from the flesh to the word, is apparent in almost every major writer of the twentieth century. The extremes may be more noticeable in the greater writers. Indeed, an author such as T. S. Eliot—certainly one of the eminent men of letters in the twentieth century—tended as a young man to write more concretely with hard objects and few generalizations. Yet Eliot's very accomplishment may have led him to philosophical discursiveness as he and his time grew older. The young poet who had been most attached to the empirical world, who had most completely refused to state his meanings, became an older man of letters who wished to be theological and philosophical. The positions of a poet in youth and in old age may contradict each other, but the development from one to another may not be surprising. Early in the century Eliot set his direction, and writers great and small followed. The dedication to concreteness may have been particularly American, perhaps in revolt against the era of slogans during World War I. Certainly the tendencies were characteristic of the most notable American winners of the Nobel Prize—Eliot, Faulkner, and Hemingway. Even if the manifestations of the change are greatly different in the three, the changes in style are similar and significant. The best works of Eliot, Hemingway, and Faulkner between 1910 and 1935 were almost uniformly imper-

1. William Faulkner, "On Privacy: The American Dream: What Happened to It," *Harper's Magazine,* 211 (July 1955), 34.

sonal; the writer took himself out of his work and made almost no statements of intent or meaning; he presented his characters through their own thinking or in the stark simplicity of objective narrative or dramatic fiction and poetry. He distrusted a vocabulary of religion, morality, or patriotism. Characters who spoke of abstract values were hypocrites; those who had values did not speak of them; to speak was to negate.

This objective and impersonal literature was in many ways a reaction to an age of verbomania and logorrhea. Slogans, glorified statements, magniloquent claims of virtue and victory idealized and sentimentalized the War and in the process ruined the language. Woodrow Wilson's florid rhetoric first stirred the country and then turned banal and stale as "a morsel of rancid butter" devoured by one of T. S. Eliot's alley cats.[2] Lionel Trilling has written that Wilson is Hemingway's Widow Douglas—"the pious, the respectable, the morally plausible." [3] In 1919 Robert Frost decided that the President talked "like a fraud," [4] and later he described him as "the whole world's mistake. . . . He missed a mark that wasn't there in nature or human nature." [5] After the world was not saved for democracy and the war had not ended all wars, those who had been swayed "in the wind" of Wilson's rhetoric "like a field of ripe corn" [6] turned cynical, avoided the old specious rhetoric, and developed contempt for Wilson's ideals.[7]

The user of empty words became one of the most common kinds of characters in literature written after Wilson and the sentimental patriots had deadened the language. The talker—orator, politician, or intellectual—declined to villain. John Crowe Ransom advised

2. T. S. Eliot, "Rhapsody on a Windy Night," *The Complete Poems and Plays: 1909–1950* (New York: Harcourt, Brace and Company, 1952), p. 15.

3. Lionel Trilling, "Hemingway and His Critics," in Carlos Baker, *Hemingway and His Critics: An International Anthology* (New York: Hill and Wang, 1961), p. 65.

4. Elizabeth Shepley Sergeant, *Robert Frost: The Trial by Existence* (New York: Holt, Rinehart and Winston, 1960), p. 226.

5. Sergeant, p. 299.

6. Eliot, "The Boston Evening Transcript," p. 16.

7. Frederick J. Hoffman, *The Twenties: American Writing in the Postwar Decade* (New York: Viking Press, 1955), p. 336.

young girls vigorously twirling their skirts and "travelling the sward" to listen to "teachers old and contrary/Without believing a word." [8] J. Ward Moorehouse in John Dos Passos's *U. S. A.* builds his career and financial and political empire on the false and shallow words of advertising. The wonder of Fitzgerald's Great Gatsby is that he has retained mystery partly in his silence amid those whose noise is an indication of insincerity. In contrast, at his parties there were "enthusiastic meetings between women who never knew each other's names." [9]

In *Pale Horse, Pale Rider,* a short novel about a young couple in love during World War I, Katherine Anne Porter contrasts the almost wordless sincerity of Adam and Miranda with the false vocabulary of a shallow patriot. One scene depicts the two main styles or languages of our time. Watching "a long, dreary play," Adam and Miranda hold hands; their "steady and noncommittal" eyes meet once, "but only once"; Adam watches "the monotonous play with a strange shining excitement, his face quite fixed and still." Before the third act, the curtain rises and reveals "a Liberty Bond salesman" standing before "an American flag improperly and disrespectfully exposed, nailed at each upper corner." Adam and Miranda do not hold hands as they listen to

> the same old moldy speech with the same old dusty backdrop. Miranda tried not to listen, but she heard. These vile Huns—glorious Belleau Wood—our keyword is Sacrifice—Martyred Belgium—give till it hurts —our noble boys Over There—Big Berthas—the death of civilization —the Boche—

As this "local dollar-a-year man" approaches "the home stretch" of his speech, as Adam puts it, the young couple hear only the worn fragments of rhetoric:

> these dead have not died in vain—the war, the *war,* the WAR to end WAR, war for Democracy, for humanity, a safe world forever and

8. John Crowe Ransom, "Blue Girls," *Two Gentlemen in Bonds* (New York: A. A. Knopf, 1927), p. 13.

9. F. Scott Fitzgerald, *The Great Gatsby* (New York: Charles Scribner's Sons, 1925, 1953), p. 40.

> ever—and to prove our faith in Democracy to each other, and to the world, let everybody get together and buy Liberty Bonds and do without sugar and wool socks—was that it? Miranda asked herself, Say that over, I didn't catch the last line. Did you mention Adam? If you didn't I'm not interested.[10]

Such professional patriotism succumbed when it reached the battlefront, but it left a sour taste in the mouth of the soldier and of the writer after the war.

The particularity, sensuousness, and restraint of twentieth-century literature begins with an unprecedented distrust of rhetoric. Edith Wharton pondered "how the meaning had evaporated out of lots of our old words, as if the general smash-up had broken their stoppers." [11] It was as if people suddenly grew old in their attitudes toward language. "You live with words a long time," Jack Burden says in Robert Penn Warren's *All the King's Men.* "Then all at once you are old, and there are the things and the words don't matter any more." [12] Beliefs may be entangled with things and facts—incarnated perhaps—and words which do not refer directly to experience of the senses consequently become false. The good do, and liars talk. "It is not hard to love men for the things they endure," a Civil War soldier says in Warren's same novel, "and for the words they do not speak." [13] Mere words are distrusted because they are spoken by those who do not know the facts or have real feeling. Even the professional user of words—the man of letters—was skeptical of language. Ezra Pound defined the good writer as one who "uses the smallest possible number of words." [14]

When silence is impossible for characters who feel truly and deeply, they speak factually, briefly, cryptically. Often the tone of voice

10. *The Collected Stories of Katherine Anne Porter* (New York: Harcourt, Brace & World, Inc., 1965), pp. 292–293.

11. Quoted in Hoffman, p. 49.

12. Robert Penn Warren, *All the King's Men* (New York: Random House, 1946, 1953), p. 367.

13. Warren, p. 199.

14. Ezra Pound, "The Serious Artist," *Literary Essays of Ezra Pound,* Edited with an Introduction, by T. S. Eliot (London: Faber and Faber Limited, 1954), p. 50.

used becomes colder and more scientific when the content is emotional and profound. Characters in a novel by C. P. Snow talk about the most emotional and romantic matters in a "flat, sensible, methodical voice" and in "the dry, analytic language of the day." [15] In World War II among the students at Devon School in John Knowles's *A Separate Peace,* "Exposing a sincere emotion nakedly . . . was the next thing to suicide." [16] Much of this kind of inhibition results from the temper of the time, but perhaps Americans are usually more restrained in expressing feelings than most peoples. "The characteristic attitude of American poets," David Bulwer Lutyens has written, "is similar to that of Americans generally—a suspicion of abstraction." [17]

Words during modern war become "a normal part of the mechanism of deceit," [18] and "the emotional aspects of modern thought" become "a veritable orgy of verbomania." [19] Partly in reaction to the cheapening of language, Eliot, Hemingway, Faulkner and many other good writers of the time began to strive toward what C. K. Ogden and I. A. Richards called "a gesture language." [20] More than ever before, poets were aware that the word was not the thing and that even rather concrete words might suggest different things to different persons. "A genuine poet, in his moments of genuine poetry," writes R. G. Collinwood, "never mentions by name the emotions he is expressing." [21] The poet's distrust of general statement was shared by philosopher and scientist. T. E. Hulme wrote,

15. C. P. Snow, *The New Men,* The Scribner Library (New York: Charles Scribner's Sons, 1954), pp. 233, 228.

16. John Knowles, *A Separate Peace* (New York: The Macmillan Company, 1960), p. 38.

17. David Bulwer Lutyens, *The Creative Encounter* (London: Secker & Warburg, 1960), p. 32.

18. C. K. Ogden and I. A. Richards, *The Meaning of Meaning: A Study of The Influence of Language upon Thought and of The Science of Symbolism* (New York: Harcourt, Brace and Company, 1946), p. 17.

19. Ogden and Richards, p. 40.

20. Ogden and Richards, p. 15.

21. Quoted in Cleanth Brooks, *The Hidden God: Studies in Hemingway, Faulkner, Yeats, Eliot, and Warren* (New Haven: Yale University Press, 1963), p. 71.

It is essential to prove that beauty may be in small, dry things.
The great aim is accurate, precise and definite description. The first thing is to recognize how extraordinarily difficult this is.[22]

For primitive peoples, an anthropologist argued, narrative speech had been "primarily a mode of social action rather than a mere reflection of thought." [23] Primitive language "is a mode of action and not an instrument of reflection." [24] Here ethnologist and semanticist describe exactly the language and style which Ernest Hemingway and many other writers wished to achieve. "It does not matter what men say in words," Alfred North Whitehead wrote in *Science and the Modern World,* "so long as their activities are controlled by settled instincts. The words may ultimately destroy the instincts. But until this has occurred, words do not count." [25]

Whitehead links medieval decorative sculpture—and the poetry of Chaucer, Wordsworth, Whitman, and Frost—with the processes of science: "The simple immediate facts are the topics of interest, and these reappear in the thought of science as the 'irreducible stubborn facts.' " [26] He could also have cited Eliot's objective correlative and the one eighth of an iceberg which rose out of the water in Hemingway's prose. The immediate fact and the avoidance of the generalization was also the aim of Pound and the imagists. Their objectives were "Dircct treatment of the 'thing' whether subjective or objective" and "To use absolutely no word that does not contribute to the presentation." [27] Abstraction was regarded as a cause of the declines of civilizations. At this time Joseph Wood Krutch viewed history as a series of collapses which mankind can

22. T. E. Hulme, *Speculations: Essays on Humanism and the Philosophy of Art,* Edited by Herbert Read (London: Routledge & Kegan Paul, Ltd, 1924, 1949), pp. 131–132.

23. Bronislaw Malinowski, "The Problem of Meaning in Primitive Languages," in Ogden and Richards, p. 313.

24. Malinowski, p. 312.

25. Alfred North Whitehead, *Science and the Modern World,* Lowell Lectures, 1925 (New York: The Macmillan Company, 1925), p. 5.

26. Whitehead, p. 23.

27. Pound, "A Retrospect," p. 3.

survive only "because naïver creatures, incapable of understanding the problems and hence not feeling the need to solve them, have appeared somewhere upon the face of the globe." [28]

The dedication of Eliot, Hemingway, and Faulkner to the fact, the thing, and the image represents the proclivities of nearly all good writers in the early years of the twentieth century. Arthur Mizener has written,

> The ordering form of Mr. Eliot's verse derives immediately from Ezra Pound's imagism. Pound's imagism is only one manifestation of an almost mystical theory of perception which is one of the remarkable phenomena of our time. From James's "represent" through Joyce's "epiphanies" and Mr. Eliot's "objective correlative" to Hemingway's "the way it was," our writers have been dominated by a belief that every pattern of feelings has its pattern of objects and events, so that if the writer can set down the pattern of objects in exactly the right relations, without irrelevances or distortions, they will evoke in the reader the pattern of feelings. Whatever the limitations of this view—and we have hardly considered seriously yet what they may be—it suited Mr. Eliot's talent, with its great powers of visual and aural perception.[29]

If the style of the writer was attempting to create the beauty of "small dry things," obnoxious and despicable and futile characters in the literature of the twenties might be ignorant of the "small dry things" and therefore incapable of speaking except in discursive generalities and abstractions. Such characters were seldom given extensive roles. The most prominent bore of this kind is probably Dawson Fairchild in Faulkner's *Mosquitoes.* Others are Robert Cohn and Gino in Hemingway, and, to some extent, the old man in Eliot's "Gerontion." More typical characters are those who intellectualize and abstract but still think—though they seldom speak—in beautifully concrete imagery, which reflects their desire if not their ability to appreciate the beauty of "small dry things." Prufrock, Quentin Compson, and Darl Bundren speak this kind of language—images of desire rather than of the known and loved.

28. Joseph Wood Krutch, *The Modern Temper: A Study and a Confession* (New York: Harcourt, Brace and Company, 1929), p. 236.

29. Arthur Mizener, "To Meet Mr. Eliot," *The Sewanee Review,* 65 (1957), 40.

T. S. ELIOT

2

Eliot and the Objective

In his early criticism, T. S. Eliot was a maker of memorable phrases. Even those which are somewhat obscure or ambiguous in meaning have become standards and touchstones of modern literature and criticism. Nearly all of Eliot's best-known critical statements deal in some fashion with problems which have been most crucial and peculiar to modern literature. His attitudes toward the "objective correlative," "the dissociation of sense and sensibility," and the "impersonality" of the poet have defined the poet's personal relationship to his poem and to his characters and have described the ways of the poet in revealing his own emotion. These terms define in various ways the uses and the limitations of language. Eliot stated his primary concern with language in terms of contemporary problems: "The poet," he wrote, "must become more and more comprehensive, more allusive, more indirect, in order to force, to dislocate if necessary, language into his meaning." [1]

Eliot's criticism in principle and his poetry in practice severely limited the province of the poem and the prerogatives of the poet. As the technical device of the novelist's use of a third-person sub-

1. Eliot, "The Metaphysical Poets," *Selected Essays,* New Edition (New York: Harcourt, Brace and Company, 1932, 1950), p. 248.

jective narrator eliminated the author from many modern novels, Eliot's critical principles eliminated the poet from the poem—or at least excluded many aspects of the poet's whole being. The failure of language after it had been assaulted by the bad taste of the half-educated prevented the poet from expressing personal feelings, sentiment, and values. Eliot excluded from his poetry what the novelists of the twenties left out of their novels, what the authors of second-rate sentimental fiction and poetry are primarily concerned with.

In "Tradition and the Individual Talent" Eliot began by eliminating the poet himself: Tradition enables the poet to surrender himself "at the moment to something which is more valuable. The progress of an artist is a continual self-effacement, a continual extinction of personality." [2] One intention here is the exclusion of sentimentality, because when the poet is removed "*significant* emotion . . . has its life in the poem and not in the history of the poet." [3] Eliot equates emotion and personality in the same essay when he defines poetry as "an escape from emotion . . . an escape from personality." [4] Again, "the poet has, not a 'personality' to express, but a particular medium, which is only a medium, and not a personality, in which impressions and experiences combine in peculiar and unexpected ways." [5]

Personal biography, beliefs, and sentiments are sacrificed in the interest of poetry "as a representation (a 'general symbol') of universally significant meaning." [6] Only the object, the character, the materials of the poem itself remain. Abstract and sentimental poetry and impressionistic criticism are to be shunned. Abstract words are those with "a meaning which cannot be grasped by appeal to any of the senses." [7] Here Eliot has imposed the greatest limitation and severest restraint upon the poet and the poem. He can only

2. Eliot, "Tradition and the Individual Talent," *Selected Essays,* pp. 6–7.

3. "Tradition and the Individual Talent," p. 11.

4. "Tradition and the Individual Talent," p. 10.

5. "Tradition and the Individual Talent," p. 9.

6. Allen Austin, "T. S. Eliot's Theory of Personal Expression," *PMLA,* 81 (June 1966), 307.

7. Eliot, "The Perfect Critic," *The Sacred Wood: Essays on Poetry and Criticism* (London: Methuen & Co., 1948, Sixth Edition), p. 8.

select and present. The poet himself cannot react, interpret, or control the reactions and interpretations of the reader except through the facts and the images. "The end of the enjoyment of poetry," Eliot wrote, "is a pure contemplation from which all the accidents of personal emotion are removed; thus we aim to see the object as it really is. . . ." [8] This resembles some of the tenets of imagism, but the object or the image for Eliot is not a mere object or image. It has a meaning, and it arouses an emotion according to one's reaction and according to its association with the tradition, with other objects and images in literature and in the common knowledge.

The poet, then, like Thomas Middleton, "has no message; he is merely a great recorder." He is "without fear, without sentiment, without prejudice, without personality." [9] Even belief is excluded from "the activity of a great poet, *qua* poet." [10] Values apparently may rest implicit in the object and the image; the creator of art may (perhaps must) have ends and values, but these rest outside the poem in a mysterious way. Eliot did "not deny that art may be affirmed to serve ends beyond itself; but art is not required to be aware of these ends, and indeed performs its function, whatever that may be, according to various theories of value, much better by indifference to them." [11] That the distinction between image and meaning may be overemphasized, however, is indicated by Eliot's inconsistency. The question seems to be in part a matter of the obviousness versus the objectivity of literature, the explicit versus the implicit. "The Experiment in Criticism" seems to make this clear: in philosophical poetry, Eliot writes, "the poet *believes* in some theory . . . and makes poetry of it"; in metaphysical poetry, "the poet makes use of metaphysical ideas and theories." [12] In both kinds of poetry there is meaning, not mere or pure poetry. In bad poetry or good poetry, then, the poet may select and write in terms

8. "The Perfect Critic," p. 14–15.

9. Eliot, *For Lancelot Andrewes: Essays on Style and Order* (Garden City: Doubleday, Doran and Company, Inc., 1929), p. 124.

10. Eliot, "Shakespeare and the Stoicism of Seneca," *Selected Essays,* p. 118.

11. Eliot, "The Function of Criticism," *Selected Essays,* p. 13.

12. Quoted in E. P. Bollier, "T. S. Eliot and John Donne: A Problem in Criticism," *Tulane Studies in English,* 9 (1959), 112.

of theory; but in good poetry, the governing theory itself does not appear in the poem, and especially not in abstraction in the poem.

The theory of the objective correlative may be interpreted in many ways, but whatever it is, it primarily excludes. The work of art as art is a self-sufficient vehicle. The first statement about the objective correlative, made in "Hamlet and His Problems," began with the problem of emotion: "The only way of expressing emotion in the form of art is by finding an 'objective correlative'; in other words, a set of objects, a situation, a chain of events which shall be the formula of that *particular* emotion; such that when the external facts, which must terminate in sensory experience, are given, the emotion is immediately evoked." [13]

For a term and a definition that seem at first glance to be clear enough, the objective correlative has been interpreted in an astonishing number of ways. There is, first of all, the question of the relationship between the objective correlative and the work of art as a whole. The words *set*, *situation*, and *chain* seem to refer to the entire work. René Wellek has made the best statement of this interpretation: the objective correlative, he writes, "seems to mean simply the right kind of work, the right plot, the whole world of the play or novel and its set of symbols." [14] George T. Wright takes a similar view: "All the conventions and devices of poetry—the plot, the characters, the imagery, the verse form—exist to be manipulated in such a way as to provide in their totality the 'formula' of the poet's feeling." [15] Most critics, however, have taken the objective correlative to be in some way merely a part of the whole work, something less than its totality. Eliot's use of plurals (*objects, events, facts*) seems to suggest that one work may contain several objective correlatives, that the objective correlative may be separately embodied in numbers of things within a single work. For Hugh Ross-Williamson it is a line, a part, an image. An example

13. Eliot, "Hamlet and His Problems," *The Sacred Wood*, p. 100.

14. René Wellek, "The Criticism of T. S. Eliot," *The Sewanee Review*, 64 (1956), 419.

15. George T. Wright, *The Poet in the Poem: The Personae of Eliot, Yeats, and Pound* (Berkeley and Los Angeles: University of California Press, 1962), p. 79.

of the objective correlative thus might be Prufrock's "I have measured out my life in coffee spoons." [16] Grover Smith defines the objective correlative as an image or a series of images which express emotion.[17] Robert Wooster Stallman takes a similar view.[18] For F. O. Matthiessen, Eliseo Vivas, and Allen Austin it is both situation and images.[19] Vivas believes that it is an impossible term. It offers "us as an explanation the fact to be explained." [20] He also, it seems to me, denies the possibility of connotation: "exactly how," he asks, "can feelings, something subjective, attach to images, something quite objective?" [21] Even if we do not know the psychological process, the "how," we know factually and aesthetically that they do.

There is also a question of whose emotion is involved in the objective correlative. Matthiessen, Vivas, and Stallman define it as the "poet's own emotion." [22] But Allen Austin contends that "the important emotion is that of the character, not that of the poet," and that the "core of Eliot's meaning" is the "necessity of a motive for the character's emotion." [23] Ernest Philip Bollier in a discussion of Eliot's attitude toward Donne's sermons defines the term by implication as the writer's obligation to "subordinate his personality to his subject." [24]

16. Hugh Ross Williamson, *The Poetry of T. S. Eliot* (New York: Putnam, 1933), p. 49.

17. Grover Smith Jr., *T. S. Eliot's Poetry and Plays: A Study in Sources and Meaning* (Chicago: University of Chicago Press, 1956), p. 213.

18. Robert Wooster Stallman, "The New Critics," in Stallman, *Critiques and Essays in Criticism 1920–1948* (New York: The Ronald Press Company, 1949), p. 502.

19. F. O. Matthiessen, *The Achievement of T. S. Eliot: An Essay on the Nature of Poetry* (New York: Oxford University Press, 1958), pp. 58, 62, 64–65; Eliseo Vivas, "The Objective Correlative of T. S. Eliot," in *Critiques and Essays in Criticism,* p. 396; Allen Austin, "T. S. Eliot's Objective Correlative," *The University of Kansas City Review,* 26 (Winter 1959), 133–134. Professor Austin's study is especially clear and helpful.

20. Vivas, p. 392.

21. Vivas, p. 392.

22. Austin, p. 136.

23. Austin, pp. 136, 140.

24. Bollier, p. 108.

Whatever the term objective correlative refers to, its artistic principles are definable and clear. Whether the emotion is embodied in the entire work or in particular images or in language, Eliot is indicating how literature effectively conveys feeling. Some object correlates with something which should not be overtly expressed in the obvious, the sentimental, the explicit. The writer creates or selects images, characters, situation, plot, even a style and language —a vehicle—in which emotion is implied, connoted, related to sensuous experience. In turn, the reader's tradition and his knowledge of literature—all his experience enables him to perceive the facts, the sensuous objects, and to supply what is implicit. In its broadest terms, then, the objective correlative represents the most significant aspect of the creation of literature and of sensitive reading.

The relationship between the objective correlative and the concept of the dissociation of sensibility is close. Both deal with emotion and with the choice of image, vehicle, style to embody the emotion. The great poets, Eliot suggests, "feel their thought as immediately as the odour of a rose." [25] They incorporate "their erudition into their sensibility: their mode of feeling . . . [is] directly and freshly altered by their reading and thought." [26] The best poetry results from "direct apprehension of thought, or a recreation of thought into feeling." [27] The relationship between sense and sensibility is psychologically almost inexplicable. Presumably when the poet's sense (his rational thinking) and his sensibility (his emotion and feeling) are properly associated, he apprehends images in the phenomenal world, and without self-consciousness his mind functions as a whole mind in simultaneously apprehending, feeling, and ideating. The "perfectly equipped" poetic mind "is constantly amalgamating disparate experience." [28] The ill-equipped poetic mind is somehow "unbalanced"; it may use "refined" language to express "crude" feelings; it thinks and feels alternately rather than simultaneously.[29] It is unable, therefore, to embody emotion in a

25. Eliot, "The Metaphysical Poets," *Selected Essays,* p. 247.
26. "The Metaphysical Poets," p. 246.
27. "The Metaphysical Poets," p. 246.
28. "The Metaphysical Poets," p. 247.
29. "The Metaphysical Poets," pp. 247–248.

satisfactory objective correlative. Poetry written by a dissociated mind would tend to be didactic and sentimental or perhaps excessively rational and intellectual—the poetry would be mere emoting or mere versified philosophy or moralizings. A mind which separates sense and sensibility substitutes "reflection or rumination for metaphysical wit." [30] Both the dissociation of sense and sensibility and the objective correlative, then, are closely related to language and style. Eliot in his early criticism was fundamentally concerned with the poet's method of expression. If the image did not exist for its own sake, it was the poet's medium—the means of communication without violating the aesthetic sensibility.

Many other statements which do not employ catch phrases reflect Eliot's primary interest in the way in which a poem must be implicit, not explicit. At times he seemed to deny that a great poet should as poet be interested in values: "I should say that in one's prose reflexions one may be legitimately occupied with ideals, whereas in the writing of verse one can only deal with actuality." [31] Poetry not dealing with actuality might be described in the words of John Crowe Ransom as "a poetry which stops with words instead of going through words to their objective referents; a verbal poetry." [32] The difficulty seems to be not only empty rhetoric, the writer's failure to embody his art properly in form and image, but also the decay of language: Eliot describes it as

> the vague jargon of our time, when we have a vocabulary for everything and exact ideas about nothing—when a word half-understood, torn from its place in some alien or half-formed science, as of psychology, conceals from both writer and reader the utter meaninglessness of a statement, when all dogma is in doubt except the dogmas of sciences of which we have read in the newspapers, when the language of theology itself, under the influence of an undisciplined mysticism of popular philosophy, tends to become a language of tergiversation.[33]

30. "The Metaphysical Poets," p. 247.

31. Eliot, *After Strange Gods: A Primer of Modern Heresy* (New York: Harcourt, Brace and Company, 1934), p. 30.

32. John Crowe Ransom, "T. S. Eliot: The Historical Critic," in Leonard Unger, *T. S. Eliot: A Selected Critique* (New York: Rinehart & Company, Inc., 1948), p. 57.

33. *For Lancelot Andrewes,* pp. 14–15.

Words have lost their definite meanings and gained indefinite ones.[34] Changes have sentimentalized language: "when we do not know enough, we tend always to substitute emotions for thoughts." [35]

The emotion of the poet is also objectified and made impersonal by the use of dramatic devices. Before Eliot began to write criticisms of the art of the drama and before he wrote his own plays, he was making much use of the form of the dramatic monologue. He has never written a great deal of criticism about the dramatic monologue and dramatic devices in poetry outside of plays. But he has maintained that great poetry is dramatic.[36] He seems to have wavered in his attitude toward the dramatic monologues of Browning. In an early statement he commented that "Browning wrote dull plays, but invented the dramatic monologue or character"—suggesting by contrast that Browning's achievement in dramatic poetry was substantial.[37] Much later in *On Poetry and Poets,* Eliot suggests that perhaps Browning did not make his dramatic poems sufficiently objective and impersonal:

> when we read a dramatic monologue by Browning, we cannot suppose that we are listening to any other voice than that of Browning himself.
>
> In the dramatic monologue, then, it is surely the second voice, the voice of the poet talking to other people, that is dominant.[38]

In Eliot's early poems the poet stood somewhat aloof from the character he created in a dramatic poem. He did not use his characters to embody "ideas" as the stage was being used for that purpose.[39] Instead, he presented "*dramatic action*" and the character's introspection. The poet was present in the poem and perhaps in the character, but not personally, not in any way that could be known by a reader. As Eliot wrote in his essay "John Ford," "a dramatic poet cannot create characters of the greatest intensity of life unless

34. "The Perfect Critic," p. 9.
35. "The Perfect Critic," p. 10.
36. Eliot, "A Dialogue on Dramatic Poetry," *Selected Essays,* p. 38.
37. Quoted in Matthiessen, pp. 155–156.
38. Eliot, "The Three Voices of Poetry," *On Poetry and Poets* (New York: The Noonday Press, 1957), p. 104.
39. Eliot, "The Possibility of a Poetic Drama," *The Sacred Wood,* p. 67.

his personages, in their reciprocal actions and behaviour in their story, are somehow dramatizing, but in no obvious form, an action or struggle for harmony in the soul of the poet." [40]

A poet writing a dramatic poem, then, embodies his own "action or struggle" in the poem in much the same manner that he embodies an emotion in an objective correlative. And there is a parallel between the writing of a dramatic poem and associating properly sense and sensibility in poetry. Emotion of character is embodied in the thought and action of drama as sense and sensibility are contained within the object or set of objects of the objective correlative.

All these terms and poetic processes, despite their multiple meanings and uses, are closely related. And all of them are generally useful in examining the techniques of many modern writers, Eliot's subject matter and his style in his poetry as well as his critical explanations are directly related to Hemingway's work, especially his objective and uniquely impersonal style. Even when Eliot has not established the pattern for other writers, he has, perhaps more than any other artist and critic, sensed the attitudes of the time. In his critical statements it is easy to see many artists' beliefs, reactions, and methods. If Eliot in his criticism was "trying to defend the kind of poetry he . . . [was] writing, or to formulate the kind that he . . . [wanted] to write," [41] he was also defining and defending modern literature and formulating the kind of poetry and fiction which the modern author wished to write.

40. Eliot, "John Ford," *Selected Essays,* pp. 172–173.
41. Eliot, "The Music of Poetry," *Selected Essays,* p. 17.

3

The Early Eliot: Poetry without a Poet

THE poems in *Prufrock and Other Observations* and *Poems, 1920* are, above all, poetry without a poet. Even when there is an autobiographical basis for the characters of the narrative or the dramatic poetry, the significance of the likeness between persona and poet should be of interest only to the biographer, not to the reader of the poetry. That is to say, Eliot is not the poetic subject, and when the poet and his persona share a journey, knowledge of a scene, or even an attitude, the correspondence is not of primary poetic interest. Some day, perhaps, a speculative biographer may reach some conclusions about how Eliot is like J. Alfred Prufrock or the old man in "Gerontion," but this will be of little or no help to the reader or the critic of the poems. These are elementary principles, but the tendency to see the poet in his poetry is a flaw in the reading of Eliot or any other poet.

The extent of Eliot's removal of himself from his early poems, the degree of objectivity, and many of his techniques in attaining a personality for the poem and an impersonality for himself still need some definitions. The first two volumes establish a number of patterns or forms: the pristine dramatic soliloquy or monologue in which every thought belongs to the character; the aloof, factual, and often obscure

narrative without explanation and with emotional values which may run to the sympathetic or to the ironic; a few slight character sketches which would not be altogether out of place in a volume by Edwin Arlington Robinson; scenes which stress imagery of urban slums and which have no significant personae; satirical portraits of aristocrats in Boston and in Europe; and lyric poems written mysteriously in the first person in a restrained manner that avoids subjective lyrical emotions. Whatever the pattern or form, these poems all have in common a remarkable restraint, a lack of exposition and sentimentality. They omit altogether what the poet thinks. Such characters as J. Alfred Prufrock not only find it impossible to say what they mean but also comfortable not to have to say what they do not believe. And the narrative poems and sketches of scenes or episodes are as stark as the dramatic ones. "Sweeney among the Nightingales," for example, is as brutal and objective as Hemingway's "The Killers"—and its meanings are much more obscure.

The lack of narrative exposition and of explicit detail has contributed to critical debates which extend to more and more possible interpretations and less and less certainty. A debate about the age, social status, and identity of Pipit in "A Cooking Egg," for example, provides an almost infinite number of explanations—all offering something but none fully satisfying. Although there is much confusion about who the people are and what happens, the greater difficulty is not fact but significance. In most of the early poems it is easier to tell what happens than to tell why. Eliot also is obscure because he seems to be subjective, lyrical, personal, while he may actually be remote and detached. A lyric which apparently reveals the personality of the poet may be a good example of Eliot's own critical theory of the impersonality of the poet. The vertical pronoun intrudes into a few of the poems, but in a mysterious and obscure fashion. The poems with "I" remain impersonal, and the reader dares not equate "I" with the poet. Eliot has asked, "what great poetry is not dramatic?" [1] An "I suppose" ironically lightens the tone of "Whispers of Immortality," but seems to provide little content and no

1. Eliot, "A Dialogue on Dramatic Poetry," *Selected Essays*, New Edition (New York: Harcourt, Brace and Company, 1932, 1950), p. 38. The poems referred to and quoted may be found in Eliot, *The Complete Poems and Plays*

lyrical subjectivity. After two stanzas which indicate how "Webster was much possessed by death," the poet writes:

> Donne, I suppose, was such another
> Who found no substitute for sense,
> To seize and clutch and penetrate. . . .

In "The Hippopotamus" one stanza is written in the first person, but it is still impersonal, as if an unidentified observer were a witness to a catastrophe in a ballad or to a comic prophetic vision in the Old Testament:

> I saw the 'potamus take wing
> Ascending from the damp savannas,
> And quiring angels round him sing
> The praise of God, in loud hosannas.

Again, "Sweeney Erect" introduces the first person in exalted rhetoric which repeats the imperative mood of verbs and ironically calls upon a painter to re-create the past as a contrast to Sweeney, a "Gesture of orang-outang."

> Paint me a cavernous waste shore
> Cast in the unstilled Cyclades,
> Paint me the bold anfractuous rocks
> Faced by the snarled and yelping seas.
>
> Display me Aeolus above
> Reviewing the insurgent gales
> Which tangle Ariadne's hair
> And swell with haste the perjured sails.

But Eliot's imperative verbs and his first-person indirect objects seem much more ironically rhetorical than personal. The voyager in "Melange Adultère de Tout" shares Eliot's background and occupations, but certainly the poem yields no personal and biographical reflections. "Mr. Eliot's Sunday Morning Service" could be the title of an acutely personal religious meditation, but Eliot presents merely the actions of the conductors of the service, the activities just outside the

---

1909–1950 (New York: Harcourt, Brace and Company, 1958). Poems will be footnoted only when there are special problems.

church windows, and the deeds of the Church Fathers and Sweeney. His poem (and his religious service) studiously avoids giving his subjective and personal interpretations of what he sees or what he recalls.

Language is a subject in many of Eliot's early poems. A poem may suggest the need for a more perfect union between the word and the sensuous fact it represents. Or a poem may portray a character who cannot cut through the phlegm of language to the hard sensuous object. "Whispers of Immortality" represents most of the ways in which Eliot deals with the sensuous, the abstract, and the union of the two. As Grover Smith Jr. has written, "The juxtaposition of body and thought . . . shows the ability . . . [of] Donne and his contemporaries . . . to 'feel their thought as immediately as the odour of a rose.' "[2] The uncorseted Grishkin, the purely sensual, "Gives promise of pneumatic bliss."

> And even the Abstract Entities
> Circumambulate her charm;
> But our lot crawls between dry ribs
> To keep our metaphysics warm.

Union between the sexual and the ideal is not accomplished. The modern has either the "dry ribs" or Grishkin, and even if he should have both, the two remain separate and distinct. Consummation is not achieved; "possessed by flesh, we take refuge in abstractions to conceive any life beyond the physical."[3] Separate, the two aspects of life are meaningless.

The abstractness of language may circumambulate Sweeney's physical grossness as well as the charm of Grishkin. And again the nearly explicit statement of meaning is cast in an ironic literary quotation from a former age—this time from Emerson. "Sweeney Erect" consists of three different sections organized around the antithesis between abstraction and concreteness: the first ten lines concretely evoke the classical; the next ten objectively describe Sweeney: "Gesture of orang-outang/ Rises from the sheets in steam." The last part

2. Grover Smith Jr., *T. S. Eliot's Poetry and Plays: A Study in Sources and Meaning* (Chicago: University of Chicago Press, 1956), p. 41.

3. George Williamson, *A Reader's Guide to T. S. Eliot: A Poem-by-Poem Analysis* (New York: The Noonday Press, 1953, 1960), p. 96.

of the poem narrates a hysterical episode in a house of prostitution. But before the last section the wisdom of Emerson intrudes in a stanza as separate from the body of the poem as the didactic conclusion of a poem by Bryant:

(The lengthened shadow of a man
  Is history, said Emerson
Who had not seen the silhouette
  Of Sweeney straddled in the sun.)

Eliot's line is an exaggeration of Emerson's contention that "An institution is the lengthened shadow of one man. . . ." [4] All Emerson's examples were heroes, and Eliot suggests that history is also based on the crudest men as well as the heroic. Emerson's falsely optimistic view of man is stated as a general principle, but Eliot's disagreement appears only in his presentation of object and character, this "withered root of knots of hair." The primary accomplishment of the poem is its creation of person and event, but Eliot has also rejected Emerson's discursive manner as well as his optimism.

If Eliot objectively presents the depravity of man and the church in the Sweeney poems and "The Hippopotamus" while refusing to state his own views, and quotes Emerson's abstractions while stating none of his own, he also writes in two poems about the Word (meaning Christ, as in the first chapter of John) and the word (an element in language) and contrasts the two. The old man in "Gerontion" thinks of Christ and of "The word within a word, unable to speak a word,/ Swaddled in darkness./ In the juvescence of the year/ Came Christ the tiger." Though figuratively "swaddled" like the Christ child in the manger, the word is not capitalized—indicating perhaps that the persona never is able to believe religiously in the incarnation of the Word as Christ. He therefore resembles the self-castrated and heretical early Church Father Origen in "Mr. Eliot's Sunday Morning Service." who wrote (according to St. Epiphanius) around six thousand treatises.[5]

4. Ralph Waldo Emerson, "Self-Reliance," *The Complete Works,* Centenary Edition (Boston: Houghton Mifflin Company, 1903), II, 61.

5. Ernest Schanzer, " 'Mr. Eliot's Sunday Morning Service,' " *Essays in Criticism,* 5 (April 1955), 154.

In the beginning was the Word.
Superfetation of γδ ε̃γ,
And at the mensual turn of time
Produced enervate Origen.

The Word (Christ) is "the silent Word"; [6] but abstract words have hidden the truth of the Word; religion, one might say, lost its images, its objective correlative. The words of the early controversies did not reflect the factual truth of Christ. The old man thinking and Eliot sitting in a church service could not experience the truth of religion sensuously, could not "feel their thought [or religion] as immediately as the odour of a rose." John Donne, in "Whispers of Immortality," did not in the later and modern fashion confuse word and fact, did not substitute abstractions for the sensuous images of experience. Donne did feel his thought or religion "as immediately as the odour of a rose."

Donne, I suppose, was such another
Who found no substitute for sense,
To seize and clutch and penetrate;
Expert beyond experience,

He knew the anguish of the marrow
The ague of the skeleton;
No contact possible to flesh
Allayed the fever of the bone.

Religious terms in Eliot's early poetry are false because they are several degrees removed from experience and reality, and the moral vocabulary of the poems is heavily ironical. In "Sweeney Erect," for example, the ladies are morally indignant at Sweeney and the epileptic:

The ladies of the corridor
   Find themselves involved, disgraced,
Call witness to their principles
   And deprecate the lack of taste
Observing that hysteria
   Might easily be misunderstood. . . .

6. Schanzer, p. 154.

All of the many words for truth in *Poems, 1920* are in some way false or abstract. They are words desired but not believed by the character; they are impersonal to the poet; they are so far removed from reality that neither poet nor character nor reader knows quite what they mean; they have abstract connotations and uncertain denotations.

In four parallel stanzas in "A Cooking Egg" the speaker says that in Heaven he shall not want Honour, Capital, Society, and Pipit. The ambiguous "shall not want" may mean that he shall have and not need to wish for these good things. Or he may not be capable of desiring the meaningful values. The friends he will seek out in Heaven are Sir Philip Sydney, Coriolanus, Sir Alfred Mond, Lucretia Borgia, Madame Blavatsky. His limitations are apparent in his abstract talk and in his belief that truth in Heaven will be provided by such false ideals as these two frustrated heroes, a capitalist, a murderess, and a Russian Theosophist. Actually, despite his mouthing of the words of truth, the poem provides no evidence that the speaker has any moral identity, that he is innocent, good, or evil. Wanting Honour, Capital, Society, and Pipit, the speaker has demonstrated that even in Heaven he would search for these in the wrong persons. He lacks virtues; he is not aware of guilt. Toward the end of the poem he longs for the innocence of childhood:

> But where is the penny world I bought
>   To eat with Pipit behind the screen?
> The red-eyed scavengers are creeping
>   From Kentish Town and Golder's Green;
>
> Where are the eagles and the trumpets?

The alternate lines of the speaker's last stanza violently juxtapose trivialities of tea parties and tea shops with images of masses of people weeping because the meanings and innocence of childhood are covered by mountains.

>   Buried beneath some snow-deep Alps.
> Over buttered scones and crumpets
>   Weeping, weeping multitudes
> Droop in a hundred A. B. C.'s.

Even in some of the exact imagery of Eliot's early poems confusion is ultimately supposed to prevail. The owner of Gerontion's house, for example, that "jew" who "squats on the window sill," was "Spawned in some estaminet of Antwerp,/ Blistered in Brussels, patched and peeled." The failure to capitalize *jew* probably suggests commercial character more than race or religion. *Spawned* indicates the lowly and animal nature of his conception, but only the tone is clear in such words as *Blistered*, *patched*, and *peeled*. How a person is literally "patched and peeled," we cannot know exactly. On the other hand, the words are so concrete that we cannot know figuratively what they denote in regard to the jew's relationships with others. In some instances emotional value is more significant than the exact denotation of an object. The old lady who "keeps the kitchen" in "Gerontion" pokes the "peevish gutter"; but one cannot know what she pokes. It has been taken as a stove, an eaves trough, a drain.[7] But the point is not what the object is; the point is the peevishness, the futility—the adjective transfers from the object to the old woman.

Poems, 1920 is difficult and obscure despite the interpretations seemingly provided by such quotations as that of Emerson in "Sweeney Erect" and allusions such as that to Ruskin when Burbank meditates in Venice on "Time's ruins, and the seven laws." The poems *Prufrock and Other Observations* are in general less obscure, perhaps less sinister, and more satirical. Usually a poem in this first volume focuses upon setting—often a city slum scene—or upon character—often an aristocrat. Eliot wrote his best poetry in *The Waste Land*, which wonderfully treats all social classes in many kinds of settings. Three poems in the first volume—"Preludes," "Rhapsody on a Windy Night," and "Morning at the Window"—are mainly experiments in techniques and imagery. In the sense of the objective correlative which correlates image and emotion, these poems suggest little besides phrases in Eliot's other poems and a

7. Taylor Culbert, "Eliot's 'Gerontion,'" *Explicator,* 17 (October 1958), 20. John Abbot Clark, "On First Looking into Benson's Fitzgerald," *The South Atlantic Quarterly,* 48 (April 1949), 260. Williamson, p. 107.

dirty and crowded city life, what Grover Smith has called "the down-at-heels, almost sinister atmosphere of a meaningless society." [8] The sensuous images in these three poems anticipate and echo almost all of Eliot's best poems before *Ash-Wednesday*. They have sources in literature and Eliot's experience, they evoke pity and memory, they are constructed with time sequence and order. They depict "the problem of relating consciousness to externality." Eliot's selection of images and characters and his failure to invest them with the possibility of anything greater than a frustrated yearning make these his most nihilistic poems. Though there is a "yearning after significance," [9] the shadowy souls in these poems are more degraded than those in "Prufrock" and *The Waste Land*, "because their consciousness embraces only what their senses can confront." [10]

Three social satires from *Prufrock and Other Observations* are restrained vignettes of the life of Boston aristocrats: "The Boston Evening Transcript," "Aunt Helen," and "Cousin Nancy." In the first two a narrator appears in the first person, but without enough identity to be significant. Aunt Helen herself and the emptiness of her life may be seen only in the clutter and paraphernalia of people and her house at the time of her wake:

> The dogs were handsomely provided for,
> But shortly afterwards the parrot died too.
> The Dresden clock continued ticking on the mantelpiece,
> And the footman sat upon the dining-table
> Holding the second housemaid on his knees—
> Who had always been so careful while her mistress lived.

The most complex and provocative of these three satires is "Cousin Nancy." Miss Nancy Ellicott rides "to hounds/ Over the cow-pasture."

> Miss Nancy Ellicott smoked
> And danced all the modern dances;

8. Smith, p. 21.
9. Hugh Kenner, *The Invisible Poet: T. S. Eliot* (New York: McDowell, Obolensky, 1959), p. 35.
10. Smith, p. 22.

And her aunts were not quite sure how they felt about it,
But they knew that it was modern.

The last three lines of the poem ironically compare Miss Nancy to older transcendental and Victorian traditions. While she rides and smokes and dances, books in her library keep watch:

  Upon the glazen shelves kept watch
Matthew and Waldo, guardians of the faith,
The army of unalterable law.

Whether Miss Nancy's shallowness is more ridiculous than Matthew Arnold and Ralph Waldo Emerson's ineffectual guardianship of faith is a matter for conjecture. The adjective *glazen* seems to attach itself to their dull-eyed manner of keeping watch, and Miss Nancy's superficiality may suggest that the faith has not been well guarded. The familiarity in the use of the first names seems to reveal contempt—the poet's as well as Miss Nancy's. Eliot's use of the line from Meredith's "Lucifer in Starlight" ("The army of unalterable law") in conjunction with the character of Miss Nancy suggests that the law has been drastically altered or broken. In Meredith's poem itself, Lucifer sinks before "the stars/ Which are the brain of heaven. . . ." That is, evil now succumbs before the natural order instead of the old theological "revolt from Awe." And after the time of Matthew and Ralph Waldo, no faith at all provides meaning in the trivialities of Miss Nancy's dizzy social life.

"Mr. Apollinax," another satire, has been neglected. It is one of Eliot's most obscure poems and one of the best. The narrator is characterized only by his thoughts about the central character, Mr. Apollinax, who may be the most vigorous and worthy soul created by Eliot before the *Ariel Poems* and *Ash-Wednesday*. The mysterious Mr. Apollinax visits the United States and attends Boston tea parties at "the palace of Mrs. Phlaccus, at Professor Channing-Cheetah's." His listeners are charmed, though they do not know what he means. They notice his "pointed ears" and decide that he is "unbalanced." The speaker is reminded of mythical figures, Priapus, the old man of the sea or Proteus, and a centaur. Mr. Apollinax laughs "like an irresponsible foetus," and the observer looks "for the head of Mr. Apollinax rolling under a chair."

Various critics have described Mr. Apollinax as vital and "reminiscent of . . . [the] god of the fertility cults," "devilish" and "baffling" "shy and crude, intellectual and animal," a "shocking" sensualist.[11] Whatever he is, Mr. Apollinax is set apart from his acquaintances in Boston and from Eliot's gallery of sterile characters. His separation is like that of a supernatural being, a god, or an artist. Fertility symbol or lecher, good or evil, he has a great vitality and exuberance unique in his surroundings. He is "submarine and profound" rather than mundane and shallow or superficial. Whether prophet or devil, at least he exists.

Impressed by the strangeness of this visitor, the narrator looks "for the head of Mr. Apollinax rolling under a chair"—like the head of John the Baptist brought in on a platter in "Prufrock." Mr. Apollinax reminds the observer of an executed criminal or a martyred saint—perhaps of both. Good or evil, he merits consideration. But the other people at this tea are capable only of surprise. Professor and Mrs. Channing-Cheetah could neither execute nor merit execution as saint or sinner. Only their sense of propriety would be shocked at seeing a rolling head.

Despite the mystery, Mr. Apollinax is the most sharply delineated character in Eliot's early poems except for the characters in the dramatic monologues—J. Alfred Prufrock, the young man and the older lady in "Portrait of a Lady," and the old man in "Gerontion." "Mr. Apollinax" is one of Eliot's most excellent poems; it lacks the complexity of the dramatic monologues only because the speaker has no distinctive identity. He only sees and describes and states his expectations at this unusual social gathering.

Language, imagery, character, impersonal and dramatic presentation of the poem through the point of view of a sensitive but lost and deficient soul—the techniques of "The Love Song of J. Alfred Prufrock," "Portrait of a Lady," and "Gerontion" make these the best poems in Eliot's first two volumes. Eliot is best as a dramatic

11. D. E. S. Maxwell, *The Poetry of T. S. Eliot* (London: Routledge & Kegan Paul, 1952), pp. 52–53. Elizabeth Drew, *T. S. Eliot: The Design of His Poetry* (New York: Charles Scribner's Sons, 1949), pp. 26, 27. Williamson, p. 83. Smith, p. 29.

poet, and these are the poems which are clearly and meaningfully dramatic monologues with well-developed characters. Many of the speakers in the other poems before *The Waste Land* are vague and inadequately characterized.

The distinction between the moral position of the characters in Eliot's dramatic monologues and that of the personae in the monologues of Browning provides a good perspective on Eliot's techniques and meanings. The moral position of Browning's characters, indeed their identity, is easily apparent. The evil Bishop of Saint Praxed's does not doubt himself. The Duke of Ferrara is a cruel tyrant. Eliot's characters, on the other hand, struggle for identity and some kind of meaningful moral position. Browning's men and women know clearly what they are and what they wish to say; Eliot's characters search for a language, for something to stand on, and for a word which might express what they hope they might wish to say. These personae have not yet achieved goodness or evil worthy of definition. That Eliot is a poet of the twentieth century rather than the nineteenth or the seventeenth is apparent because technique and meaning do not lead to resolution. The ambiguity, the lack of final comprehension in terms of a certain standard, is exactly the point made.

The dramatic conflict and the struggle are greater in the soul of one of Eliot's characters than the turmoil in one of Browning's. In "My Last Duchess" the conflict is external, between people; the Duke of Ferrara knows exactly what he stands for. Prufrock wishes to stand for something, to face meaning, to make some kind of statement about what the world is. Even to say it means nothing would be a kind of relief. But his affliction is not only that belief is closed to him, but that disbelief is also. The style of the poems reveals the characters' wavering, and the devices in the poetry must be read as the characters' modes of thinking, part of their manner of expressing themselves. The style is the characters', not the poet's. An example is anticlimax, which creates humor in "Prufrock" and "Portrait." Eliot does not artificially impose a comic anticlimax upon the character in order to evoke a wry grin from the reader at the character's expense. Instead, Prufrock himself takes refuge in anticlimaxes because he has just enough of a sense of humor and just enough wisdom to avoid serious questions by deliberately resorting to the trivial. He self-consciously recognizes his own evasions and still avoids any kind of commitment. Overwhelming questions or the answers to them can lead only to despair. So when Prufrock confronts significant meaning, he abruptly breaks the continuity of his thought. Streets

> follow like a tedious argument
> Of insidious intent
> To lead you to an overwhelming question . . .
> Oh, do not ask, "What is it?"
> Let us go and make our visit.

With a wry grin, Prufrock himself has evaded and dodged. This device is used many times with minor variations in the poem, and every time it indicates the character's manner of thinking. In a way, it lays bare his very soul. The young man in "Portrait of a Lady" thinks in similar fashion:

> —Let us take the air, in a tobacco trance,
> Admire the monuments,
> Discuss the late events,
> Correct our watches by the public clocks.
> Then sit for half an hour and drink our bocks.

Thus he avoids intimacy, friendship, love, and takes refuge in public things. After chitchat about monuments and late events, he avoids words and meanings.

Prufrock, the man in "Portrait," and the old man in "Gerontion" avoid all actions. They are antitheses of those who can act in modern literature, such as Faulkner's Caddy Compson and Addie Bundren, Hemingway's Frederic Henry, and Eliot's Mr. Apollinax. Eliot's early dramatic monologues depict modern damned and doomed intellectuals, abstractionists such as Darl Bundren and Quentin Compson, and many characters in the poetry of Allen Tate and especially in that of John Crowe Ransom. Curiously, all these lost souls do not think purely in terms of abstract and intellectual language and words. Prufrock and others like him think in beautifully concrete imagery. There are two explanations for this paradox: the beautiful imagery of Prufrock and the other intellectuals ultimately reveals preoccupation with triviality, flight from reality. They use sensuousness as a "substitute for sense"; the character desires concreteness of fact because he does not have a concreteness of belief. Thus the artist can create an abstract intellectual who thinks in concrete and poetic imagery and language. Only the old man in "Gerontion" ineffectually confronts abstraction and vacillates between sensuous imagery and a vocabulary of belief.

Images in Prufrock's mind lead him unintentionally to questions which he does not wish to face. The "one-night cheap hotels" and "sawdust restaurants" might suggest social issues or even the subject of the place of man in the world. The nature of Prufrock and man is such that images make him desire significance, but the state of the world is such that he avoids them when they occur almost accidentally. The reader can never know exactly what overwhelming question Prufrock was about to face, because he does not let his mind think that far. The argument is "tedious" and the intent is "insidious" because these hostile abstractions lead Prufrock to think in terms he is accustomed to deny.

After the possibility of an overwhelming question has been evaded, Prufrock turns to thoughts of a tea party as a form of escape. He sees women walking back and forth aimlessly in a room. Of course they are talking: lazily, perhaps, his mind conjectures their subject of conversation: Michelangelo. Prufrock has again, almost accidentally, hit upon an image which would force him to deal with meaning and to take some kind of stand upon it. This accounts for his abrupt transition to thoughts of "the yellow fog." He dodges. Almost out of desperation he turns from what could become meaningful thoughts of figures in the paintings to what he hopes will be merely an idle observation. In the fog Prufrock almost succeeds in his attempt to escape overwhelming questions.

Throughout the poem Prufrock wavers. From momentous questions which he cannot entirely ignore and which he does not dare try to answer he moves to casual observations which momentarily enable him to forget his plight. Even a single image or allusion may bring alternate despair and comfort. A kind of preoccupation with a casual reminiscence about Shakespeare gives him comfort when he almost despairs that he cannot face the serious questions of Prince Hamlet. Hamlet despairs over his own indecision; Prufrock habitually attempts to escape thoughts of the need for a decision. Mermaids sing from the sea, and from their songs Prufrock might learn love and meaningful answers, but instead, he is preoccupied with the mere beauty of his own thoughts about them.

> We have lingered in the chambers of the sea
> By sea-girls wreathed with seaweed red and brown
> Till human voices wake us, and we drown.

Drowning, Prufrock symbolically shares the fate of that later intellectual Quentin Compson. He contentedly passes into an oblivion which gives him ease because he no longer has to exist.

The most significant distinction between "The Love Song of J. Alfred Prufrock" and "Portrait of a Lady" is that the conflict in the first is wholly within the character and that in the latter the conflict is between two Prufrockian souls, one a little more deserving of salvation than the other. In three separate scenes in three different seasons (December, spring, October) a young man visits a lady apparently somewhat older than he is. Desperately she strives to create a meaningful relationship where one cannot exist. The language of her first conversation, in December, reveals her desires. She chooses personal and religious terms: Chopin is "intimate"; "his *soul*/ Should be *resurrected* only among *friends*" (italics mine). She talks about qualities, friendship, meaning, and life.[12] But the young man thinks without saying a word in the poem, and he takes "the air in a tobacco trance."

In the second scene the lady again speaks of abstractions: friends, life, youth, peace, prevailed, give, sympathy. Her abstraction and her desperation are shown by what she actually does to life, "Slowly twisting the lilac stalks." Her faint hopes, however, slowly give way to despair because the young man can only think and listen, because he cannot speak or love. Ironically, it is in the spring that she first

12. See Keith Wright's excellent study of how the lady's obsession is portrayed by parallel repetitions of *friend* and its various forms, "Word-Repetition in T. S. Eliot's Early Verse," *Essays in Criticism*, 16 (April 1966), 202.

recognizes that her life will continue empty: "I shall sit here serving tea to friends. . . ." The young man cannot give her friendship and life. He takes his hat and asks, "How can I make a cowardly amends/ For what she has said to me?"

In October the lady despairs, and she and the young man separate. Talk is no longer a means of expressing hope for a close relationship. She merely suggests that he write to her and expresses her puzzlement over their not becoming friends. In the last stanza he sits "pen in hand"

> Doubtful, for a while
> Not knowing what to feel or if I understand
> Or whether wise or foolish, tardy or too soon. . . .

He cannot act meaningfully, and he cannot even express his despair in words.

"Gerontion" is clearly a dramatic monologue. The style is not the poet's but the character's. The meditations of the old man wander from an initial impulse provided by a boy who reads to him. That Eliot may be in some way personally related to the spiritual problems of the old man is indicated by the recurrence in many poems of the subject of belief and disbelief. But to establish any closer relationship is impossible because Eliot is not the persona. To read the character's thoughts or his acts as those of the poet makes the poem didactic, abstract, personal rather than impersonal. The tone of the passage on history is indeed hortatory. It is also desperate and almost neurotic in its repetitiousness, particularly of the words *think* and *gives*. The old man's admonishments to himself to think indicate his unwillingness to think—his incapacity. And caesuras which are late within each line and which precede his imperatives emphasize his desperation. To attribute this style to the mind of Eliot rather than to the old man would be to make the poet violate all of his critical principles. The poem would contain biography; it would not be impersonal; it would not contain an objective correlative; and it would indicate the poet's dissociation of sense and sensibility, separation of image and meaning. The distinction between Eliot the poet and the old man could hardly be stated with greater clarity than

Eliot himself has put it in *The Sacred Wood*: "It is not in his personal emotions, the emotions provoked by particular events in his life, that the poet is in any way remarkable or interesting.[13] Again, "Impressions and experiences which are important for the man may take no place in the poetry, and those which become important in the poetry may play quite a negligible part in the man, the personality." [14]

Not to see precisely the dramatic nature of a poem is to run the risk of misreading. Stephen Spender, however, reads "Gerontion" as

> an objective poem. It is in complete contrast to the preceding subjective poems. It no longer expresses the disgust and horror of one man at symptoms which one might after all believe to be purely subjective. It is written in the belief that the decline of civilization is real, that history is, as it were, now senile.[15]

One should say that the old man in the poem speaks in his belief that history is senile; only biography—evidence outside the poem—could make the poem a statement of the views of T. S. Eliot. Indeed, Spender ignores the dramatic quality of the poem: that the character attributes his own sterile senility to history. Harvey Gross makes the same mistake about the same passage. "Eliot," he writes, "drops the dramatic mode and proposes, in a sustained conceptual passage, an attitude toward history. The tone is hortatory; the argument closely reasoned. . . ." Again, "Eliot certainly maintains in *Gerontion* a deterministic attitude toward history." [16] The determinism and the hortatory tone, on the contrary, are the character's. The reader has little more evidence that Eliot shares his view of history than he has that Shakespeare shares Macbeth's ambition.

13. Eliot, "Tradition and the Individual Talent," *The Sacred Wood: Essays on Poetry and Criticism* (London: Methuen & Co., 1948, Sixth Edition), p. 57.

14. "Tradition and the Individual Talent," p. 56.

15. Stephen Spender, "T. S. Eliot in His Poetry," in Leonard Unger, *T. S. Eliot* (New York: Rinehart & Company, Inc., 1948), p. 270.

16. Harvey Gross, "*Gerontion* and the Meaning of History," *PMLA,* 73 (June 1958), pp. 300, 303.

The very rhythm and patterns of language in the following figure indicate the speaker's despair and desperation.

After such knowledge,* what forgiveness?* *Think* now
History has many cunning† passages, contrived† corridors
And issues, deceives† with whispering† ambitions,*
Guides us by vanities.* *Think* now
She *gives*, when our attention is distracted†
And what she *gives*, *gives* with such supple confusions†
That the giving famishes the craving.† *Gives* too late
What's not believed* in, or if still believed,*
In memory only, reconsidered† passion. *Gives* too soon
Into weak† hands, what's thought can be dispensed with
Till the refusal propagates a fear.*† *Think*
Neither fear*† nor courage* saves us. Unnatural vices*
Are fathered by our heroism.* Virtues*
Are forced upon us by our impudent crimes.*
These tears are shaken from the wrath†-bearing tree.

Gives—repeated with stark and simple subject (she); or the subject is assumed, omitted to emphasize the verb. A strong caesura precedes or follows every *Gives.*

Three times the old man chides himself to think. Eliot achieves great emphasis by placing the repeated imperative verb at the end of the sentence and just after a strong caesura.

These caesuras and run-on lines also indicate the desperately irregular rhythm of the character's meditations.

*Abstractions which are poetic mainly because they characterize the persona's abstract and tortured mind.

†Words which describe anguish, doubt, anger, and suspicion. They describe the character's own mental state as much as they do his view of history.

The abstractions of the character's meditations are impossible, wishful, or false as the character is defeated, frustrated, and lost. And only a moral weakling in the good literature of this time would use such a vocabulary. The strong—like Frederic Henry, Addie Bundren, Caddy Compson and possibly Mr. Apollinax—condemn such language or avoid it. The old man in "Gerontion" can use the words of virtue; but he cannot know truth because he is deprived of his bodily senses: he has lost his "sight, smell, hearing, taste and touch. . . ."

In *After Strange Gods* Eliot wrote that in prose "one may be legitimately occupied with ideals, whereas in the writing of verse one can only deal with actuality." [17] Eliot's early poems deal only with actuality. Some characters are preoccupied with ideals or the need and the search for them. Thus in a curious fashion, the characters' false language becomes poetic and dramatic and psychological actuality; and meaningless abstraction is the subject matter. The poet may wish for a more perfect union between thought and feeling, but no character in the poems attains it except possibly Mr. Apollinax. The personae cannot connect experience and belief. Almost no person in the poems can simultaneously use the word and know the thing it represents. Eliot's world is peopled mainly by thinkers such as Prufrock and the grossly physical such as Sweeney. Few there be who can know both belief and the material world. The poet is so completely outside the poem that he refuses to know personally for his character or to comment.

17. Eliot, *After Strange Gods: A Primer of Modern Heresy* (New York: Harcourt, Brace and Company, 1934), p. 30.

4

The Waste Land—Enjoyment of the Poetry

"It is a test," T. S. Eliot has contended, "that genuine poetry can communicate before it is understood." [1] The reader may know the events or the facts, for instance, before he knows what they mean. This is a simple explanation of a mysterious process, but it is consistent with Eliot's further explanation that "it is not necessary to understand the meaning first to enjoy the poetry, but . . . our enjoyment of the poetry makes us want to understand the meaning." [2] The "maturing artist" has the impersonality "of the poet who, out of intense and personal experience, is able to express a general truth, retaining all the particularity of his experience to make of it a general symbol." [3] Communication, enjoyment, impersonality, and particularity—the terms which Eliot emphasizes suggest that many poems may be appreciated without much of the ponderous learned apparatus which has been added to them. The art of a work of literature is much more difficult to discuss than its philosophical

1. Eliot, "Dante," *Selected Essays* (New York: Harcourt, Brace and Company, 1932, 1950), p. 200.
2. "Dante," p. 229.
3. Eliot, "Yeats," *On Poetry and Poets* (New York: The Noonday Press, 1957), p. 299.

meanings. Possibly there are works which contain art too difficult (or perhaps even too obvious) to discuss, works which provoke one who contemplates them merely to appreciate and enjoy. Possibly *The Waste Land* is such a work of art. The art of the poem lies first in the surface fact and the actions of the characters rather than in mythological explanations.

Communication and understanding—the two words may suggest the difference between a child's delight over a poem like Blake's "The Tyger" as contrasted to an intellectual reader's comprehension of the theological and symbolical implications. The deeper reader, of course, may understand the poem better and enjoy it more after it is thoroughly understood—but only if his study and intellect lead him back to something like the pleasure of the child. Before attaining a full understanding of *The Waste Land*, one must become entangled in paraphrase, sources, mythologies, anthropology, theology, transitions, influences, evaluations, and symbolic equations. But these should be a means to attain the fullest pleasure in the poetry, not the end of the critical process. As a work of art, the poem consists of images, language, and characters; awareness of these exactly as they are presented is necessary before there can be communication or understanding.

If *The Waste Land* is great poetry by Eliot's own standards, it must be impersonal and dramatic. If it is impersonal, it must not be primarily a lyrical presentation of the poet's own emotions. The poet as poet must not be the major character or the narrator of his poem; his "self-sacrifice" contributes to his "continual extinction of personality." [4] It is easy to forget that the personages, Eliot says, "in their reciprocal actions and behaviour in their story, are somehow dramatizing, but in no obvious form, an action or struggle for harmony in the soul of the poet." [5] How they dramatize his struggle may be undeterminable, and certainly how they do so has no effect whatsoever on the art and the reader's appreciation of the work. Parallels between the poet and his major narrator, Tiresias, may be

4. Eliot, "Tradition and the Individual Talent," *The Sacred Wood: Essays on Poetry and Criticism* (London: Methuen & Co., 1948, Sixth Edition), p. 53.

5. Eliot, "John Ford," *Selected Essays*, p. 173.

numerous, but the character as a part of a work of art must stand or fall on his own merit. The parallels are part of biography, not part of the poetry. Indeed, the reader's associations of himself with Tiresias are much more important than any likeness which he can establish between character and poet.

Although Eliot's note on Tiresias attempts "as an afterthought," perhaps, "to supply the poem with a nameable point of view," the poem has no single "pervading zone of consciousness." [6] The poet is not himself in the poem. Eliot, one interpreter has written, "is putting both himself and his readers into the poem, identifying them in the immediate context with 'Stetson' and more indirectly with humanity in general. We do indeed recognize the prophetic voice of the poem as that of the poet." [7] Other critics who seem to understand the over-all dramatic nature of the poem identify the first-person pronoun as Eliot in a line like the following: "There I saw one I knew, and stopped him, crying: 'Stetson!' " [8] Eliot and his readers discuss how Tiresias "melts" into another, "uniting all the rest." [9] But this too is an abstract statement about meaning. It diminishes the poetic individuality of any character speaking or acting at any particular moment. And certainly a reading of the poem should not allow the character to melt into the poet. George T. Wright correctly argues that, "although the protagonist's quest is essentially the same quest as Eliot's, it is inside the poem instead of outside, and at no particular point in the poem is Eliot participating in the emotions of his personae." [10] F. O. Matthiessen effectively defines the necessity of the poet's absence from the poem: "Eliot's

6. Hugh Kenner, *The Invisible Poet: T. S. Eliot* (New York: McDowell, Obolensky, 1959), p. 149.

7. Kristian Smidt, *Poetry and Belief in the Work of T. S. Eliot* (London: Routledge and Regan Paul, 1949, 1961), p. 91.

8. Lloyd Frankenberg, *Pleasure Dome: on reading modern poetry* (Boston: Houghton Mifflin Company, 1949), p. 67. F. O. Matthiessen, *The Achievement of T. S. Eliot* (New York: Oxford University Press, 1958), p. 22. Genevieve W. Foster, "The Archetypal Imagery of T. S. Eliot," *PMLA*, 60 (1945), 571.

9. Eliot, *The Complete Poems and Plays 1909–1950* (New York: Harcourt, Brace and Company, 1958), p. 52.

10. George T. Wright, *The Poet in the Poem* (Berkeley and Los Angeles: University of California Press, 1962), p. 84.

observations are not primarily of physical objects; his most sustained analysis is applied to states of mind and emotion. But he holds none the less that permanent poetry is always a presentation of thought and feeling 'by a statement of events in human action or objects in the external world.' "[11] In this sense, "external world" is the exact antithesis of the internal and personal world of the poet himself. The "external world" in *The Waste Land* is "something which the reader is to know through his mind, but is to know primarily as an actual physical experience, as a part of his whole being, through the humming pulsating evidence of his senses."[12] This "pulsating evidence" derives from the reader's perception of the characters' actions and environment because nothing of the personality of the poet intrudes into the poem.

The Waste Land is "a fact, factum," in Robert Frost's words, "a thing done or made. . . . 'The fact is the sweetest dream that labor knows.' "[13] Now it is extremely ironic that the poem has been understood before it has really communicated. The reader must give up some of his intellectual understanding if the poem is to communicate its art. The characters know what they are doing; and they are not aware of the mythological implications of their actions. Myth and theme are what the reader may comprehend after contemplation. The first level of poetic appreciation of *The Waste Land* is to understand what the character thinks and knows. The most basic level of understanding dramatic poetry (whether it is read silently or presented orally to a communal group) is a sympathetic comprehension of the situation and attitude of the person in the poem. Yet the failure to communicate may be the fault not of the poem but of the half-educated and over-educated audience. Most of the criticism of the poem and even of Eliot's own notes represents an abstraction which is characteristic of our age, and in so far as annotations fail to consider the dramatic art of the poem, they are a betrayal of its characters, its imagery—in short, its objective correlative. The poet here obeyed his own critical precepts and strictures—remained

11. Matthiessen, p. 58.
12. Matthiessen, p. 43.
13. Sidney Cox, *A Swinger of Birches: A Portrait of Robert Frost* (New York: New York University Press, 1957), p. 121.

impersonal, objective, dramatic, concrete. Then in annotations added later to his own poem he was the first to lead his readers astray by making the poem abstract, personal, and mythical.

Discussing the first section of the poem without reference to Jessie L. Weston's *From Ritual to Romance* and all the other mythologies may at first seem to belabor the obvious. On the contrary, such an analysis should reveal what should be the first esthetic effect of a reading but what remains in part still publicly unsaid.

The first part of the poem, "The Burial of the Dead," is artistically meaningful even without knowledge of such intellectual abstractions as the burial of the Fisher King and the fact that the title is derived from a section of a prayer book. The first words of the body of the poem may be spoken by the main narrator, perhaps Tiresias. Whether or not the main narrator is the poet is dramatically irrelevant. The first speaker, on the other hand, may be a chorus of Waste Landers (note the plural in line four: "Winter kept us warm"). The poetry and the drama derive from their obvious despair. They live in such a caged-in and desperate situation that they wish to die.

The speaker and the chorus of Waste Landers may be visualized as dramatis personae somewhat like the stage manager in *Our Town*. They are the spokesmen for those who live in this country, and they are at the same time fellow citizens of those who are active in the life of the place. Their debilitation makes them unaffected by what usually seems to be beauty in the world—April, lilacs, "spring rain," the April showers and May flowers of traditional verse. They prefer "forgetful snow" because they would regard any love of beauty in this diseased world as a naïve moongazing romanticism. Their "memory and desire" are unavailing. Oblivion is preferable to those who know that memory and desire, the abstractions of another time or other people, can bring no romance or pleasure.

Under the supervision of the stage manager, the inhabitants of this land begin speaking in strange and revealing soliloquies. Each character knows only the facts as he relates them. He may not hear the other personae speak, and he may not know the full meanings of his own speech. It is not merely that the characters refuse to face meaning as Hemingway's characters do in *The Sun Also Rises* and

A Farewell to Arms but mainly that they do not know what the meaning is. To them "Life has no meaning; history has no meaning; there is no answer to the question: 'What shall we ever do?' " [14]

One woman remembers how summer surprised her and her companion. In his recording of the poem, Eliot reads her words in an enervated monotone of sadness and ennui. Lost in self-contemplation, she and her friend had not expected summer or anything from the natural world to intrude on their consciousness. But despite the surprise as they came over the Starnbergersee, they were not startled out of their passiveness. They drank coffee and talked, and that is all they knew to do. Seeking identity, one woman claims to be a German and to be from Lithuania. She remembers a homeland, but she cannot make such a generalization as calling it childhood or a homeland. The line is uttered with certainty, but she does not know the implications of what she has said any more than Frederic Henry will interpret the concrete phenomena he sees. Again, the chatter is more meaningful to the reader than to the character.

The next speaker remembers a scene in childhood, a visit to her cousin, a ride on a sled, fright on the steep slope, the security and fear at the same moment as the cousin told her to hold on tight, the thrill of the ride. She remembers that she felt free in the mountains, but freedom remains for her a meaningless generalization. Although it is closer to a statement of need than anything yet spoken in the poem, it is still a mere groping for meaning. The fact is that the freedom has vanished and cannot be regained even in the mountains. Probably the speaker is among mountains now, and she has no freedom. Dramatically, what she really desires and needs but cannot define is authority and belief—freedom from guilt. The need is perfectly apparent to the reader of the poem, but the character cannot articulate it. This person resembles the Sibyl of Cumae in the epigraph. Now aged in spirit, she remembers childhood as a different time. Now she can only wish to die or to return to the time of greater innocence which she had once known in the mountains.

The next line ("I read, much of the night, and go south in the

14. Allen Tate quoted by Cleanth Brooks, "The Waste Land: An Analysis," in B. Rajan, *T. S. Eliot: A Study of His Writings by Several Hands* (London: D. Dobson, 1949), p. 15.

winter") may be spoken by Marie or perhaps by another anonymous Waste Lander. The characters read and therefore live only vicariously—or not at all. Sleepless at night, she leads a neurotic and unnatural life. Dissatisfaction is indicated by the inconsistency with the first speaker, who views April as a cruel month and likes the oblivion of winter and "forgetful snow." This character's restlessness leads her south in the winter as she flees the snow, but migration still does not enable her to enjoy spring or April or a youthful life.

These fragments are not so confusing as they are dramatically revealing. The emptiness and the ennui are apparent rather than obscure. Read with imagination and visualization, *The Waste Land* is not difficult. Presented in a dramatic reading to an audience which had never read anything about the poem, it might be almost as easy to understand and as beautiful as a ballad or the folksong of a bard or a scop. It properly belongs to an oral tradition of poetry.

After these fragments of conversation, the main narrator speaks again. He describes a conglomeration of fantastic natural images that are as contorted and as agonized as the souls of those who have just spoken. The psychological and spiritual agony of the characters is reflected in physical objects—"roots that clutch" and branches that grow in fantastic and weird shapes from "stony rubbish." The Biblical and mythical origins for these images are less important poetically and dramatically than the mental conditions which the images reflect. The point of the description is the terrible desire of the main narrator for "shelter," "relief," "sound of water." But the only possibility is shadow under a red rock, and it is a poor shadow at that, because in the physical desert or the desert of the mind the red would be itself a torrid color, providing more heat than cooling shadow. Small hope lies in the desert. The searching character moves ever toward the east. His shadow strides behind him in the morning as he walks eastward and rises to meet him in the evening as he walks always toward a possible sunrise. But walking is futile, as hiding under the red rock is also. Walking in the desert, he can survey only a world full of dust; hiding under the red rock, he sees only the same diminished desolation and fear, now a "handful of dust."

But surely the poem loses all apparent meaning when Eliot next quotes from a Wagnerian opera in German? Perhaps not. The meaning is likely to be lost if one puzzles over the source and context of the quotation, the translation of the German, and the elaborate meanings. The poem and its tone may communicate if the reader considers the effect and forgets the complexities. Ernie Kovacs in one of his strange and experimental television programs might have succeeded in presenting a brief scene from Wagnerian opera without translation or explanation. And even some of the weird recent music may be slightly analogous. Kovacs popularized on television the techniques of association discovered in modern psychology, in the modern novel, and by Eliot in modern poetry. Even one who does not know German may perhaps grasp with ease something of the meaning by guessing at cognates—*Frisch* for *fresh, Wind* for *wind*, *Irisch* for *Irish*, *du* for *thou.* To any reader familiar with the King James version of the Bible or the talk of Quakers, the verbal ending of *weilest* suggests meaning, contrast, simplicity, and older and different speech and mood. The quotation from Wagner, then, may concretely indicate a change to a lighter and happier mood if the reader will take it simply. The brevity of the lines, the use of short words, and the high pitch of the vowel sounds may also suggest a less ominous tone:

Frisch weht der Wind
Der Heimat zu
Mein Irisch Kind,
Wo weilest du?

It seems that the joy in the words and the music of the bit of Wagnerian opera should carry over to the next speech by the hyacinth girl. But, again by contrast, the joy has given way to an undefined despair. The girl knows only that her companion gave her hyacinths and that his gesture has never been fulfilled. The hyacinths were given in an innocent past; she remembers that she was called the hyacinth girl; but the relationship and the token gift came to nothing. As a result of her memory, her dramatic mood here is one of longing. This relationship has been no more meaningful and rewarding than the life of the Sibyl of Cumae.

Here approximately in the middle of the first section of the poem the characters come closest to meaning and understanding. But the opportunity dissipates immediately, and even the wonderful moment of first giving culminates in nothing more significant than the token gift. True, they came back almost in rapture from the "Hyacinth garden"; her arms were full and her "hair wet"; but her companion was never able to speak; his eyes failed; he "was neither/ Living nor dead"; and he "knew nothing." Dramatically, the main point is that he was incapable of making love, seducing, or proposing. The hope of love of any sort fades away into incomprehensible sadness and confusion, revealed in the low and sorrowful sounds of a line of German: "*Oed' und leer das Meer.*" The very sounds communicate a tone and mood exactly antithetical to the passage beginning "*Frisch weht der Wind. . . .*" Such low-pitched and long vowels and slow labials may convey a mood even without translation.

The living exist in the first part of *The Waste Land* without meaning, and in the next section a similar character seeks relief through the cheap fortune-telling of Madame Sosostris. The frequenters of her establishment know her to be "the wisest woman in Europe," and in the vernacular she tells a mean fortune "With a wicked pack of cards." Even the language indicates the loss of normal values, and the shallowness of the characters when wicked comes to mean "excellent" in slang.

Eliot and his critics may be able to interpret the fortune because of their knowledge of the allusions of the cards in this deck. But obviously the person whose fortune is told does not know the mythical derivation of the "drowned Phoenician Sailor," "Belladonna, the Lady of the Rocks," "The man with three staves," the "Wheel," and

> the one-eyed merchant, and this card,
> Which is blank, is something he carries on his back,
> Which I am forbidden to see.

Understanding of the derivation of the cards is no more necessary here than it is necessary for a poker-player to know the history of the cards he uses. The first thing to understand is the mystery and the tawdriness of this fortune-telling. Here in general are the supernatural, the occult, the mysterious, the unknown. And even the illiterate knows of the guilt involved in the mysterious burden of humanity, a common image in *Pilgrim's Progress*, folklore, Christian hymns, and any guilty psyche. "Fear death by water" may suggest all the fertility legends of Miss Weston's book and of the world, but first it means that Madame Sosostris has told her client that he should be careful not to drown.

The first section of *The Waste Land* consists of two kinds of poetry: the objective and dramatic presentation of vignettes of characters whose confusion is immediately apparent; and an omniscient narrator's objective description of appropriate natural and urban backgrounds for these characters. The first setting, a desert, occurs in the middle of the first section; the second, a desert of civilization, occurs at the end:

> Unreal City,
> Under the brown fog of a winter dawn,
> A crowd flowed over London Bridge, so many,
> I had not thought death had undone so many.
> Sighs, short and infrequent, were exhaled,
> And each man fixed his eyes before his feet.
> Flowed up the hill and down King William Street,
> To where Saint Mary Woolnoth kept the hours
> With a dead sound on the final stroke of nine.

Knowing that Dante's description of limbo is Eliot's source adds depth, but the reader does not need to know Dante to interpret the scene if he has ever paused in a busy city to muse on the futile bustle of the mob or even if he has heard a friend return from a large metropolis to marvel about the confusion of the subways.

Tiresias's or the main narrator's description of the city is directly related to the prophecies of Madame Sosostris. The "crowds of people, walking round in a ring" which she saw as a dire omen becomes a reality in the narrator's description of the "Unreal City." The Madame's prophecies of death ("Fear death by water") and intrigue and the fear of crime ("One must be so careful these days") and conspiracy are objectified in the last part of "The Burial of the Dead." The narrator himself, perhaps the most admirable character and the most desperate seeker after truth in the poem, seems to be an accomplice in murder. In his mind he cannot let the corpse lie; fearfully he asks whether it has come to light and warns that the Dog may dig it up. He is troubled by fear and guilt. The last line, mostly in French (" 'You! hyprocrite lecteur!—mon semblable,—mon frère!' "), is generally read as a direct address from the poet to the reader. It may be. But if it is, dramatically and artistically that must be a secondary and incidental interest. The French, possibly whispered, establishes the relationship between the two men, perpetuates their alliance in crime. The word *lecteur*, usually read as a direct address to the reader which places him also in the Waste Land, may mean "reader," but it may in this case also mean "old professor," which might be a form of familiar address between these two associates in guilt. The speaker, then, reminds Stetson that these two international hoodlums in London have a common guilt. To reduce the French to its lowest English equivalent, it might mean dramatically, "You! You're in this too, buddy!"

The words of vegetation in this passage (*planted*, *garden*, *sprout*, *bloom*) suggest the fertility myths of the poem, but again these words may be read on a literal level. Assuming that Stetson and the speaker are associates in crime, it is expected and even necessary that they speak indirectly as they talk on King William Street among a crowd. To preserve secrecy, they must use these euphemisms, which may suggest also a jargon, a sort of murderers' argot. Hugh Kenner rightly sees the literal level of the poem when he compares Stetson and his friend to "two Englishmen discussing their tulips, with a note of the terrible intimacy with which murderers imagine themselves being taunted." [15]

"The Burial of the Dead" presents the facts of *The Waste Land* as Benjy Compson's first section of *The Sound and the Fury* presents the facts of Faulkner's novel. The first task in both works is simply determining what happens. Once the reader has read the first part of either work intelligently, he is prepared to read the other parts and to see what happens. He has been given the exposition. Then he may increase his appreciation of the work by reading criticism and by making his own interpretations. But no matter how true

15. Kenner, p. 162.

those critical abstractions and generalizations are, any reader must remember that they are all implicit, that they are not the literal level of the work, and that the literal level (the facts, the people, the things) is just as vital a part of the work as any interpretative generalization. Indeed, *The Waste Land* is not a work of art if we discuss only its meanings and do not enjoy the vehicle, the imagery, the drama. Eliot wrote an excellent concrete and dramatic poem. But following the tendencies of our time and the proclivities of critics, his readers have been making the poem more and more mythical and moralistic ever since it was written.

5

Eliot's Substitute for Sense

AFTER T. S. Eliot turned to Anglo-Catholicism, royalism, and classicism in 1928, his poetic power began to wane. Because the subject of his later poetry treats a great and noble religious faith, a believer wishes to regard it as great and noble poetry. And presumably genuine Waste Landers, except those masochistically cultivating their own anguish, would like to find in the later poetry not only art but also the end of the search for grounds for belief. Obviously, however, poetry must first be regarded as art, and it is not to be praised or condemned mainly on other grounds.

The development of Eliot's religious beliefs, his political views, and his literary tastes seems to have been a slow intellectual and spiritual change rather than a sudden blinding light. The years from 1927 through 1930 were crucial for Eliot in both spiritual belief and poetic development, and the poems published in those years are more varied in technique and in manner than any other poems he ever wrote. They are a bridge between "Gerontion" and *The Waste Land* on the one hand and the *Four Quartets* on the other.

Apparently Eliot was writing very different kinds of poems alternately within the same period if we may judge date of composition by date of publication and if we consider the vast differences in poetic manner between the *Ariel Poems* and *Ash-Wednesday*. During each year from 1927 through 1929 Eliot published one of the *Ariel Poems* and one of the first three parts of *Ash-Wednesday*. Then in 1930 he published the last of the *Ariel Poems* and *Ash-Wednesday* in six parts, three previously unpublished. Internal evidence and poetic technique may suggest that the *Ariel Poems* preceded *Ash-Wednesday;* on the other hand, Eliot arranged his collected poems chronologically and placed the *Ariel Poems* after *Ash-Wednesday*. The *Ariel Poems* contain concrete imagery; *Ash-Wednesday* is discursive and abstract; three of the *Ariel Poems* are dramatic, spoken by personae; "Animula" and *Ash-Wednesday* are lyrical, spoken by the poet, or at least there is not a shred of evidence that the speaker is someone other than Eliot himself; three of the *Ariel Poems* have particularity of time and place; *Ash-Wednesday* is so general that one cannot prove it to be set in mortal time rather than in purgatory beyond the grave. If Eliot composed the separate poems of *Ash-Wednesday* in the order in which they were published, he mysteriously and distinctly alternated between his old manner in one group and a new technique in another —a puzzling but not impossible kind of development for a poet. Internal evidence alone might argue that Eliot published the *Ariel Poems* in an annual volume of Christmas poems, but wrote those with concrete imagery and personae first. The order of composition thus would be (1) "Journey of the Magi," (2) "A Song for Simeon," (3) "Marina." "Animula," which is more lyrical than dramatic, was published before "Marina" possibly because the poems are arranged in order from the more skeptical to the more optimistic. Perhaps Eliot wrote four poems for the Christmas series, published only one a year, and turned to the different poetry of *Ash-Wednesday* only after he had written all four. Only thus can we find a systematic development in the poet; if the conjecture is wrong, Eliot in the manner of a new convert alternated or vacillated between two sets of techniques if not two kinds of beliefs between 1927 and 1930.

Regardless of the dates of composition, the changes in technique are demonstrable and significant. Presumably the spiritual desire in *The Waste Land* is universal, but the poet gains universality not by a general and vague blurring of setting; instead, he uses a wide range of particular landscapes. The characters in the first part of *The Waste Land* remember a shower of rain at the Starnbergersee, visits at the archduke's, and coffee in the Hofgarten. Crowds on King William Street hear the "dead sound on the final stroke of nine" of Saint Mary Woolnoth. The refuse on the Thames, the Cannon Street Hotel, the desert wastes of the journey to Emmaus —these and other places are vividly created. But in *Ash-Wednesday* places have no particularity in geography or in landscape: "three white leopards sat under a juniper-tree." Neither animals nor the tree have distinctive features. Even the color of the leopards seems to be only allegorical rather than albino and sensuous. This imagery is even more general and auditory than that which Eliot had criticized in Milton's "L'Allegro" and "Il Penseroso": "It is not a particular ploughman, milkmaid, and shepherd that Milton sees [as Wordsworth might see them]; the sensuous effect of these verses is entirely on the ear, and is joined to the concepts of ploughman, milkmaid, and shepherd." [1] Even more than Milton was, Eliot here is interested in concepts—of three, of leopards, of a juniper-tree.

The speaker of *Ash-Wednesday* proffers his love "To the posterity of the desert," and the wasted land in this poem is marked by no red rocks, no mountain mouths of "carious teeth," in short, no concrete poetry. The most concretely described place in the poem is the stair in the third part. "The symbol of the stair," F. O. Matthiessen has written, "is perfectly concrete whether or not we identify it with Dante's purgatorial mount." [2] And F. R. Leavis: "The third poem of the sequence offers an admirable example of the way in which Mr Eliot blends the reminiscent (literary or conventional) in imagery with the immediately evocative. The

1. Eliot, "Milton I," *On Poetry and Poets* (New York: The Noonday Press, 1957), p. 159.

2. F. O. Matthiessen, *The Achievement of T. S. Eliot* (New York: Oxford University Press, 1958), p. 65.

'stairs' of this poem (they have a 'banister') have their effect for a reader who recognizes no reminiscence."[3] And D. E. S. Maxwell compares the figure of the stairway to "the word's distractions" and the "ugliness" created in "the mood of the Sweeney poems."[4]

A close look at the stair, however, reveals little more than a foreboding spiritual indefiniteness and vagueness. There are two stairs, each with at least a first and second turning. The second stair (only the second and third appear in the poem) has a banister, on which a "shape" is "twisted." "Under the vapour in the fetid air" this shape struggles "with the devil of the stairs who wears/ The deceitful face of hope and of despair." Even in this most concrete section of *Ash-Wednesday,* Eliot seems to be attempting to convey an idea of a spiritual state in general terms. Certainly the images are not particular enough to enable one to visualize the color of the stair, the materials of which it is made, the new or the worn condition of whatever kinds of treads it may have, and the shape, texture, color, odor of the banister. Instead of creating images which enable the reader to feel his thought "as immediately as the odour of a rose," Eliot here presents only the concept of a twisting stairway; and instead of feeling a real twinge of fear at the devil, one perceives only the concept of the devil. Indeed, Eliot has described the devil abstractly as wearing "The deceitful face of hope and of despair." Here one does not feel the thought of the devil as immediately as he senses the odor; he must himself create the odor itself from the thought. Eliot's aim is, in the terms of Edgar Allan Poe, "a suggestive indefinitiveness of meaning, with the view of bringing about a definitiveness of vague and therefore of spiritual *effect.*"[5]

The most concrete image which describes a place in *Ash-Wednesday* appears in the passage on the stair. One flight

3. F. R. Leavis, *New Bearings in English Poetry: A Study of the Contemporary Situation,* Ann Arbor Paperback (Ann Arbor: University of Michigan Press, 1932, 1964), p. 125.

4. D. E. S. Maxwell, *The Poetry of T. S. Eliot* (London: Routledge & Kegan Paul, 1952), p. 143, fn. 2.

5. Edgar Allan Poe, "Marginalia," *The Works of Edgar Allan Poe,* ed. Edmund Clarence Stedman and George Edward Woodberry (New York: Charles Scribner's Sons, 1914), VII, 379.

> was dark,
> Damp, jaggèd, like an old man's mouth drivelling,
> beyond repair,
> Or the toothed gullet of an agèd shark.

This concreteness is unusual for this poem; indeed, it is almost incongruous in the passage; it resembles the scenery of *The Waste Land* and the "Dead mountain mouth of carious teeth that cannot spit. . . ." The drivelling saliva in the mouth of the old man is as uncomfortable and sensuous as the dryness of the mouth of rotting teeth. Again, Eliot proves how much easier it is for him to figure hell than even purgatory, not to mention paradise.

After the third poem of *Ash-Wednesday* Eliot treats place even more generally as a concept rather than a cluster of sensuous images:

> Who walked between the violet and the violet
> Who walked between
> The various ranks of varied green . . .
> Who then made strong the fountains and made fresh the
> springs
> Made cool the dry rock and made firm the sand. . . .

And the images of sea and land are more general than ever before in Eliot's poems.

> Where shall the word be found . . .?
> Not on the sea or on the islands, not
> On the mainland, in the desert or the rain land. . . .

In the *Ariel Poems,* places have sensuous particularity, not only because the personae remember personal experiences vividly, but also because the poet adds sensuous imagery which makes his reader visualize the particular place (and its meaning) as immediately as the odor of a stable in "Journey of the Magi." Camels lie down "in the melting snow" while the riders regret their memories of "The summer palaces on slopes, the terraces. . . ." Later the Magi come

> to a temperate valley
> Wet, below the snow line, smelling of vegetation;

> With a running stream and a water-mill beating the darkness,
> And three trees on the low sky,
> And an old white horse galloped away in the meadow.
> Then we came to a tavern with vine-leaves over the lintel,
> Six hands at an open door dicing for pieces of silver,
> And feet kicking the empty wine-skins.

Odor, sound, motion, sight, number of hands, kind of coins or money, and emptiness of a particular kind of container for wine—all these devices make one feel the frustration of the Magus. His journey is a different order of poetry from that of the journey up the stair of *Ash-Wednesday*—and better. The room (and therefore the world) of the soul in "Animula" and the ship of the speaker in "Marina" are also created in concrete and visual terms rather than in abstractions.

How, then, one must ask himself, is the poetry of a particular place with a proper name better than that of a place with a common name and without images? No one has better demonstrated the difference between discursiveness and creation than Eliot has in his poems or better defined it in his criticism. Particular places may accomplish poetically the same thing as concrete language, which T. E. Hulme says, "endeavours to arrest you, and to make you continuously see a physical thing, to prevent you gliding through an abstract process." [6]

Ash-Wednesday is the least dramatic poem written by Eliot before the *Four Quartets*. The lyrical and subjective first-person pronoun is more dominant than in any other major poem which Eliot ever wrote. Only Helen Gardner has adequately defined the extreme personality of the poet, the subjectivity. In *Ash-Wednesday,* she writes, "one is too conscious of the author's presence." Not a single word suggests a speaker other than the poet: "the author speaks in his own person, without the use of a 'persona' such as Gerontion, or the various masks which the poet of *The Waste Land* adopts. . . ." [7] For the first time in Eliot's career the poetry does

6. T. E. Hulme, *Speculations: Essays on Humanism and the Philosophy of Art,* ed. by Herbert Read (London: Routledge & Kegan Paul, Ltd., 1924, 1949), p. 134.

7. Helen Gardner, *The Art of T. S. Eliot* (New York: E. P. Dutton & Co., Inc., 1950), p. 122.

not eliminate the poet's personal feelings. The "continual self-sacrifice . . . continual extinction of personality" which Eliot demanded in *Sacred Wood* is not achieved or even attempted.[8] Indeed, according to Miss Gardner, "The symbols and images he employs have the arbitrariness of the individual's inner world, and have hardly emerged into the self-explanatory world of art." [9] Whether the objective correlative is the form of an entire work or an image or a series of images, *Ash-Wednesday* is without an objective correlative.

With merely a name and an image Eliot could create vivid characters in his early poems. Excluding fully developed characters such as J. Alfred Prufrock and Sweeney and Burbank, there are many brief but sharp portraits, such as that of "Mr. Silvero/ With caressing hands, at Limoges/ Who walked all night in the next room. . . ." Or "The person in the Spanish cape," who

Tries to sit on Sweeney's knees

Slips and pulls the table cloth
Overturns a coffee-cup
Reorganized upon the floor
She yawns and draws a stocking up. . . .

The character comes through clearly in specific details even when some obscurity exists. Whether Mr. Silvero caresses porcelain or pervertedly strokes his male friends, he is a contemptible sensualist and neurotic.

Not so in *Ash-Wednesday*. The Lady in this poem is the most developed character besides "I." Like other personae in Eliot, she has been interpreted variously: as "personal memory," the Virgin, a nun, a "Jungian personality development," and Mary Magdalene.[10] The variety of explanations reflects—not the critical translation of concrete life into meaning—but a new vagueness of characterization in Eliot's poetry.

The poet addresses her directly, and he tells us that she is good

8. Eliot, *The Sacred Wood: Essays on Poetry and Criticism* (London: Methuen & Co., 1948, Sixth Edition), p. 53.

9. Gardner, p. 122.

10. Gwenn R. Boardman, *"Ash Wednesday:* Eliot's Lenten Mass Sequence," *Renascence,* 15 (Fall 1962), 28, 32.

and lovely, that "She honours the Virgin," that she "is withdrawn/ In a white gown, to contemplation. . . ." that she walks in the garden "between the violet and the violet . . . between/ The various ranks of varied green/ Going in white and blue . . ./ Talking of trivial things. . . ." But the reader can only assume that she glides in some dignified fashion appropriate to her spiritual status; for all Eliot says, she might even limp or stalk, or pace neurotically like Mr. Silvero. Truly, as Helen Gardner says, "the figures in *Ash-Wednesday* are not persons." There are no personae; the poetry is not impersonal, not dramatic. But even Miss Gardner attributes some of her own imagination to *Ash-Wednesday*. The characters, she says, "are like figures seen for a moment through the window of a swiftly moving train, where an attitude or a gesture catches our attention and is then gone forever, but remains to haunt the memory. Much of the imagery has this fleeting vividness; it is not fixed with the precision of the earlier poetry, and it is only occasionally that the brilliant exact wit of the earlier comparisons is found. . . ." [11] Actually the train moves faster than Miss Gardner says; the character does not gesture; the most vivid detail is the symbolic color of her clothes; the attitude must be assumed; it is not created by the poet except in very general terms. Grover Smith writes that the Lady, "by a daring and rather mysterious identification, . . . becomes indistinguishable from the Virgin." [12] Perhaps. But only on the philosophical and thematic level; on the human level she is certainly vague, actually indistinguishable from any striking, noble, and admirable female.

The characters in the *Ariel Poems* are treated much more specifically than the allegorical personae of *Ash-Wednesday,* but less so than in Eliot's poetry before 1927. The most dramatic aspect of the three dramatic poems is the speaker's tension and his confusion about the "sense of ambiguity between" dying and birth—a theme of each of the poems.[13] Strangely, Eliot's poetic development as well as his increasing faith may be revealed in the gradual decrease

11. Gardner, pp. 100–101.

12. Grover Smith Jr., *T. S. Eliot's Poetry and Plays: A Study in Sources and Meaning* (Chicago: University of Chicago Press, 1956), p. 136.

13. Elizabeth Drew, *T. S. Eliot: The Design of His Poetry* (New York: Charles Scribner's Sons, 1949), p. 118.

of tension in these characters. In the first published poem, "Journey of the Magi," the speaker endures more anguish than Simeon and the father in "Marina." The Magus confronts hostile peoples on his journey to the birth of the Christ child, and animosity toward his new belief among his own people after his return. Within himself he dramatically wavers between a comprehension of the meaning of the birth of the Messiah and confusion because the birth leads to death and because he has not seen the Resurrection. The trials of the Christian are figured in terms of conflict between the individual and society. The person-to-person relationship prominent in the dramatic tensions of Eliot's early poems has developed into a conflict within a social order. This change itself is a trend from objectivity to subjectivity. The old man in "Gerontion," for example, meditates on such particular persons as his Jewish landlord, Mr. Silvero, Hakagawa, and Fräulein von Kulp. The Magus, in contrast, remembers classes of persons: silken girls, camel men, "Six hands at an open door dicing for pieces of silver," and "an alien people."

In "A Song for Simeon," the second poem of the Ariel group, the character is even more introspective and subjective. An old man who has been told that he will see the Christ child before he dies, Simeon either has already seen the Christ or he is at the moment of his meditation in the presence of the Christ. Necessarily ignorant of the meanings of the Crucifixion and Resurrection, he thinks neither of the people who will be saved nor of the Messiah himself. Simeon meditates upon his own life, and his introspection is shown by his awareness that for him the coming of the Messiah means death and the possibility of rest. Simeon's antagonists are neither particular individuals as in the early poems nor such classes as the camel men and the alien people of the "Journey of the Magi." He does remember "this city," "the poor," and Israel. Spiritually he has not attained much vision. Although he is created dramatically, he is not able to embody his world in images as specific as Prufrock's.

The final dramatic poem of the *Ariel Poems* is "Marina," "the only purely joyous poem Eliot has ever written." [14] This is his last attempt at a dramatic monologue, his only effort in a short dramatic

14. Drew, p. 127.

poem to present a moment of ecstasy in the relationship between two people. The situation is that an old man has regained his long-lost daughter. The subject of the poem is abstract: the ecstasy of spiritual life, the salvation of the soul, and the rediscovery of the past. The surface of the work, a man's finding his long-lost daughter, is a credible dramatic and human vehicle. As in "A Song for Simeon," however, the tension is wholly within the speaking character, who remembers vividly his past trials in explicit images. The daughter appears only passively in the poem. She is apparently living but unconscious:

> This form, this face, this life
> Living to live in a world of time beyond me; let me
> Resign my life for this life, my speech for that unspoken,
> The awakened, lips parted, the hope, the new ships.

A dramatization of an ecstatic state of the soul perhaps cannot be embodied in a human relationship as real as that between the young man and his neurotic older lady friend in "Portrait of a Lady" or that between the typist and the young man carbuncular in *The Waste Land.* Although "Marina" falls short of these, spiritual ecstasy in the poem is more dramatic and concrete than in any other poem written by Eliot after 1927, including *Ash-Wednesday* and the *Four Quartets.*

Stylistically Eliot's interest in the abstract word and in discursive poetry begins in *Ash-Wednesday.* Before his declaration of faith he had written satirically (in "Mr. Eliot's Sunday Morning Service") about the difference between the vital word, the Christ, and the sterile words of theological dogma. In a painting, he had seen the reality of the Word.

> But through the water pale and thin
> Still shine the unoffending feet. . . .

In his service he heard only the endless unreal mouthings of "enervate Origen" and of the "masters of the subtle schools." When Eliot himself turned to the faith, he was faced with the need for a new theological language. No longer did he satirize sterile priests in dramatic and narrative poetry; instead, he found himself in the place of the priest. But the penance of *Ash-Wednesday* does not contain a single image of the Christ so concrete as that of the "unoffending feet." The words and the Word are traditional, abstract, general, unspoken.

> If the lost word is lost, if the spent word is spent
> If the unheard, unspoken
> Word is unspoken, unheard;
> Still is the unspoken word, the Word unheard,
> The Word without a word, the Word within
> The world and for the world;
> And the light shone in darkness and
> Against the Word the unstilled world still whirled
> About the centre of the silent Word.
>
> O my people, what have I done unto thee.
>
> Where shall the word be found, where will the word
> Resound? Not here. . . .

Eliot's use of imagery develops from the extremely concrete in the early poems to generality in *Ash-Wednesday* and some concreteness in the *Ariel Poems.*

Some critics have persisted in finding sensuousness and exactness in the imagery. In Part V of *Ash-Wednesday,* D. E. S. Maxwell argues, "The imagery that evokes the assiduous distractions of the world is transposed from the general to the particular. . . ." [15] And F. O. Matthiessen finds in the poem a peculiar combination of vagueness and definiteness: "The way in which Eliot secures both definiteness of statement and indefiniteness of suggestion by building his imagery upon an objective structure can be seen in the third poem in *Ash-Wednesday. . . .*" [16] The poem contains "Exact description of memories of the varied loveliness of the New England coast," and Matthiessen feels "the very sensation of his distraction" almost as immediately as the odor of a rose.[17] Grover Smith also

15. Maxwell, p. 144.
16. Matthiessen, p. 65.
17. Matthiessen, p. 64.

praises the poem's "brilliant texture of . . . imagery." [18] Helen Gardner sees "sharpness" in the images in the poem.[19] Elizabeth Drew finds patterns of images of "sound and silence," "movement and stillness," "disintegration and reintegration," "light and darkness," "loneliness and companionship." [20] And in the third part of the poem, Miss Drew believes, "the 'clear visual images' . . . give perfect 'sensuous embodiment' to the allegorical content." [21] Herbert Howarth believes that *Ash-Wednesday* has concreteness similar to that in *The Waste Land:* "Perhaps in the poems of the twenties, *The Waste Land* and *Ash-Wednesday,* there is an avoidance of abstractions, just as there is the cultivation of the vivid, perfect pictorial image. . . ." [22]

Other critics, however, are unable to find "perfect pictorial" imagery in the poem. For Hugh Ross Williamson the imagery is "occasionally trite"; [23] the syntax in Part IV is "purposefully vague" [24] Hugh Kenner is pleased that "The . . . language is emptied of irrelevant specificity. . . ." [25] In contradiction to Eliot's argument that the poet may feel his thought as immediately as the odor of a rose, Helen Gardner asserts that the roses are omitted in this poem because they might be distracting: "The poet seems not to wish to linger on any particular image, which might by its vividness, aptness, or unexpectedness interrupt the stream of meditation and distract us from his essential theme." [26] Does she mean that the beauty of poetry should not distract the reader from philosophical content? For a similar reason, apparently, Eliot uses "stock

18. Smith, p. 158.

19. Gardner, p. 119.

20. Drew, p. 98.

21. Drew, p. 109.

22. Herbert Howarth, *Notes on Some Figures Behind T. S. Eliot* (Boston: Houghton Mifflin, 1964), p. 219.

23. Hugh Ross Williamson, *The Poetry of T. S. Eliot* (New York: Putnam, 1933), p. 171.

24. George Williamson, *A Reader's Guide to T. S. Eliot: A Poem-by-Poem Analysis* (New York: The Noonday Press, 1953, 1960), p. 177.

25. Hugh Kenner, *The Invisible Poet: T. S. Eliot* (New York: McDowell, Obolensky, 1959), p. 267.

26. Gardner, p. 101.

images" and "traditional symbols." [27] Only one critic, I believe, has judged the imagery of the poem vague and disapproved of the vagueness. "The poem," Theodore Morrison asserts, "is disappointing at its crucial moment, where we have to accept assertion instead of experience—instead of those vivid images and conveyors of experience which Mr. Eliot has elsewhere contrived." [28]

To find "perfect pictorial" imagery in *Ash-Wednesday,* I suggest, is to rewrite it; no critic should imagine the sensuousness for the poet. On the other hand, to argue that specificity is irrelevant and to regard vividness, aptness, and particularity as interrupting the poetry—these are strange critical principles. The art of *Ash-Wednesday* is perhaps defensible, but not in terms of Eliot's own early criticism and certainly not on the grounds of a deliberate and admirable vagueness of language.

In Part I of the poem there are a few concrete objects, but no sensuous images. In parenthesis in the first stanza Eliot asks, "Why should the agèd eagle stretch its wings?" Is the eagle in flight? Perhaps. The line may suggest the concept of a once-strong man or poet or soul now questioning whether he should try again. Eliot presents no optical vision of a grounded and aged eagle with bedraggled feathers. The eagle may be airborne in slow flight, unable or unwilling to make a vigorous flight of speed and power. Imagery is vague when an eagle is not visible and when it may be either in flight or on the ground.

What might be taken as sensuous image in *Ash-Wednesday* is really neither sensuous nor image, but actually a statement of a concept in terms of a traditional metaphor or figure. Other figures in Part I similar to that of the eagle, other statements about conditions, are the following:

> . . . trees flower, and springs flow. . . .
> . . . these wings are no longer wings to fly. . . .
> The air . . . is now thoroughly small and dry. . . .

And these lines exemplify much of what the critics regard as

27. Gardner, p. 103.

28. Theodore Morrison, "*Ash Wednesday:* A Religious History," *The New England Quarterly,* 11 (June 1938), 278.

imagery in the poem; in strong contrast to Eliot's early poetry, these lines are characteristic of his later style.

Later in the poem the lady

> made strong the fountains and made fresh the springs
> Made cool the dry rock and made firm the sand. . . .

This is the subject matter of *The Waste Land,* but not the imagery. The fountains, the spring, the dry rock, and the sand are general conditions of nature without particularity. By contrast, the wastes of the earlier poetry are created with particularity and with dramatic intensity which belongs to the personae: "the torchlight red on sweaty faces," "The road winding above among the mountains," "Sweat is dry and feet are in the sand," "Dead mountain mouth of carious teeth that cannot spit," and "red sullen faces sneer and snarl/ From doors of mudcracked houses." Nothing in *Ash-Wednesday* ever makes any place so concrete for the purgatorial spirit as were the furnishings of the room of the typist home at tea-time and the five particular kinds of litter as well as other and more obscene "testimony of summer nights" on the banks of the Thames.

The concreteness of the best images attaches to a figurative comparison rather than to the object actually expressing Eliot's meaning in the poem:

> the stair was dark,
> Damp, jagged, like an old man's mouth drivelling, beyond repair,
> Or the toothed gullet of an aged shark.

Unfortunately for the meaning of the poem, one senses the darkness of the stair more than its other qualities. In itself the comparison to the mouth of the old man is as vivid as any passage of *The Waste Land,* but the characteristics of the mouth do not extend the vivid concreteness of the stair. That is to say, how are the stairs jagged? How is one to visualize or to feel tactually the dampness and the drivelling of a stairway? Is there water on the floor, or is it seeping through the walls? Similarly, in visualizing the shark's gullet, one sees the shark well but forgets its likeness to the stair.

The best images of the poem do not embody, make concrete,

the major theme of the poem—purgatorial penance. The old man's mouth and the toothed gullet of the shark in the passage belong in the Waste Land more than they belong in a poem of penance. They suggest Hell and the tortures of Hell more than they describe a soul working its way to salvation through purgatory.

The best images of the poem fail in another way by praising the beauties of the flesh more concretely than they praise the wonders of the spirit. In Part III of the poem, the speaker remembers a figure like Pan and the pleasures of the flesh.

> And beyond the hawthorn blossom and a pasture scene
> The broadbacked figure drest in blue and green
> Enchanted the maytime with an antique flute.
> Blown hair is sweet, brown hair over the mouth blown,
> Lilac and brown hair. . . .

Although the sensuousness conveyed here is a bit general compared to many passages in the early poems, the hair has specificity. It is blown, blown in shape and position until it covers the mouth; it is brown; it belongs to an outdoor world of the wind; and its natural perfume is suggested by its being lilac. But the concrete fleshliness of the hair and of the passage suggest not purgatory, not the refinement of the spirit, but the very fleshly world and the lusts for which the soul is suffering purgatory.

In Part VI of the poem, the last, the speaker for an entire stanza dwells on his memories of the past. The imagery runs the gamut of all the senses: sight, taste, tactual feeling, sound, and odor. Again, however, he succeeds only in creating a physical world of the flesh, and the world of the spirit in this poem of purgation remains vague, abstract, general. One might almost conclude that the spirit is unwilling while the flesh is strong. Whatever the reason, Eliot was not able to make his poetry of belief so concrete as his poetry of doubt. Apparently, considering the problems of the modern language which Eliot himself defined well, the poetic vehicle which embodies a sensuous impression comes to a believing poet with much greater difficulty than to the skeptical poet and the poet of the flesh—if it comes to the modern believing poet at all.

The different *Ariel Poems* exhibit imagery with a wide range in concreteness and abstractness. The most concrete as well as the most damatic is the first, "Journey of the Magi." The speaker, the Magus, first recalls how hardships made the Wise Men regret soft pleasures of the past, such as "the silken girls bringing sherbet." But his account of the hardships of the journey is especially poetic in the way he re-creates his difficulty in his speech. Stark nouns and active present participles and ugly adjectives—these combined with numerous *and*'s (two per line), regularly spaced caesuras, and the monotony of his list communicate the feeling of the Magus. The reality of the journey is comparable to that of a marching army in *A Farewell to Arms.*

> Then the camel men cursing and grumbling
> And running away, and wanting their liquor and women,
> And the night-fires going out, and the lack of shelters,
> And the cities hostile and the towns unfriendly
> And the villages dirty and charging high prices. . . .

After this account of all the difficulties of the long journey in the winter, the speaker re-creates two particular places, "a temperate valley" and "a tavern with vine-leaves over the lintel,/ Six hands at an open door dicing for pieces of silver/ And feet kicking the empty wineskins."

Only in the last stanza of "Journey of the Magi" does the Magus turn from the arduous travels to the question of the significance of the birth of Christ. But his meditations years after his journey are wholly dramatic, and rhythms of his speech are strange as well as personal to him:

> but set down
> This set down
> This: were we led all that way for
> Birth or Death?

The contrast between the exactness of the imagery describing the journey and the generality and abstraction of the last stanza is perfectly appropriate to the theme of the poem. The Magus never knows the full meaning of the birth which he witnessed; he has not witnessed the life of Christ, the Crucifixion, and the Resurrection.

Although "Journey of the Magi" is the most dramatic of the *Ariel Poems* and the imagery is most relevant to theme and most concrete, "Animula" and "Marina" are also concrete. ("A Song for Simeon" is as dramatic as these two but almost as devoid of images as *Ash-Wednesday.*) The "simple soul" of "Animula" sees concrete objects: "the sunlit pattern on the floor/ And running stags around a silvery tray. . . ." These embody the sensuous imagery of this world but also suggest a Lost Paradise, a previous existence of the soul like that in Wordsworth's "Intimations Ode." And the suggestion by the image of a mythical and spiritual world beyond the ken of the child does not diminish the sensuousness. "Marina" is notable for the dramatic and spiritual ecstasy of the old man who has found his long-lost daughter. Most of the images of the poem are somewhat general. There are, however, some glimpses of hard reality: "Bowsprit cracked with ice and paint cracked with heat." And as in "Animula" vivid details suggest the inexplicable: "And scent of pine and the woodthrush singing through the fog."

Eliot's discursiveness in *Ash-Wednesday,* his lack of imagery, the new lyrical subjectivism instead of the objectivity of drama—these characteristics are not all of the poetry. The general style of the poem has not been described. Critics have called it names. The "beauty of its sound" "is capable of making an instantaneous impression." [29] The poem suggests "renovated decorums of the impersonal English language." [30] Quotations of prayers in the poem "are snatches of familiar phrases which attain a powerful impact because of their familiarity and also because they are used as entreaties of a soul in travail." [31] Finally, the style is based upon "liturgical language and rhythms"; [32] it "shows an extraordinary relaxation; it is highly repetitive, and much of the repetition has an

29. Matthiessen, p. 114.

30. Kenner, p. 262.

31. Sister M. Cleophas, *"Ash Wednesday:* The *Purgatorio* in Modern Mode," *Comparative Literature,* 11 (Fall 1959), 334.

32. Genevieve W. Foster, "The Archetypal Imagery of T. S. Eliot," *PMLA,* 60 (1945), 580.

incantatory effect." [33] Statements of this kind do not help the inquiring reader. The critics have said what they felt, but they have not shown the cause of the feeling in the poem itself, and their labels do not help the reader to share the pleasure. Granted that the poem is liturgy, what is the poetry in liturgy? Even one who shares Eliot's Christian faith and who has read *Ash-Wednesday* carefully and then read of the liturgy in the poem may still be unable to answer the question. If the best poetic quality of *Ash-Wednesday* lies in its liturgy, the critics in on the secret have named the accomplishment but not defined it.

33. Gardner, p. 101.

6

The Word without Flesh in the *Four Quartets*

T. S. Eliot's last substantial poem, the *Four Quartets* (or its four parts) is regarded by various critics as his "masterpiece," [1] "a precarious unobtrusive masterpiece," [2] a poem which is "unique and essentially inimitable," [3] "the ideal of poetic language which best suits his genius," [4] "Mr. Eliot's finest poetry to date," "his greatest poem," [5] "the greatest of his poems and among the great poems of his time" (the poetry is so exciting to this critic that he believes that "the lines fondled" him), [6] "some of the most moving

1. Philip R. Headings, *T. S. Eliot,* Twayne's United States Authors Series (New York: Twayne Publishers, 1964), p. 119.

2. Hugh Kenner, *The Invisible Poet: T. S. Eliot* (New York: McDowell, Obolensky, 1959), pp. 301–302.

3. Helen Gardner, *The Art of T. S. Eliot* (New York: E. P. Dutton & Co., Inc., 1950), p. 55.

4. C. L. Wrenn, "T. S. Eliot and the Language of Poetry," *Thought,* 32 (Summer 1957), 245.

5. M. C. Bradbrook, *T. S. Eliot* (London: Longmans, Green and Co., 1950, 1951), p. 27. John Crowe Ransom, "Gerontion," *The Sewanee Review,* 74 (Spring 1966), 391.

6. Herbert Howarth, *Notes on Some Figures Behind T. S. Eliot* (Boston: Houghton Mifflin, 1964), pp. 120–121.

poetry that English literature has known," [7] "creative theology," [8] "a great lyric of history," a poem which contains "the most satisfying sequence of negations in the English language," [9] "a cold aspic of abstractions" but "probably the best abstract ruminative verse ever written," [10] "one of the great defenses of poetry in the English language," [11] "probably the best poem of our time." [12]

Other critics see the poem or parts of it in very different terms: as, in part, an apology for Eliot's earlier racial views,[13] "mere talkativeness" "spoiled by argument," [14] "simply rather a bad poem," [15] "philosophical abstraction without poetic content," "a long, very bad piece of writing," [16] "a versified tractate," [17] "all too much a long muttering, with few flashes of vivid speech," [18] a poem of "abstract generality." [19] Much of it is written in a "new 'flat' style,"

7. B. Rajan, "The Unity of the Quartets," in B. Rajan, *T. S. Eliot: A Study of His Writings by Several Hands* (London: D. Dobson, 1949), p. 95.

8. Grover Smith Jr., *T. S. Eliot's Poetry and Plays: A Study in Sources and Meaning* (Chicago: University of Chicago Press, 1956), p. 282.

9. Eric Thompson, *T. S. Eliot: The Metaphysical Perspective* (Carbondale: Southern Illinois University Press, 1963), p. 115.

10. John Frederick Nims, "Greatness in Moderation," *Saturday Review,* 46 (October 19, 1963), 27.

11. Thompson, p. 81.

12. Randall Jarrell, "Introduction," William Carlos Williams, *Selected Poems,* The New Classics Series (New York: New Directions Books, 1949), p. xiii.

13. Oscar Cargill, "Mr. Eliot Regrets. . . ," *The Nation,* 184 (February 23, 1957), 172.

14. David Daiches, "Some Aspects of T. S. Eliot," *College English,* 9 (December 1947), pp. 121, 122.

15. Donald Davie, "T. S. Eliot: The End of an Era," *The Twentieth Century,* 159 (April 1956), 350.

16. Karl Shapiro, *In Defense of Ignorance* (New York: Random House, 1960), pp. 55, 56.

17. Rossell Hope Robbins, *The T. S. Eliot Myth* (New York: H. Schuman, 1951), p. 183.

18. Edmund Wilson, " 'Miss Buttle' and 'Mr. Eliot,' " *The New Yorker,* 34 (May 24, 1958), 149.

19. F. R. Leavis, *Education and the University: A Sketch for an 'English School'* (London: Chatto & Windus, 1943), p. 99.

"like having a lyric plus a prose commentary on that lyric in a single poem. . . ." [20]

The *Four Quartets,* then, is regarded by some as Eliot's masterpiece and by others as the worst of his major efforts. Language, style, and imagery are major points of contention. The adverse critics generally use little praise in damning the abstruseness, and the praisers find a variety of defenses. One remarkable justification of the poem maintains that the abstractions of philosophical poetry become more perceptual than the sensuously apprehensible. "Eliot has found a way," one anthology argues, "to make the most abstruse material concrete and immediate" in this "lyrical and reflective poetry." [21] The abstractions, Herbert Howarth maintains, lose their abstractness in a mysterious way: "They are unexpected; they are a powerful attempt to express the lack of sensation, the lack of care about sensation; they have, one might almost say, the sensation of nonsensation." [22] And for Rajan, Eliot makes "philosophic terms more solid and tangible than objects." [23] He has thus transcended semantics: if the word *apple* for a semanticist is not the thing apple, Eliot's philosophic terms are more "solid and tangible" than an apple or indeed than iron. And for Raymond Preston the same transsubstantiation miraculously occurs. In context in the *Four Quartets* an "apparently abstract" statement "can stand as solid as stone. . . ." [24]

A few critics do not need to prove that the abstract can be concrete. They find passages of outstanding particularity in the poem. For D. E. S. Maxwell, "Idea and image are, in the poetry, inseparable," [25] and the sea in "The Dry Salvages" is more directly

20. Curtis B. Bradford, "Journeys to Byzantium," *The Virginia Quarterly Review,* 25 (Spring 1949), 219.

21. M. L. Rosenthal and A. J. M. Smith, *Exploring Poetry* (New York: The Macmillan Company, 1955), p. 701.

22. Howarth, p. 220.

23. Rajan, p. 82.

24. Raymnod Preston, *"Four Quartets" Rehearsed: A Commentary on T. S. Eliot's Cycle of Poems* (New York: Sneed & Ward, 1947), p. 22.

25. D. E. S. Maxwell, *The Poetry of T. S. Eliot* (London: Routledge & Kegan Paul, 1952), p. 167.

observed than in the "Fire Sermon" in *The Waste Land*. Elizabeth Drew sees "the clearest pictures" in the poem.[26] The "return to imagery in *The Dry Salvages,*" Helen Gardner asserts, "comes with wonderful power and force. . . ." [27] Other arguments describe artistic achievements which are due to the poet's deliberate avoidance of particularity in the poem. Eliot circumvents "the image in the elusive pursuit of essence." [28] The place in "Burnt Norton" is not particular because its vague universality allows it to depict the " 'private world' of each one of us." [29] Similarly, the images are not so much beauty as they "are evocative of inarticulate spiritual feelings," [30] and consequently "truth and beauty are not formally one." The "blurred, greyed, flickered images" are regarded as appropriate to content.[31]

Objections to discursiveness and vagueness are brief but numerous. Karl Shapiro protests "the metaphysical abstraction," the "diction devoid of both image and music." [32] For John Frederick Nims, the "longing for beyondness" in the poem "is quixotic: like wishing to live without a body." [33] The lack of particular imagery seems to be the cause of the distaste of Clive Sansom: "There are long stretches which are too much the product of the purely intellectual, philosophizing part of the mind, and are rhythmical prose rather than poetry." [34] Rossell Hope Robbins regards the poem as "propagan-

26. Elizabeth Drew, *T. S. Eliot: The Design of His Poetry* (New York: Charles Scribner's Sons, 1949), p. 154.

27. Gardner, p. 40.

28. A. Kingsley Weatherhead applies Allen Tate's words to Eliot. *"Four Quartets:* Setting Love in Order," *Wisconsin Studies in Contemporary Literature,* 3 (Spring-Summer 1962), 33.

29. Gardner, p. 58.

30. Anthony Thorlby, "The Poetry of 'Four Quartets,' " *The Cambridge Journal,* 5 (February 1952), 294.

31. Arnold D. Drew, "Hints and Guesses in *'Four Quartets,'* " *University* of *Kansas City Review,* 20 (Spring 1954), 173

32. Shapiro, pp. 55, 56.

33. Nims, p. 27.

34. Clive Sansom, *The Poetry of T. S. Eliot* (Text of a Lecture to the Speech Fellowship, 18 May 1946; London: Oxford University Press, 1947), p. 27.

da" rather than a description of an "objective world." [35] D. S. Savage has a similar objection: "the moralist in Eliot has developed somewhat at the expense of the aesthete," and the "generalized image" suggests "strained impotence." [36] David Daiches describes the poetry after *The Waste Land* as exhibiting "a more relaxed style, a less concentrated use of imagery, even a more discursive and argumentative diction." [37]

This brief summary of an amazing quantity of scholarship and criticism suggests unresolvable dissension about the poetry of the *Four Quartets.* Judgments have been confirmed and sentences passed. But there are some serious problems in the criticism. The *Four Quartets,* I believe, has not been adequately examined in terms of Eliot's own early criticism. His career altogether reverses itself. Whether good or bad, the art of his later poems is almost an exact contradiction of his early theory and practice. Indeed, if he could have read his own late poetry early in his career without knowing that it was his own, the *Four Quartets* would have been a good example of what he was revolting against. "What Eliot's theories and examples tried to demonstrate," E. P. Bollier writes, "was that poetry could be personal without being confessional, passionate without being emotional or sentimental, intellectual without being philosophical." [38] The fact and the object and the persona were the sole concerns of the better literature written during Eliot's early career. The fact or the object could be regarded as a possible representation of an abstract faith or evil, although one could never be able to articulate exactly what the object and the fact represented. "Ideas are, then, in things"; Frederick Hoffman summarized, "there are no ideas *but* in things. This does not mean that ideas do not belong in poetry; only that they do not *overtly* belong there but should be developed from the particulars talking among them-

35. Robbins, p. 182.

36. D. S. Savage, "The Orthodoxy of T. S. Eliot," in Leonard Unger, *T. S. Eliot* (New York: Rinehart & Company, Inc., 1948), pp. 138, 141.

37. Daiches, p. 120.

38. E. P. Bollier, "T. S. Eliot and John Donne: A Problem in Criticism," *Tulane Studies in English,* 9 (1959), 105.

selves."[39] Thus Eliot strove "to reunite thought and feeling—to transform an 'observation into a state of mind. . . .' "[40]

In *On Poetry and Poets* Eliot described the hopelessness of trying to find a language to deal with religious feeling. "When religious feeling disappears, the words in which men have struggled to express it become meaningless."[41] The generalization is sweeping. Only the objects were left. They might implicitly convey a religious feeling which could not be articulated. This statement denies the possibility of the very vocabulary of the *Four Quartets.* By describing a particular object, the poet might convey through art; he could not assert. Thus Eliot had argued in 1917 that "the abstract thought of nearly all poets is mediocre enough, and often second-hand."[42] And belief was like abstraction. Eliot doubted "whether belief proper enters into the activity of a great poet, *qua* poet."[43] The objective correlative itself was at least in part an attempt to suggest feeling through object and art vehicle, whether image or form. Without an object, the "poetry tends to create a self-sufficient world of words, which does not even 'depend upon some world which it simulates.' "[44] The world of the *Four Quartets* is not created in images. The late Eliot tried to make the reader think the ideas. Poetry should create "a particular ploughman, milkmaid, and shepherd" rather than "concepts of ploughman, milkmaid, and shepherd."[45] A concept is an abstraction rather than poetry, an idea rather than a feeling derived from an actual person.

Based on Eliot's early principles, then, a poet might give up image in a dramatic or narrative poem, might give up personae in a lyric

39. Frederick J. Hoffman, *The Twenties: American Writing in the Postwar Decade* (New York: Viking Press, 1955), p. 181.

40. William Van O'Connor, *Sense and Sensibility in Modern Poetry* (Chicago: The University of Chicago Press, 1948), p. 3.

41. Eliot, "The Social Function of Poetry," *On Poetry and Poets* (New York: The Noonday Press, 1957), p. 15.

42. Eliot, "Reflections on Contemporary Poetry," *The Egoist,* 4 (October 1917), 133.

43. Eliot, "Shakespeare and the Stoicism of Seneca," *Selected Essays,* New Edition (New York: Harcourt, Brace and Company, 1932, 1950), p. 118.

44. Northrop Frye, *T. S. Eliot* (Edinburgh: Oliver and Boyd, 1963), p. 32.

45. Eliot, "Milton I," *On Poetry and Poets*, p. 159.

poem. He could not, however, give up particular image and drama and individual personae and still have poetry. Without these three things, he would have only rhythm and argument and concept and philosophy. He would have the *Four Quartets*. Now the disputes come because many critics do not accept Eliot's early principles. Indeed, some accept them for the early poems and deny them for the later ones. Eliot himself apparently underwent a great change. In his second essay on Milton, he argued that the poet was right in not being concrete and particular in treating his subject: "This limitation of visual power, like Milton's limited interest in human beings, turns out to be not merely a negligible defect, but a positive virtue, when we visit Adam and Eve in Eden. Just as a higher degree of characterization of Adam and Eve would have been unsuitable, so a more vivid picture of the earthly Paradise would have been less paradisiacal." [46] Again Eliot in 1947 is justifying the kind of poetry coming from his workshop. In contradiction to the standards of his own early criticism, he is admitting that earthly imagery cannot describe the good and spiritual and paradisiacal so well as it does the earthly and the evil. One who accepts his early tenets must still believe that in his second essay on Milton and in the *Four Quartets* Eliot is confronting the limitations of poetry of belief in our age. He is really defending a poetry of belief on religious rather than artistic grounds.

One real critical question, then, is the degree of concreteness in the *Four Quartets*. How carnal is the incarnation of the spirit? Strange as it may seem, the theory and the practice of the literature of the twenties might be expressed in religious terms: there had to be a new incarnation if any spirit were to be apprehended just as the Logos, the Word, was made flesh so that the Divine might be apprehensible to the world of the flesh. Jesus Christ came into the world not merely to suffer in the place of man but also to enable man to perceive God through fleshly evidence. And this is the essential process of poetry as well as of religion and of the mystical literature which tends "to conceive divine love in human terms." [47] Elizabeth Drew correctly sees Incarnation as the key to the success-

46. Eliot, "Milton II," *On Poetry and Poets*, p. 178.
47. Bollier, p. 114.

ful imagery of the *Four Quartets.* "Capitalized, Incarnation is to our Christian civilization, the ultimate symbol of the union of sense and spirit, the resolution of the paradoxes of life and death, time and the timeless; a symbol of totality, of wholeness, to which all time-experience is relative." [48] One standard by which art may be measured, then, though not the only one, is the degree to which the carnal, the flesh, the world of objects and the senses, is suggested in the images. Yet the Christian poet wishes to convey more than the world of the senses. He redoubles his complexity, attempts to add depth and mystery. Even the disbeliever still longing for some sort of faith may wish him success. By association, by tradition, by the suggestive and haunting nature of the image itself the spirit may be suggested in the carnal.

How ready to hand are the images for man's depravity! The sensuous image, being fleshly, can exactly represent the evils of the flesh, which in turn are perfect symbolic representations of more abstract evils of the soul. Apprehensible images are worldly, yet the poet finds that they are the only available means of symbolizing God and the mystical union of the soul with the divine. The whole point about mystical experience is that it is not physical or sensuous. Only two methods are open to the mystical poet: he must sensuously use the tainted flesh, or he must seek to convey the inexpressible by abstraction, without symbol and image. And the difficulty of this latter process is that it omits a necessary level of poetic experience.

The wonder of the better poetry of the *Four Quartets* is that Eliot does occasionally convey the sense of the divine through the use of fleshly images. The failure of the poem is that he seldom accomplishes so much.

Concreteness and particularity may be revealed in images (objects, things, the sensuously apprehensible), in personae, and in places. Obviously, a poem may contain these three and still be general and lack concreteness. How may the critic determine the degree of particularity? He often feels specificity and asserts its presence even when his judgment is so subjective that it cannot be communicated to his reader or a fellow critic. Elizabeth Drew, for

48. Drew, p. 187.

example, refers to "the wonderful complex imagery" [49] of the following lines:

> The crying shadow in the funeral dance,
> The loud lament of the disconsolate chimera.

The tone coloring, the sound, of the lines may be more wonderful than the imagery. Who can recreate in his auditory imagination the cry of the imaginary chimera? And if the lament of the beast is not heard, does the line contain an image at all? If Miss Drew hears the cry, she cannot suggest the nature of the hearing to another reader.

Places, personae, and images—these are the poet's opportunities for concreteness. The theme to be objectified in the poetry is the mystical union of the soul with God. In the *Four Quartets* Eliot bases his theme on the works of Saint John of the Cross and on Heraclitus. These may be background, good preparation for the reading of the poem; but they are in a sense only preliminaries. They stand outside the poem and separate from it, and the ultimate knowledge of the poem is simply a matter of understanding and appreciating the way Eliot's art expresses his meaning. Themes and images are organized on the basis of paradoxes and oxymorons which make the flesh spiritual and the spiritual fleshly. The main point to comprehend about the theme is that in this world it is never wholly comprehensible. Ultimate meanings in poetry are unutterable just as in theology words cannot describe the Word of God. The poet would like to yoke by paradox together worlds so separate that they never can possibly unite. "Then, since the order whereby the soul acquires knowledge is through forms and images of created things, and the natural way wherein it acquires this knowledge and wisdom is through the senses, it follows that, for God to raise up the soul to supreme knowledge, and to do so with sweetness, He must begin to work from the lowest and extreme end of the senses of the soul. . . ." [50] Matter without spiritual im-

49. Drew, p. 161.

50. Saint John, *Ascent of Mount Carmel, The Complete Works of Saint John of the Cross,* trans. E. Allison Peers (London: Burns, Oates & Washbourne, Ltd., 1934), I, 139.

plications does not exist in terms of the religious theme of the poem. Spirit without matter is impossible in this world and in the poetry of this world. Spirit and matter, consequently, must always exist together in some kind of tension. The *Four Quartets* treats rhythms of the spiritual, of Gods, spirits, the occult, the heavens, astronomy, astrology. And these in turn are represented by the rhythms and cycles of the natural world: the seasons, the times of the day, different places, the four elements, the body, flowers, plants, and animals. As these rhythms blend, they are joined in paradox, in hundreds of seemingly irreconcilable things: fact/fantasy; matter/spirit; here/not here; timeless/time; occupation/no occupation; never/always; hope/despair; end/the unending; loitering/hurried; soundless/wailing; England/nowhere; pole/tropic; frost/fire; and so on.

Of the five senses, hearing is probably the most effective one in a poet's attempts to make the Divine apprehensible to man. The ear may perceive most sharply and exactly and still communicate to the mind little information about the totality of a thing. A touch in complete darkness conveys texture, moisture or dryness, temperature, and direction or position. Smell shares some of the mystery of sound. The smell of sulphur, for example, traditionally suggests the demonic. But smell is an underdeveloped sense in the human being. A sound may register sharply upon the mind while the source of it is not perceived at all. For this reason, perhaps, sound is the sense impression which is most often used as evidence of the supernatural. Some knowable thing clearly exists and makes the perceiver sharply aware of its presence, but the other qualities of the thing remain as unknown to us as God. Sound, then, is used to suggest the supernatural (ghost or God) in drama, poetry, and motion pictures. In cheap television horror shows the presence of the mysterious is suggested by weird sound effects. The mournful sound of the breaking string in Chekhov's *The Cherry Orchard* is an almost perfect example of the creation of mystery through sound.

Music and psychology may help to explain how sounds may reveal something of the transcendant to man. The ancient concept of the music of the spheres suggested that "the universal life must reveal itself as something audible rather than visible."[51] Melody, wrote Sir Thomas Browne, is "an Hieroglyphical and shadowed lesson of the whole World and creatures of God."[52] And music, according to Herbert Spencer, suggests "an incomprehensible secret," "indefinite expressions of an unknown ideal life."[53] The mystic and the materialistic psychologist may at least agree on the difficult subject of the suggestiveness of music even when they do not agree on the cause. Music, says Victor Zuckerkandl, "does cross a decisive frontier; . . . we find its most essential nature in this crossing, this transcendence—all who have ever thought about music are of one mind, as indeed they are too in finding that this transcendence occurs nowhere else in the same way, with the same directness."[54] And finally, music or sound is directly related to religious symbol: "Great as the difference between musical tone and religious symbol may be, in this one essential point they are alike: in both, a force that transcends the material is immediately manifested in a material datum."[55]

The psychological effect of music and the suggestions of the supernatural by music are subjects of basic significance in the study of the *Four Quartets.* Eliot's awareness of the explicit connection between poetry and sound or music is indicated in the very title of the poem, in the forms of the parts, in the verse rhythms, and (the main subject here) in the imagery.

Mystical poetry may suggest the supernatural in its treatment of sounds while at the same time the images of the poetry suggest the particularity of certain sounds and the rhythm of the tone coloring may attempt to convey the sound also. If a poet could achieve harmony of image, poetic sound, and the sound described—and if all of these might suggest mystical union of the soul with God—surely the poem would be a great one for any age. In the *Four Quartets* the use of certain images of sound to suggest the transcen-

51. Victor Zuckerkandl, *Sound and Symbol: Music and the External World,* trans. Willard R. Trask, Bollingen Series XLIV (New York: Pantheon Books, 1956), 2.

52. Quoted in Zuckerkandl, p. 147.

53. Quoted in Zuckerkandl, p. 5.

54. Zuckerkandl, p. 4.

55. Zuckerkandl, p. 69; see also pp. 42, 71, 23.

dent is one of the most significant achievements. Those used most frequently are bells, birds, the sea, and the horn. Such dissimilar artists as Thomas Wolfe ("The bell rang under the sea." "Far-forested, the horn-note wound.") and William Wordsworth (the birds, the tabor's sound, cataracts, Trumpets, Echoes—all in the third stanza of the "Intimations Ode") have used the same kinds of images to suggest concrete sensuous experience of the ineffable. There are other precedents and parallels: bells have been used to summon gods, to accompany sacred rites, and to drive off demons and evil spirits.

Eliot concentrates upon the image of the bell in six different passages of the *Four Quartets*, four of them in "The Dry Salvages." The bells which are not in this section of the poem appear more as concepts than images. In "Little Gidding" the thoughts of Charles I and Milton and others of the past do not "ring the bell backward," a signal of alarm.[56] In "Burnt Norton," "Time and the bell have buried the day." Associated with time and mortality, destroyers of life and "the day," the bell here seems to be a funeral bell, and the image of its sound, its tolling, is not so apparent as its meaning. Images of the actual sounds of bells, then, occur only in four brief passages in "The Dry Salvages":

> And under the oppression of the silent fog
> The tolling bell
> Measures time not our time, rung by the unhurried
> Ground swell. . . . (I 36–39)

> And the ground swell, that is and was from the beginning,
> Clangs
> The bell. (I 48–50)

> There is the final addition, . . .
> In a drifting boat with a slow leakage,
> The silent listening to the undeniable
> Clamour of the bell of the last annunciation. (II 13, 16–18)

> [Sailors unable to hear] the sound of the sea bell's
> Perpetual angelus. (IV 14–15)

56. George S. Tyack, *A Book about Bells* (London: William Andrews & Co., 1898), p. 252.

In every one of these passages the bells are mediums between the mortal and the immortal. The forces which ring the bells are not the ordinary and expected motions of the sea. The bells here ring to a ground swell, a phenomenon caused by an earthquake or a long-continued gale, so long indeed that it has the eternity of God —"that is and was from the beginning." Rung more by supernatural than natural forces, Eliot's bells are known and unknown, heard and not heard. The very sounds suggested are extremely effective in the tone coloring and in the onomatopoeia of "tolling," "clangs," "clamour," and perhaps "perpetual angelus." But the bells are also obscured to the mortal, who may not perceive immortal truth directly. The fog not only hides the bell but also oppresses its sound. Unseen and remotely heard, the bell may suggest not only the impossibility of communicating directly with the immortal but also the presence of the divine in the physical world. Eliot's bells, then, in both obscuring and revealing the divine share the paradox of the incarnation and of the world of the spirit.

Like the imagery of the bells, that of the birds in the *Four Quartets* is a link between two worlds. But meaning predominates and does not spring directly from the sensuous fact. Even when there is the suggested rhythm of the song of the bird, the didactic message prevails over any musical sound of a bird call:

> Quick, said the bird, find them, find them. . . .

And

> Go, said the bird. . . .
> Go, go, go said the bird. . . .

Reflectively, the speaker of the poem admonishes himself to "Wait for the early owl," perhaps suggesting no more than the traditional meaning of wisdom. In a passage on sounds associated with the sea, Eliot merely mentions the seagull; and the vague image perhaps conjures up visual mystery, but no sound so effective as the hideous suggestions of mortality in the description of the sea-fowl in Melville's *Billy Budd*:

> So near the hull did they come, that the stridor or bony creak of their gaunt double-jointed pinions was audible. As the ship under light airs

passed on, leaving the burial spot astern, they still kept circling it low down with the moving shadow of their outstretched wings and the cracked requiem of their cries.[57]

The most effective image of a bird in the poem presents soundless flight:

> After the kingfisher's wing
> Has answered light to light, and is silent. . . .

Strangely, the antithesis of silence here is not sound but reflected light, an image of vision. The mystery evolves not from an exact perception of a physical image but from a weird combination of two kinds of perception, perhaps more meaningful than exact. The strangest images of birds in the poem are that of "the dark dove with the flickering tongue" and that when "The dove descending breaks the air. . . ." These associate the appearance of the Holy Ghost in the form of a dove and the German Luftwaffe over London during World War II. Thematically, the awesomeness of God is associated with the death-dealing fires of war planes. Psychologically, the association may be realized more on the intellectual level than on the levels of emotion and visual perception. Eliot's use of the sounds of birds is never so effective as his use of bells to link mortal with the eternal. Sensuously, not one of the birds in the poem is so well realized as the "full-throated ease" of Keats's nightingale, which suggests the volume of sound as well as the visual image of the pulsing throat of the singing bird. Or so particular and euphonious as "The murmurous haunt of flies on summer leaves." And no sound of a bird in the *Four Quartets* is so haunting as the "plaintive anthem" which

> fades
> Past the near meadows, over the still stream,
> Up the hill-side; and now 'tis buried deep
> In the next valley-glades. . . .

57. Herman Melville, *Billy Budd, Sailor: (An Inside Narrative)*, Ed. by Harrison Hayford and Merton M. Sealts Jr. (Chicago: The University of Chicago Press, 1962), p. 127.

Perhaps one way to measure the degree of concreteness and incarnation in the *Four Quartets* is to compare the poem with Eliot's earlier poems and with other works on similar subjects. If the imagery of bells is Eliot's greatest sensuous accomplishment in the poem, if that of birds might have been as good, other images are extremely vague. One of the most concrete passages is the description of the Mississippi River, which Eliot had known as a child in St. Louis. "The Dry Salvages" begins with the general assertion that the speaker does "not know much about gods," and the river is introduced immediately as a "strong brown god"—one whom the speaker presumably does know. It does have human or superhuman attributes: it is "sullen, untamed and intractable,/ Patient to some degree. . . ." The river passes from the godly to an abstraction in the mind of civilization and in that of the poet without ever becoming a river. It is a "problem confronting the builder of bridges./ The problem once solved, the brown god is almost forgotten/ By the dwellers in cities"—and by the poet. Only the "rhythm" of the stream is present in the domestic urban world.

The godliness of the river is much more apparent to Huckleberry Finn and to the convict in Faulkner's "Old Man" than it is to the speaker of Eliot's poem. The superhuman quality is simply asserted discursively in the *Four Quartets*, but it is an experienced narrative fact to Faulkner's convict. That difference might be simply the difference of literary form, the subjectivity of a lyric and the event of a novel. But Faulkner's convict regards the river as truly supernatural in the most elemental sense of the word. Only the thin planks of the bottom of the boat separate him from this super-reality of the river. He "seemed to feel run through the very insentient fabric of the skiff a current of eager gleeful vicious incorrigible wilfulness. . . ." The personifications are frightening as well as intimate. The convict is not so far removed from the river as Eliot's "dwellers in cities." But Eliot's failure is that the river seems no more real to him as poet than it did to the unperceptive "worshippers of the machine" whom he condemned.

The same contrast is apparent in Mark Twain's great novel of the Mississippi. Huck Finn and Jim not only pass through a night in darkness on the flooding river, but also know it tactually in serenity. They swim in the river, sit on its sandy bottom, and watch

> the daylight come. Not a sound anywheres—perfectly still—just like the whole world was asleep, only sometimes the bullfrogs a-cluttering, maybe. The first thing to see, looking away over the water, was a kind of dull line—that was the woods on t'other side; you couldn't make nothing else out; then a pale place in the sky; then more paleness spreading around; then the river softened up away off, and warn't black any more, but gray; you could see little dark spots drifting along ever so far away—trading scows, and such things; and long black streaks—rafts. . . .[58]

Because of the reality of the sensuous experience of the river, Huck and Jim know it first hand. By assertion Eliot argues that the unnamed river of the *Four Quartets* "is within us. . . ." Truly the river is within Huck Finn because he knows and names its realities and senses the abstractions. He does not state the meanings as propositions.

In Eliot's earlier poetry he had demonstrated that he knew the difference between a river and a meaning. The Thames of *The Waste Land* in its poetic quality resembles the rivers of Mark Twain and William Faulkner rather than the abstraction of the *Four Quartets*. The river of the earlier poem is charged with all the symbolic meanings Eliot intended to give the Mississippi, but the meaning is conveyed through tactual images ("sweats," "oil," "tar"), images of sound and motion ("drift," "wash"), and many images of sight:

> The river sweats
> Oil and tar
> The barges drift
> With the turning tide
> Red sails
> Wide
> To leeward, swing on the heavy spar.
> The barges wash
> Drifting logs
> Down Greenwich reach
> Past the Isle of Dogs.

58. Mark Twain, *The Adventures of Huckleberry Finn* (Hartford: The American Publishing Company, 1899), p. 161.

And the poetic creation of a stream is also successful in "Journey of the Magi," when the Magus remembers "a running stream and a water-mill beating the darkness." Truly the contrasts between the different kinds of imagery of streams in Eliot's early poems and his later ones illustrate the difference between (in his own critical terms) feeling thought "as immediately as the odour of a rose" and "abstract thought" without poetic embodiment.

The next stanza of "The Dry Salvages" turns to the sea and begins with the suggestion that it will be more objectively treated: "The river is within us, the sea is all about us. . . ." But the images become only slightly more concrete while the thought remains obtrusive. Particulars such as "The starfish, the hermit crab, the whale's backbone" are "hints of earlier and other creation" more than sensuous embodiments of the hints. The "torn seine,/ The shattered lobsterpot, the broken oar,/ And the gear of foreign dead men" are a clutter which resembles that on the Thames in the summer of *The Waste Land*: "Empty bottles, sandwich papers,/ Silk handkerchiefs, cardboard boxes, cigarette ends/ Or other testimony of summer nights." But the hint of generality is more obvious in the sea of "The Dry Salvages." There are fewer objects in the sea; the objects are described as "our losses"—a specific interpretation rather than embodiment; and the poet's vision fades into generality in "the gear of foreign dead men." What gear? What kind of foreigners? Indeed, what men? None so particular as the suggestion of discarded prophylactics ("testimony of summer nights") or as Mr. Silvero or Sweeney or the young man carbuncular.

One paradox of the literature created by the young men of letters early in this century was that they created abstract men of mind, thinkers rather than doers, but created them in a vivid poetic reality. They expressed their inadequacy in beautiful imagery, the Quentin Compsons, Darl Bundrens, Ransom's spectral lovers and his friar, Eliot's Prufrock and the old man in "Gerontion." It was almost a stretching of credulity to present such sharp perceptions in such bloodless walking dead men. The unbeliever in the early Eliot is transformed to a heroic but suffering figure in the later poems, but the late protagonist who has experienced salvation apprehends the sensuous world (the incarnation) less successfully than did the earlier lost characters. Those who presumably are saved at least seem to be unable to sense the world of the spirit.

Excluding the subjective first person, there are strikingly few characters in the *Four Quartets*. Those who appear are characterized as plural generalities: voyagers, seamen, fishermen, people, passengers, faces, women, old men, sons, and husbands. The plurals and the classifications represent types, concepts, generalities. Others appear as allegorical and religious figures without particularity: a Lady, the Queen of Heaven, a saint, a broken King, a dead master (who is so generalized that he has been identified by critics as a conglomerate portrait of many poets or by others who disagree on which one of many poets he is), a healer, a wounded surgeon, a dying nurse, a ruined millionaire, and so on.

One of Eliot's tasks in the *Four Quartets* is to present the Incarnation, the embodiment of the spiritual in the sensuous. Presumably, then, his supreme attempt as a Christian poet in this poem should be his portrait of Christ, the Incarnate God. In the poem Christ appears as a surgeon:

> The wounded surgeon plies the steel
> That questions the distempered part;
> Beneath the bleeding hands we feel
> The sharp compassion of the healer's art
> Resolving the enigma of the fever chart.

Here Eliot points out the necessity of suffering before salvation (to oversimplify), but the problem is that the suffering is more apparent than the salvation. Indeed, the difficulty of the Christian life is not so apparent in the stanza as unpleasant pain almost needlessly inflicted on the patient by this ungodlike Christ. The words *plies, steel, questions, sharp, fever chart* convey the carelessness and impersonality of a bored and overworked physician more than godliness. That little compassion which exists in the surgeon is merely asserted. Surely the surgeon is no God, no Christ Incarnate. How disillusioned Eliot's Magus would be after he had made a journey to see this Christ! If in one sense the spirit is not incarnate, in another the figure of the surgeon is too worldly to convey the meaning. To find the Christ Incarnate in Eliot's poetry, one must turn back to the Journey to Emmaus in *The Waste Land*.[59] The narrative, the dramatic situation, and the imagery—all convey the anguish of the impossibility of knowing the risen God and paradoxically the reality of an Incarnated God:

> Who is the third who walks always beside you?
> When I count, there are only you and I together
> But when I look ahead up the white road
> There is always another one walking beside you
> Gliding wrapt in a brown mantle, hooded
> I do not know whether a man or a woman
> —But who is that on the other side of you?

The *Four Quartets* is a lyrical, meditative poem written in the first person. By Eliot's earlier standards, it is personal rather than impersonal poetry. Not a word spoken by the speaker can be proved to be biographically untrue of the poet, and the biographical parallels between the lives of speaker and poet are numerous: both were air-raid wardens in London during World War II; both have ancestral backgrounds in Missouri, Massachusetts, and England; both have been poets. Although there seems to be no valid reason for differentiating between speaker and poet, critics still have considerable difficulty and many disagreements in defining the speaker and his relationship to the poet. For F. R. Leavis, "East Coker" is "personal, running even to autobiography (it is the most directly personal poem of Eliot's we have)." [60] According to Curtis B. Bradford, the protagonist "is sometimes clearly Eliot himself." [61] Anthony Thorlby "does not know what importance to attach to this invisible 'I.' " [62] Others regard the poem as impersonal and dramatic. B. H. Fussell believes that "Eliot speaks through *personae*, if only the differing voices of the anonymous 'I.' " [63] And for Hugh Kenner, Eliot mysteriously disappears more in this poem than ever before. He is "the

59. See Denis Donoghue, "T. S. Eliot's Quartets: A New Reading," *Studies*, 54 (Spring 1965), 56.

60. Leavis, p. 98.

61. Bradford, p. 216.

62. Thorlby, p. 291.

63. B. H. Fussell, "Structural Methods in Four Quartets," *ELH*, 22 (September 1955), 233.

now wholly effaced Invisible Poet, who composed the score, but is only figuratively present in the performance."[64] A conclusion of this kind seems to be possible only as a result of circuitous reasoning if the critical statement is placed side by side with a passage from the poem like the following:

> So here I am, in the middle way, having had twenty years—
> Twenty years largely wasted, the years of *l'entre deux guerres*—
> Trying to learn to use words, and every attempt
> Is a wholly new start, and a different kind of failure
> Because one has only learnt to get the better of words
> For the thing one no longer has to say, or the way in which
> One is no longer disposed to say it.

The discursive and prosaic passages without images in the *Four Quartets* have been defended in many ways. The "strength and flexibility of the metre" permits Eliot's new style;[65] the style is justified as an "attempt to approach the inexpressible, and showing the process as part of his attempt";[66] or, the "strategy . . . is to explore the more or less familiar meanings of certain words until full consciousness of the words is achieved," and "ideal associations of the meanings" result.[67]

By these standards, the *Four Quartets* is perhaps defensible as great poetry. But these are strange standards indeed for twentieth-century poetry. They contradict Eliot's own earlier theories, and they have never been stated so fully or articulated so well as the principles behind the practice of the best literary artists in this century of objectivity, impersonality, and restraint. The defenses of the *Four Quartets* move into the territories of liturgy and metrics and general ambiguity without clear and forthright admissions of change in standard. If the *Four Quartets* is great poetry by Eliot's own critical principles, the language underwent some unexpected and still undefined change in the decades between the two wars. Eliot

64. Kenner, p. 306.
65. Gardner, p. 15.
66. Anne Ridler, "A Question of Speech," in Rajan, p. 117.
67. Robert D. Wagner, "The Meaning of Eliot's Rose-Garden," *PMLA,* 69 (March 1954), 27.

himself had built up a convincing case against just such language as he uses in his later works. The generality and abstraction of his later poems should not, indeed cannot, be defended convincingly in criticism which itself is guilty of generality, abstraction, and assertion without analysis.

ERNEST HEMINGWAY

7

The Sun Also Rises and the Failure of Language

DEFEATED in his war against the Almighty and cast out of Paradise, Satan in Milton's *Paradise Lost* remembers how he fought with "fixt mind/ And high disdain, from sence of injur'd merit. . . ."

> What though the field be lost?
> All is not lost; the unconquerable Will,
> And study of revenge, immortal hate,
> And courage never to submit or yield. . . .[1]

By his own standard Satan regards himself as a just and great being:

> One who brings
> A mind not to be chang'd by Place or Time.
> The mind is its own place, and in it self
> Can make a Heav'n of Hell, a Hell of Heav'n.[2]

Wandering on the stormy heath, Shakespeare's King Lear rails until his "wits begin to turn":

1. John Milton, *Paradise Lost* in *John Milton: Complete Poems and Major Prose,* ed. by Merritt Y. Hughes (New York: Odyssey Press, 1957), p. 214.
2. Milton, p. 217.

Let the great gods,
That keep this dreadful pother o'er our heads,
Find out their enemies now. Tremble, thou wretch,
That hast within thee undivulgèd crimes,
Unwhipped of justice. Hide thee, thou bloody hand,
Thou perjured, and thou simular man of virtue
That art incestuous. Caitiff, to pieces shake,
That under covert and convenient seeming
Has practiced on man's life. Close pent-up guilts,
Rive your concealing continents and cry
These dreadful summoners grace. I am a man
More sinned against than sinning.[3]

Made impotent by World War I, Jake Barnes in *The Sun Also Rises* apparently has all the passionate longing of a vigorous male but none of the possibility of fulfillment. A mountain peak of Jake's rhetoric in a moment of supreme agony occurs when Lady Brett Ashley wires for him to come to her:

That was it. Send a girl off with one man. Introduce her to another to go off with him. Now go and bring her back. And sign the wire with love. That was it all right. I went in to lunch.[4]

Juxtaposition of passages by Milton, Shakespeare, and Hemingway produces a shocking contrast. Characters in the seventeenth-century drama and the Christian epic achieve their destinies in terms of a theological and moral order clear to the author and his contemporary reader. The character also, even an antagonist, has a high view of the rightness of his own cause. Satan and Lear can describe their terrible sufferings in utterances of agonized rhetoric. Their language expresses their views of their own plight and provides a measure of release. Jake Barnes, on the other hand, must suffer in silence: " 'Let's not talk,' " Brett tells him. " 'Talking's all bilge' " (*SAR*, p. 57). Jake is more confused and puzzled about the moral order of the world than even Satan, but no language, no rhetoric,

3. William Shakespeare, *The Tragedy of King Lear*, in *Shakespeare: The Complete Works,* ed. by G. B. Harrison (New York: Harcourt, Brace and Company, 1948, 1952), p. 1161.

4. Hemingway, *The Sun Also Rises* (New York: Charles Scribner's Sons, 1926, 1928), p. 239. Hereafter cited in text with abbreviation *SAR*.

can express his agony and provide relief. He can only endure, choke and swallow his emotions, and suggest his feelings in sardonic understatement and irony.

The theme of *The Sun Also Rises* is essentially a search for meaning despite the belief that no meaning can be significant and certain. Religion or love of God, sexual love, idealistic romance or love, patriotism or love of country—all is vanity. After belief has gone, only method remains: " 'I did not care what it was all about,' " Jake Barnes concludes. " 'All I wanted to know was how to live in it' " (*SAR*, p. 153). If this is a philosophical or moral system at all, it is entirely practical—and *a posteriori* at that. "That was morality," Jake says again; "things that made you disgusted afterward. No, that must be immorality" (*SAR*, p. 153). But Jakes does not define either morality or immorality. He arrives at no principles; "things that made you disgusted afterward" are ultimately only things. One cannot even predict the disgust. Yet "things" are the only God which Brett can believe in: giving up her young lover Romero, "deciding not to be a bitch," is "sort of what we have instead of God" (*SAR*, p. 257).

It is easy to generalize about a waste land. Not all the characters in *The Sun Also Rises* share the same beliefs and skepticisms. Although the book and the characters are expressions of the mind of Ernest Hemingway, they are not allegorical equations of aspects of his personal credo. It has been easy for reviewers to equate the moral views of Hemingway with those of his characters. The "things he writes about," according to a reviewer in *The Saturday Review of Literature*, are "scarcely worthy of the care, of the artistic integrity which he devotes to them." [5] And the *Dial*:

> If to report correctly and endlessly the vapid talk and indolent thinking of Montparnasse café idlers is to write a novel, Mr. Hemingway has written a novel. His characters are as shallow as the saucers in which they stack their daily emotions, and instead of interpreting his material —or even challenging it—he has been content merely to make a carbon copy of a not particularly significant surface of life in Paris.[6]

5. Cleveland B. Chase, *The Saturday Review of Literature*, 3 (December 11, 1926), 420.
6. *The Dial*, 82 (January 1927), 73.

These early views have persisted tenaciously. Even a recent survey of the American novel regards *The Sun Also Rises* as "a slight thing, successful . . . in teaching young people how to waste their lives." [7] Lawrence S. Morris in *The New Republic* explained the theme and the relationship of theme to technique superbly:

> The essential characteristic of our time is that it is a period without a generalization. Without a mythology, if you prefer: we have inherited a hundred mythologies, and our minds flutter among them, finding satisfaction in none. The distress we are all acutely aware of comes from our failure to realize this fact emotionally. . . . Until we are emotionally convinced that the old values are gone, we shall not begin to lay down our generalizations. We have reached the stage . . . where we must pass through Ecclesiastes before writing our Revelations. All contemporary art that is vital, that has its roots in our immediate problem, must seem destructive. It is concerned in realizing this desperate purposelessness by objectifying it.
>
> *The Sun Also Rises* is one stride toward that objectification. The clear boundaries which were formerly assumed to define motives are gone. Very well: Hemingway will not try to make use of them, and will admit in his vocabulary only words which he himself has found solid. . . . Between the lines of the hard-boiled narrative quivers an awareness of the unworded, half-grasped incomprehensibles of life.[8]

Style and language themselves become a major part of the novel. That is, the author's and the characters' very language is a part of the meaning. Since the point is a search for meaning, there is no greater certainty than sensuous images, endurance, and an unfulfilled search. The code is to have one's personal values, but not to let them show because in the absence of universal beliefs the personal may appear ridiculous. An action may be an answer to an overwhelming question, but if one meditates or articulates an answer, it proves in language to be no solution at all. A man with some kind of code or standard must hide it, as a journalist does his work: "in the newspaper business . . . it is such an important part of the ethics that you should never seem to be working" (p. 11).

Outside his fiction Hemingway was not always so implicit and

7. Edward Wagenknecht, *Cavalcade of the American Novel, from the Birth of the Nation to the Middle of the Twentieth Century* (New York: Holt, 1952), p. 369.

8. Lawrence S. Morris, "Warfare in Man and among Men," *The New Republic,* 49 (December 22, 1926), 142.

restrained. Art is often partly the implication of image or fact as contrasted to the explicitness of statement. In World War I Hemingway had a "genuine desire to serve the Allied cause." [9] In a letter he wrote, "I go to the front tomorrow. Oh, Boy!!! I'm glad I'm in it." [10] After the war he made a spectacle of himself as a wounded hero before his community and his high school in Oak Park, Illinois. He wore his uniform, carried a cane, limped, let the boys see his scars, lectured, and exhibited "a pair of shrapnel-riddled trousers." [11] Some of Hemingway's young extravagance survived the war. As a reporter for the Toronto *Star Weekly* he sounded almost like a prohibitionist in a description of a "slack lipped, white faced kid" drunk on whisky bootlegged from Canada.[12] In the *Weekly* in 1923 he condemned the European night life that he presented without comment in *The Sun Also Rises*: "a sort of strange disease," he called it, and "vulgar, ugly, sullenly dissipated," "altogether revolting." He roundly damned the absurdities of the literary life in Paris—but in the Toronto *Star Weekly* rather than in fiction. "Paris is going to pot. Seems awfully lousy. More traffic than in New York. Everybody has too much money and it's expensive as hell and after where we've been and what seen and how felt this last year there's no damn fun in drinking at a cafe with a lot of hard faced lesbians (converted ones not even real ones) and all the little fairies. . . ." [13] Later, after enjoying life as a fisherman in the Carribean, Hemingway pondered over why he should go back to the cafes and the Parisian literary life.[14]

In Hemingway's fiction and in his theories about writing he left no room for explicit statements of the author's views or those of the good characters. Like Frederic Henry, he was embarrassed by statements of value and the obscene words like "sacred, glorious,

9. Charles A. Fenton, *The Apprenticeship of Ernest Hemingway: The Early Years* (New York: Viking Press, 1954), p. 61.

10. Fenton, p. 58.

11. Fenton, pp. 70–71.

12. Hemingway, "Canuck Whiskey Pouring into U. S.," Toronto *Star Weekly,* 5 June 1920, p. 1.

13. Hemingway, "Night Life in Europe a Disease: Constantinople's Most Hectic," Toronto *Star Weekly,* 15 December 1923, p. 21.

14. Letter to Thornton Wilder, May 26, 1931. Now in Yale University Library.

and sacrifice and the expression in vain." [15] But the explicit condemnations of explicitness like this in *A Farewell to Arms* would be almost embarrassing in *The Sun Also Rises*, which is not abstract enough to condemn abstraction.

Until Hemingway abandoned the practice of being only concrete and implicit in the late 1930s, he stated the principle many times: "A Writer," he wrote in 1935, "should judge a book he finishes by the quality of the stuff he is able to cut out and still have his book intact. If he cuts out damned good stuff the chances are that what remains is better." [16] In this statement he might have had in mind his own prose or even T. S. Eliot's *The Waste Land* after it had been drastically pruned by Ezra Pound. Indeed, Hemingway's literary theory and his style might have been based on statements by Pound. "Go in fear of abstractions," Pound had written; and "Use no superfluous word, no adjective which does not reveal something." [17]

Hemingway's literary advice to the writer often seems to follow earlier dicta by T. S. Eliot. The best-known statement of the need for implicitness is embodied in the figure of an iceberg:

> If a writer of prose knows enough about what he is writing about he may omit things that he knows and the reader, if the writer is writing truly enough, will have a feeling of those things as strongly as though the writer had stated them. The dignity of movement of an ice-berg is due to only one-eighth of it being above water.[18]

The writer should "convey everything, every sensation, sight, feeling, place and emotion to the reader." [19] But the emotion is con-

15. Hemingway, *A Farewell to Arms,* Modern Standard Authors (New York: Charles Scribner's Sons, 1953), p. 191. Hereafter cited in text with abbreviation *FA*.

16. Hemingway, "He Who Gets Slap Happy: a Bimini Letter," *Esquire,* 4 (August 1935), 19.

17. Ezra Pound, *Literary Essays of Ezra Pound,* Edited with an Introduction by T. S. Eliot (London: Faber and Faber Limited, 1954), pp. 5, 4.

18. Hemingway, *Death in the afternoon* (New York: Charles Scribner's Sons, 1932), p. 192. Hereafter cited in text with abbreviation *DA*.

19. Hemingway, "Monologue to the Maestro: A High Seas Letter," *By-*

veyed only through the concrete images, never through general and abstract statements. How the reader derives from the writing the emotions which the writer wished to communicate is a difficult question. He may not, of course, derive the correct ones. If T. S. Eliot believed that the image may arouse an emotion according to one's knowledge of literature and tradition as well as according to a fund of common knowledge, Hemingway believed that the imagination, the link between image and emotion, "may be racial experience. I think," he wrote, "that is quite possible." [20] Here Eliot's and Hemingway's theories of esthetics are almost exactly the same. Eliot's definition of the objective correlative describes well the stylistic technique of both: the objective correlative, whether it be the work as a whole or the imagery of the work, is "a set of objects, a situation, a chain of events which shall be the formula of that *particular* emotion; such that when the external facts, which must terminate in sensory experience, are given, the emotion is immediately evoked." [21] The difference between the objective correlatives of Eliot and Hemingway, Carlos Baker says in a perceptive exaggeration, is that Eliot uses "complex *literary* symbols" which are read in terms of one's "cultural holdings" and that Hemingway evokes a response "to things actually seen and known by direct experience of the world." [22] Richard Adams has argued convincingly not only that Eliot influenced Hemingway generally but also that *The Waste Land* is "a typical case of direct, formative literary influence" on Hemingway and especially on *The Sun Also Rises*. "My theory," Adams writes, "is that Hemingway found what he needed in *The Waste Land* and took it." [23]

The reader of *The Sun Also Rises* must know the themes of the

---

Line: Ernest Hemingway, ed. William White (New York: Charles Scribner's Sons, 1967), p. 216.

20. "Monologue to the Maestro," p. 215.

21. T. S. Eliot, "Hamlet and His Problems," *The Sacred Wood: Essays on Poetry and Criticism* (London: Methuen & Co., 1948, Sixth Edition), p. 100.

22. Carlos Baker, *Hemingway: The Writer as Artist* (Princeton: Princeton University Press, 1952), p. 56.

23. Richard Adams, "Sunrise Out of the Waste Land," *Tulane Studies in English,* 9 (1959), 123.

novel, comprehend the implicit, and appreciate the language and the style. Hemingway's use of the modern vernacular is not mere exhibitionism. The style must be insensitive enough to communicate the characters' deliberate stoicism, their refusal to state didactically or sentimentally meanings which they only search for. The style must also represent the intensity and the wistfulness of the desire for meaning. It must be sensitive enough to be good fiction, to communicate by implication what neither reader nor author nor character dares to articulate.

Since Jake Barnes tells his own story and since Hemingway never once violates Jake's point of view, there is not one single overt expression of Hemingway's views in the entire novel. Jake and other characters do express their attitudes, but with dissimulation, stoic restraint and endurance, understatement, humor, and many kinds of irony.

Often views of the characters are expressed only indirectly and almost inadvertently. Jake's restraint is apparent early in the novel. For the first twenty pages he never mentions Brett or indicates his love for her. Then a group of homosexuals enters the cafe where he sits and Jake thinks, "With them was Brett." He quotes a little of the conversation of the homosexuals and thinks again, "And with them was Brett" (*SAR*, p. 20). Jake's angry reaction to the general situation is something he can express: "I was very angry." But his love for Brett and his anger at the company she keeps are communicated only indirectly in the repetition of the blunt factual statement: "And with them was Brett." Jake and Brett dance together and leave in a taxi, alone at last after a long separation. Jake's injury during the war prevents any physical expression of his love for Brett; his stoicism and frustration and the inadequacy of language prevent any open expression of his love and disappointment. The reader can perceive the intense emotions of the occasion only by noting Jake's actions. Alone in the dark taxi, he gazes intently toward Brett whether or not there is enough light to see her:

> I saw her face in the lights from the open shops, then it was dark, then I saw her face clearly as we came out on the Avenue des Gobelins. The street was torn up and men were working on the car-tracks by the light of acetylene flares. Brett's face was white and the long line of her neck showed in the bright light of the flares. (*SAR*, p. 25)

But the depth of Jake's emotions is indicated only by the ardency of his gaze as he turns toward her and stares. Nothing else expresses his devotion. What the reader should note is not Brett, but Jake's efforts to see her.

Words do not convey truth. Brett relies on physical sensation to communicate to Jake the fact that she lusts for Romero. The language which Brett does use is almost ridiculous enough to be funny.

> " . . . I'm a goner. It's tearing me all up inside."
>
> . . . .
>
> " . . . I can't stop things. Feel that?"
>
> Her hand was trembling.
>
> "I'm like that all through." (*SAR*, p. 190)

One possibility of this modern stoicism is silence. Another is to take refuge in enigma, irony, or the sardonic. Asked if he is "really a Catholic," Jake replies, " 'Technically' " (*SAR*, p. 127)—a strange word to answer the question. It answers without real information or commitment. It is a dodge, and Jake knows little more about its real meaning than his interlocutor. Like the English upper classes, he uses "fewer words than the Eskimo" (*SAR*, p. 149). He would like to think as superficially as he talks, but sometimes it is hard to empty the mind: "The Catholic Church had an awfully good way of handling all that. Good advice, anyway. Not to think about it. Oh, it was swell advice. Try and take it sometime. Try and take it" (*SAR*, p. 31).

The emotional reactions to the art of bullfighting are as incommunicable as those of love and religion. Those who are aficionado know that talk about genuine appreciation is impossible; it is "a very special secret." Montoya "always smiled as though there were something lewd about the secret to outsiders, but that it was something that we understood. It would not do to expose it to people who would not understand." What can be communicated is almost a physical, sensuous fact to be conveyed in something besides language. "But nearly always there was the actual touching. It seemed as though they wanted to touch you to make it certain" (*SAR*, pp. 135–136). Disapproval is also incommunicable. After Jake violates the code of the aficionado by placing Romero at the disposal of Brett, Montoya never utters a word of censure, never once speaks to Jake. On the other hand, those who are not aficionado attempt to express the feelings which they ought to have. On the photographs which they have given to Montoya they have written "the most flattering inscriptions. But they did not mean anything" (*SAR*, p. 136).

During the fiesta at Pamplona a man is killed in the running of the bulls. Jake describes how a bull "shot ahead, caught a man in the running crowd in the back and lifted him in the air. Both the man's arms were by his sides, his head went back as the horn went in, and the bull lifted him and then dropped him." Without comment or interpretation, Jake then tells how the man "who had been gored lay face down in the trampled mud" (*SAR*, p. 204). A waiter supplies an ironic comment later when he repeats over and over that it was "all for fun. Just for fun." But the waiter's humanitarianism is hard to reconcile with the views of Hemingway and those of his characters who are aficionado. Jake asks the waiter, "You're not an aficionado?" (*SAR*, p. 205). Should those who are aficionado not grieve for the dead lost in the pursuit of pleasure? Jake's own tone remains factual but also becomes elegiac: "the man who was killed was named Vicente Girones, and came from near Tafalla. . . . he was twenty-eight years old, and had a farm, a wife, and two children." Sadly the next day Jake watches the corpse leave Pamplona: "The coffin was loaded into the baggage-car of the train, and the widow and the two children rode, sitting, all three together, in an open third-class railway-carriage" (*SAR*, p. 206). In this passage Jake and Hemingway almost lose the restraint characteristic of the rest of the novel and almost lapse into a sentimental humanitarianism. Hemingway perhaps lapses into explicit condemnation of a catastrophe which is so unnecessary as that of the man running before the bulls. This passage is possibly the only one in which the style of *The Sun Also Rises* is not *afición*.

The characters in the novel live as they gamble, lose graciously, and endure silently. Mike rolls the dice for drinks, loses every roll cheerfully, and gives good tips to the bartender until he can pay only twenty francs on his last loss of thirty-six francs (*SAR*, p. 239). "There is a gaping cleavage here between manner and message.

. . ." [24] Jake and his friends celebrate at the fiesta in Pamplona, but their gaiety hides despair. "In Hemingway's waste land there is fun, but there is no hope." [25] James T. Farrell has described the manner of the characters in the novel as "calculated bravado. Their conversation is reduced to enthusiastic small talk about their escapades. And this talk, as well as their actions, is largely a matter of pose and gesture." [26] Graciousness is a part of the manner even when it has no practical result. Jake leaves fifty francs with the patronne of a bar for the prostitute Georgette (whom he had merely carried to dinner) even though he knows that the patronne will not give it to her if she does return (*SAR*, p. 24). "Calculated bravado" and even triviality may represent strength. Brett's emotions almost break through the pretty exterior at the end of the novel. " 'Oh, Jake,' " she exclaims over her frustrations, " 'we could have had such a damned good time together.' " But Jake has acquired the strength to yank her back from the abyss of self-pity, emotion, sentimentality. Brett has mentioned the disappointment of his life—love, manhood itself. But Jake's reply, the last words in the novel, is a casual and ironic statement that does not deny the possibility of depth, but treats it lightly to make it bearable: " 'Yes,' I said, 'Isn't it pretty to think so' " (*SAR*, pp. 258–259).

The Sun Also Rises describes two havens: the characters can manage to hide their desperation in humor or irony, or they can flee the confusion of the world by taking a fishing trip into the remote fastnesses of the mountains. Bill Gorton's and Jake Barnes's retreat is as idyllic as the sojourn of Frederic Henry and Catherine Barkley in the mountains of Switzerland. Only here may one sometimes say what he means. Moods mingle. Bill's language quickly turns from the satiric and ironic to a sentiment that is shocking even to himself.

24. Philip Young, *Ernest Hemingway,* Rinehart Critical Studies (New York: Rinehart & Company, 1952), p. 59.

25. Young, p. 60.

26. James T. Farrell, "The Sun Also Rises," in John K. M. McCaffery, *Ernest Hemingway: The Man and His Work* (Cleveland: World Publishing Co., 1950), p. 222.

> ". . . Anybody ever tell you you were a good guy?"
> "I'm not a good guy."
> "Listen. You're a hell of a good guy, and I'm fonder of you than anybody on earth. . . ." (*SAR*, p. 119)

Then Bill becomes embarrassed at his own sentiments, recognizes that in the outside world he could not use words of this kind without being regarded as a homosexual, and turns to crass comedy. He accuses Abraham Lincoln of being homosexual and of freeing "the slaves on a bet" (*SAR*, p. 119). On the fishing trip Jake even reads a "wonderful story" about "true love" by the romantic novelist A. E. W. Mason. In the outside world it would be as absurd as Robert Cohn's favorite, W. H. Hudson's *The Purple Land*. During the entire idyll the style is relaxed as Bill and Jake move easily from sincerity to humor to irony in their discussions of dreams and even the order of creation. This is the only time in the novel when a character may say with some sincerity, "We should not question. Our stay on earth is not for long. Let us rejoice and believe and give thanks" (*SAR*, p. 125).

Almost every reader closes *The Sun Also Rises* with a feeling that Robert Cohn is despicable, and there is some puzzlement about the cause. He seems to represent some kind of normality in the novel. He is in favor of love and manhood and country. His virtues should make him a protagonist, but he is an ass. It is his manner that ruins him. Openly and sentimentally he speaks of values and abstractions. He reminds his friends of what they wish to forget. " 'Do you realize,' " he asks Jake, " 'you've lived nearly half the time you have to live already?' " (*SAR*, p. 11). Jake, on the other hand, if he is obsessed with time, refuses to discuss it. Cohn constantly uses the words that Jake and Bill can speak only in Burguete. " 'You're really about the best friend I have, Jake' " (*SAR*, p. 40). Just a moment before he had almost hit Jake for telling him to go to hell. He has delusions of virtues where they do not exist. He refuses to believe that Brett would marry anyone she did not love, but she had twice married for some reason other than love (*SAR*, p. 40). He weeps (*SAR*, p. 49). His naïvete forces foolish abstractions into the presence of his companions and taunts them with what they have learned to forget. He resembles his mistress, who dislikes children but likes the idea of having them. " 'I always thought,' " she says, " 'I'd have them and then like them' " (*SAR*, p. 49). Cohn is obnoxious precisely because he is not able to endure in fact like the other characters. He overstates his feelings and beliefs. He has failed in everything except in his shallow use of the words of morality and truth.

Riotous pleasure does not dominate *The Sun Also Rises*. It is a symptom of an opposite mood underneath. Tension and frustration are apparent in bantering and in bitter conflict. A deadly serious search for a way to live in the world is revealed in Brett's and Jake's desires for love, in Jake's meditations, and perhaps especially in the stylistic tone of many passages. One vivid passage describes the suffering of the sick and aged Belmonte as he fights a bull before a hostile crowd.[27]

The writing throughout Book III of the novel, the section following the fiesta in Pamplona, is one of Hemingway's most interesting stylistic accomplishments. Celebrations have ended, the celebrants have departed; Jake has a bad hangover, and he prepares to return to Paris and the same old perpetual despair. The technical characteristics of Hemingway's prose seldom vary—the short sentences, the frequent *and*'s, the co-ordinated and equal sense impressions, the dominant nouns and verbs. But Hemingway's sentences are versatile, and the ending of *The Sun Also Rises* is subdued, written in a minor key, filled with a saddening tone color. Style alone reflects the frustration of Jake's hope that after a fiesta all would change. But the more the change, the more the same thing. Returning to Spain to meet Brett after she has separated from Romero, Jake's comments on the scenery reveal his bleak mood:

> I did not sleep much that night on the Sud Express. In the morning I had breakfast in the dining-car and watched the rock and pine country between Avila and Escorial. I saw the Escorial out of the window, gray and long and cold in the sun, and did not give a damn about it. I saw Madrid come up over the plain, a compact white sky-line on the top of a little cliff away off across the sun-hardened country.

27. W. M. Frohock, *The Novel of Violence in America* (Dallas: Southern Methodist University Press, 1957), p. 174.

The Norte station in Madrid is the end of the line. All trains finish there. They don't go on anywhere. (*SAR,* pp. 250–251)

"Gray and long and cold in the sun"—sad and slow-paced monosyllables—Hemingway makes use of the rhythm, the imagery, and the suggestive, almost onomatopoetic sounds of poetry. One knows that Jake doesn't give a damn about it before he says it.

Jake Barnes's despair can never have any of the flourish of Lear's and Satan's. A fall like that of an ancient hero might itself be a cause of hope, a token of order and design. Exalted rhetoric in Hemingway's novel would be inappropriate by its very nature. Tragedy has changed because the hero knows not why or by what rules he has fallen. Given the theme of search and despair, the unique style is an almost perfect vehicle to express the futility of those who have discovered the failure of meaning and language.

8

World Pessimism and Personal Cheeriness in *A Farewell to Arms*

AFTER describing every nation fighting in World War I as "cooked," a British major in Ernest Hemingway's *A Farewell to Arms* tells Frederic Henry "Good-by" cheerfully and wishes him "Every sort of luck!" Henry reflects on the contradictions in the major: "There was a great contrast between his world pessimism and personal cheeriness." [1] The major's world view epitomizes the theme and the style of this novel and even provides a good perspective on all Hemingway's fiction. *The Sun Also Rises* and *For Whom the Bell Tolls* offer the greatest contrast. In the first of these novels personal cheeriness is the only refuge in a world of utter despair. In *For Whom the Bell Tolls* individual and small groups of men sacrifice personal happiness in a magnanimous attempt to improve the conditions of the world for all men. The generalizations of *For Whom the Bell Tolls* could not possibly be embodied in a style as factual, blunt, and noncommittal as that in *The Sun Also Rises*. And the earlier novel contains little hope or regard for the general welfare which

1. Hemingway, *A Farewell to Arms,* Modern Standard Authors (New York: Charles Scribner's Sons, 1953), p. 140. Hereafter cited in text with abbreviation *FA*.

could be stated in the didacticism and optimism of *For Whom the Bell Tolls.*

The variety of critical judgments on style and theme in Hemingway's writing is always amazing. Generally the most favorable views of his late fiction belong to critics who most desire some kind of glowing view of man. The early works, on the other hand, appeal to those who prefer art for art's sake and to those who object most strenuously to the explicit or the didactic. Some of the critics of *A Farewell to Arms* have praised the novel as the best of Hemingway, and others have damned it as an example of his worst. Robert Penn Warren regards it as his best.[2] For Carlos Baker it is his best except for *For Whom the Bell Tolls.*[3] Although much of Hemingway "is the product of a somewhat uneasy attitudinizing," writes D. S. Savage, *A Farewell to Arms* is "surprisingly genuine and unforced." [4] Some extremists have viewed the novel as too immoral or, by contrast, too brazenly philosophical or even didactic. The novelist Robert Herrick and Henry Seidel Canby were repelled by the "lustful indulgence," "mere dirt," "erotic fantasy." [5] E. M. Halliday finds too many "subjective passages" and too little "objective epitome," too little "firm gaze upon outward reality." [6] David Daiches dislikes the "false simplicity" and "forced primitivism." [7] Edwin Berry Burgum does not have a high regard for the novel. "On the whole," he wrote in 1947, "this novel is written in a more awkward style than any other work of Hemingway's." [8] And Frederick Hoffman judges the novel severely: its style is "perceptibly losing hold

2. Robert Penn Warren, "Introduction," *A Farewell to Arms,* Modern Standard Authors, p. xxv.

3. Carlos Baker, *Hemingway: The Writer as Artist* (Princeton: Princeton University Press, 1952), p. 116.

4. D. S. Savage, *The Withered Branch: Six Studies in the Modern Novel* (New York: Pellegrini & Cudahy, 1952), p. 32.

5. Robert Herrick, "What Is Dirt?" *The Bookman,* 70 (November 1929), 261. Henry Seidel Canby, "Chronicle and Comment," *The Bookman,* 70 (February 1930), 643.

6. E. M. Halliday, "Hemingway's Narrative Perspective," *The Sewanee Review,* 60 (1952), 210.

7. David Daiches, "Ernest Hemingway," *College English,* 2 (May 1941), 734.

8. Edwin Berry Burgum, *The Novel and the World's Dilemma* (New York: Oxford University Press, 1947), p. 185.

of the discipline"; the love affair is created in "sentimentality and romantic softness"; conversations are "embarrassingly naïve." He objects to Hemingway's "philosophical interpretation" and "a note of softness and insincerity in the sentiments." In Hemingway's treatment of values, Hoffman says, *A Farewell to Arms* represents "a half-conversion to an ideological religion and a degeneration of moral insight and artistic integrity." [9]

Any considered view of this novel should be based on a careful examination of the unique style, the theme, and the peculiar blend of the two. Of all aspects of fiction, style is the most difficult to define and evaluate. Lists and categories of figures of speech say something about writing, but dissimilar manners of writing may contain the same kinds of figures of speech. And even if the style of a work could be exactly defined, the question of its appropriateness to a particular theme would still be exceedingly difficult. Hemingway's style has been described by Mark Schorer as "the very finest prose of our time. And most of it is poetry." [10] Burgum uses derogatory terms from several economic and social vocabularies to describe the style contemptuously as "the typical speech of the proletariat, taken over and stylized, as the last step in a process long under way in the American collegian and his elder brother, the sportsman of the mature world." [11]

The simplicity and the technical characteristics of Hemingway's prose enable the critic to describe it about as accurately as any style can be described. Even so, how Hemingway blended his manner of writing and his subject matter in *A Farewell to Arms* needs still further discussion. Indeed, the harmony between style and theme may be as perfectly demonstrable in this novel as in any work of literature. Robert Penn Warren describes "the close coordination that he sometimes achieves between the character and the situation, on the one hand, and the sensibility as it reflects itself in the style, on the other hand." [12]

9. Frederick J. Hoffman, *The Modern Novel in America 1900–1950* (Chicago: Henry Regnery Company, 1951), pp. 98–100.

10. Mark Schorer, "Mr. Hemingway & His Critics," *New Republic,* 131 (November 15, 1954), 20.

11. Burgum, p. 190.

12. Warren, p. xxvi.

Like Jake Barnes and the heroes of most of the short stories, Frederic Henry rejects all the conventional words associated with personal ideals and love of country. Henry despises the words of orators and posters and proclamations—the words made so prominent by idealists such as Woodrow Wilson:

> I did not say anything. I was always embarrassed by the words sacred, glorious, and sacrifice and the expression in vain. . . . I had seen nothing sacred, and the things that were glorious had no glory and the sacrifices were like the stockyards at Chicago if nothing was done with the meat except to bury it. There were many words that you could not stand to hear and finally only the names of places had dignity. Certain numbers were the same way and certain dates and these with the names of the places were all you could say and have them mean anything. Abstract words such as glory, honor, courage, or hallow were obscene beside the concrete names of villages, the numbers of roads, the names of rivers, the numbers of regiments and the dates. (*FA*, p. 191)

This passage has been quoted perhaps as much as anything Hemingway wrote; it is almost as well known as Faulkner's Nobel Prize Speech. Curiously, the two passages have four words in common: *glory*, *honor*, *sacrifice*, and *courage*. In 1950 Faulkner stated that it is necessary for the writer to write about these things. In 1929 Frederic Henry had been embarrassed by the same words. But Frederic denies the words more than he does the concepts they represent. He admires names of villages and rivers and numbers of roads and regiments and dates. On particular dates, numbered regiments fight battles on numbered roads and at named villages and rivers. The actions of individual soldiers might be loosely described with the abstract words that Frederic shuns. But the problem is that Henry and Hemingway cannot use these terms in telling the story of *A Farewell to Arms*.

But Frederic uses them in the very act of rejecting them. In the passage denying abstraction he is already more abstract than Jake Barnes, who was so embarrassed at the words that he did not even state his embarrassment and the words that could cause it. Mainly the words appear when Henry quotes someone who uses them abstractly and emptily. The battle police, for example, "had that beautiful detachment and devotion to stern justice of men dealing in death without being in any danger of it" (*FA*, p. 233). They know only the vocabulary, not the referents, not the "dignity" of facts and names and places. One who is positive and genuine may on occasion courageously use one of the abstract terms without embarrassment. The priest tells Henry that love means that "You wish to sacrifice for" (*FA*, p. 75). Henry assures himself that taking the stars off his uniform after his desertion is "no point of honor" (*FA*, p. 241). The concept may be real even if the word is false: Henry thinks of Catherine Barkley and people "who bring so much courage to this world" (*FA*, p. 258).

Henry's and Hemingway's embarrassment at abstract words controls the style and the meaning of *A Farewell to Arms*. If Henry were absolutely true to his principles, he could use only words that communicate sensuous impressions. Since polysyllables are usually more abstract than monosyllables, Henry uses a plain vocabulary. Many co-ordinate connectives are words which reflect abstractions and intellectual concepts. The more subtle the connector, the less likely it is to appear in the novel. Such words as *therefore*, *however*, *moreover*, *furthermore*, *consequently* appear seldom or not at all. Hemingway uses only simple subordinating connectives, the relative pronouns and *where*, *when*, *after*. Such words as *if*, *unless*, *since*, *though*, *although*, *whereas* represent conditions, causes, contrarieties—that is, sophisticated concepts, nuances, intellectualizations. And Frederic Henry never uses them. Even *but* may suggest antithesis or elementary paradox. When Henry does not avoid connectives, he usually uses *and*. His sentences are simple or compound—seldom complex. They are "staccato jabs" which "make many pages tedious" [13] for many readers who cannot accept this "great leveling democracy of the *and*." [14] Francis Hackett regards the style in places as "patent infantilism." [15] Those who read merely for plot are untroubled by the metronomic rhythm, but after the

13. Francis Hackett, "Hemingway: 'A Farewell to Arms,'" *Saturday Review of Literature*, 32 (August 6, 1949), 32.

14. Joseph Warren Beach, *American Fiction 1920–1940* (New York: The Macmillan Company, 1941), p. 101.

15. Hackett, p. 32.

odd sentences are pointed out they are disturbed by a style which makes them wish to bob their heads up and down as if they were first graders chanting in unison the words from a primer.

Because there is considerable variety within the dominant pattern, no paragraph selected to exemplify the style of *A Farewell to Arms* can be entirely representative. The shortest sentences are likely to occur when Frederic meditates or when there is great suspense or a crisis. The paragraph at the end of Book III just after his desertion illustrates the most unusual quality of the style. Fifteen sentences contain only eighty-three words—less than six words per sentence. Henry thinks about not-thinking, and the only suggestion of thought above the level of the senses is contained in the word *go*, which may suggest flight. *Go* is repeated several times, and it appears at the end of four sentences.

> I was not make to think. I was made to eat. My God, yes. Eat and drink and sleep with Catherine. To-night maybe. No that was impossible. But to-morrow night, and a good meal and sheets and never going away again except together. Probably have to go damned quickly. She would go. I knew she would go. When would we go? That was something to think about. It was getting dark. I lay and thought where we would go. There were many places. (*FA*, p. 242)

The style here is about as remote from the usual manner of the stream of consciousness as any writing one can imagine, and yet it does suggest not only the urgency of Frederic's thoughts but also the processes of his thinking. Faulkner's Quentin Compson shows his weakness by the complicated process of his thinking, his excessive abstraction, and his intellectualizing. Frederic, on the contrary, demonstrates his strength by thinking only of the facts and the necessities without interpreting them. Quentin uses sense impressions to make himself remember; Frederic uses them to forget. Quentin's brother Jason does not think with the rapid and poetic associations of stream of consciousness, and Faulkner thus suggests his practicality, his lack of imagination. But the short sentences and the practical facts of Henry's thought process indicate his extraordinary strength and will power.

If abstract words are obscene, truly obscene words may indicate virtue. During the retreat from Caporetto, Aymo gives two young girls a ride in his ambulance.

> "Don't worry," he said. "No danger of———," using the vulgar word. "No place for ———." I could see she understood the word and that was all. Her eyes looked at him very scared. She pulled the shawl tight. "Car all full," Aymo said. "No danger of ———. No place for ———." (*FA*, p. 203)

A strange vocabulary to reassure a virgin. But Aymo, here a gentle man, reassures the virgins with whorehouse talk and escorts them as he would his sisters. His words make little difference. The facts and the deeds are right.

Sometimes in *A Farewell to Arms* abstractions and generalizations become almost necessary, but the characters use various strategies to avoid them. To express the ideals and aims of a profession would be as objectionable as to describe one's patriotic fervor. Though Frederic is a man of education, his studied vocabulary is not more extensive than that of a near illiterate. He shuns mentioning his civilian ambitions and ideals. He states that he is studying to be an architect only when he is escaping from Italy and is asked what he has been doing there (*FA*, pp. 250, 289). Never is any explanation of his reasons for joining the Italian army given. There are no indications of frustrated hopes for adventure during the war. Presumably he joined the ambulance corps for some humanitarian or even patriotic motive. Hemingway himself did.[16] Soon after Catherine meets Frederic she asks him why he joined, and he answers, " 'I don't know. . . . There isn't always an explanation for everything' " (*FA*, p. 18). When another nurse asks the same question, he replies, " 'I was in Italy. . . , and I spoke Italian' " (*FA*, p. 22). When he denies the possibility of explanation, Catherine replies that she was brought up to think there were always explanations. The values have changed, but the words which once explained them have changed even more. Their conversation here is as much a discussion of language as of motive. John W. Aldridge explains the reluctance: "Abstract thoughts, like abstract words, seduce his mind

16. Charles A. Fenton, *The Apprenticeship of Ernest Hemingway: The Early Years* (New York: Viking Press, 1954), p. 61.

away from essential experience, the true nature of things. . . ."[17]

Some restraint always prevails between Catherine and Frederic. Intimate feelings and thoughts of love itself almost always must remain unexpressed and incommunicable. Their restraint in language may make their love seem more casual and gross than it is. Frederic and Catherine's parting when he returns to the front from the hospital may be one of the most restrained emotional scenes in all fiction. He uses fewer words than a teen-ager fleeing from his first trip to a brothel.

"Good-by," I said, "Take good care of yourself and young Catherine."
"Good-by, darling."
"Good-by," I said. (*FA*, p. 164)

But the refusal to state feelings is itself a sign of emotion. The throat-tightening comes simply because this is a novel and a world where the expression of sentiment is impossible no matter how real the sentiment is. Words are as inadequate as a handshake between an inhibited father and son after one has spent years in the horrors of a Buchenwald.

At times Frederic's friends and the world make it impossible for him to be silent or to use words that are meaningful only on the sensuous level. Occasionally when he is forced to speak in general terms, he picks and chooses words that are deliberately worn and trite and even vague. This too is a manner of self-defense. When he is compelled to refer to a world order, he uses the great impersonal *they*, which for him cannot have an antecedent. *Nice* and *fine* and *lovely* are words common in the novel. These counter words avoid the particular and the sentimental and the extravagant. They are so worn that they are not embarrassing when used genuinely or ironically. Catherine speaks vaguely of her "nice boy":

"I wanted to do something for him. You see I didn't care about the other thing and he could have had it all. He could have had anything he wanted if I would have known. I would have married him or any-

17. John W. Aldridge, *After the Lost Generation: A Critical Study of the Writers of Two Wars* (New York: McGraw-Hill Book Company, Inc., 1951) p. 8.

thing. I know all about it now. But then he wanted to go to war and I didn't know." (*FA*, p. 19)

Some words are so general as to be puzzling. Yet author and character do not wish definition. The priest, Frederic says, "had always known what I did not know and what, when I learned it, I was always able to forget" (*FA*, p. 14).

The positive unbeliever, curiously, can use more abstractions in his evangelical denial of his faith than a believer. The priest-baiters say such things as "I am an atheist" and "shook my faith" (*FA*, p. 7). The priest does not say "I am a believer" and "found my faith." On him is the burden of demonstration without declarations. As a friend of the priest, Henry can only change the subject. Even the priest uses concrete images when he wishes to spread the gospel to Frederic. The mountains of the Abruzzi represent home to the priest; they suggest the things of religion. Tactfully, he couches his invitation to Frederic in concrete terms. He promises "good hunting," a land that is cold and clear and dry, and a place where the peasants take off their hats and call you Lord—suggesting but not stating order and tradition.

A social historian reading *A Farewell to Arms* and deliberately searching for its subject matters would find a variety of topics: war, love, religion, mores and attitudes of a time and place. But the critic should indicate how these subject matters, if one may call them that, become integral parts of the over-all action or plot of the novel and how "subject matter," plot, and style are harmonious. In general, Hemingway's treatment of his subject matter rejects exactly the same abstractions as are shunned in the style. This is that almost perfect harmony of techniques and subject toward which all works of art aspire and which none ever perfectly attains.

Style and subject yearn for the one (singularity) and reject the many (plurality). The subject of war is one of the best vantage points from which to see the distinction between the one and the many. In pulp fiction perhaps and certainly in romantic fiction the tale-teller may not distinguish between the individual and the great and glorious cause. An almost perfect example of such a yarn is Thomas Nelson Page's "Marse Chan," where the hero's individuality is entirely submerged in his fight for God and country and cause and his love. But modern soldiers or perhaps all sane soldiers truly seen in fiction cannot wholly submerge themselves in the general cause.

Every aspect of the art and the meaning of *A Farewell to Arms* establishes a conflict between the concrete, the particular, the individual on the one hand and the abstract, the general, and the mass on the other. The larger theme is figured in several ways: the individual caught in the toils of the war; lovers trapped by their own bodies or by the mortal world in which they love; the individual's solipsism and terrible need for religion in a world without belief and without an order or a pattern which might provide evidence of something in which to believe. Plot, image, character, event —the minute details of the novel reflect the whole.

The themes of love, war, and religion dominate the patterns of meaning in *A Farewell to Arms*. Only one of these is perfectly comprehensible and without mystery—war. Love and religion remain complex, mysterious, inexplicable. An army and battle police can more definitely represent a society than love and a priest can represent the divine and the mystical. One may desert the army and make his separate peace, but he cannot withdraw from his own body without death; nor can he simply by proclamation separate himself from chaos or rule himself outside the theological order. The theme of war in *A Farewell to Arms*, therefore, because of the very nature of the problems involved, most clearly reveals the over-all design of the novel.

Only the naïve patriot in the novel may believe wholeheartedly in the cause of his country. Such a man is Gino, who provokes Frederic to think of his embarrassment at words: "Gino was a patriot, so he said things that separated us sometimes, but he was also a fine boy and I understood his being a patriot" (*FA*, p. 191). Ettore was worse—"a legitimate hero who bored everyone he met" (*FA*, p. 129). Gino provides an opportunity for Frederic to examine himself. Until the retreat from Caporetto he is more disturbed by the words than he is by the patriotism which they represent. That he himself was something of an idealist is indicated by his talk with disgruntled soldiers. As concretely as he can, he tells them that "defeat is worse" than war, and again he says, "I believe we should get the war over" (*FA*, pp. 51, 52). But the restraint of these abstractions indicates only the vaguest kind of patriotism. Even these minor symptoms of belief disappear after his desertion, and always they are made to seem insignificant in comparison with the other soldiers' hatred of the war. The triviality of Frederic's little patriotic displays is also made apparent by the contrast with his ardent feelings about his men. Personal relationships are comparable to facts, the words of the senses, the names of places. Under artillery fire, Frederic takes food to his men. Told to wait, he says, "They want to eat" (*FA*, p. 55). Here are sacrifice, honor, courage; but even to name the virtues is to diminish the force of the deed. If a character used the words, he would be a bore like Gino. A shell hits the group; and Manera, one of the most disgruntled and mutinous of the men, tenderly leads in the rescue of Frederic after he is wounded. One could say of him (like the major) that there is a great difference between his "world pessimism" and his personal loyalty.

The retreat from Caporetto reveals best the difference between the world and the individual. Different episodes in the retreat indicate a change in Frederic's view of the self, the war, and the world. The first of these, the shooting of the sergeant, is the most complex moral situation in the novel; and though it is a key to meaning in *A Farewell to Arms*, it has been ignored in almost all interpretations of the book. Henry's men invite two sergeants to ride in their ambulances during the retreat. From the moment when the two join the ambulance drivers, Hemingway begins preparing for the climactic desertion of the army by Frederic, and he juxtaposes several moral systems: the responsibilities of the individual to himself, to his group of friends, and to his general military or patriotic cause. The whole situation has been interpreted as mere selfish inconsistency on the part of Frederic: "Though he does not hesitate to kill a deserter," writes Francis Hackett, "he himself deserts when offered the same dose of medicine. . . ." [18] The medicine is the same, but the disease is not. First of all, the sergeants violate the code of a group by eating first without sharing. (Contrast Frederic's carrying food to his men during bombardment.) The sergeants enjoy the

18. Hackett, p. 33.

ride for a long time, but they are unwilling to share the ill fortunes of the group. When the ambulances are stuck in the mud, the sergeants refuse to push or to cut brush to put under the wheels. Thus they betray those who have helped them and disobey the orders of a superior officer. At a moment of desperate crisis they violate military law as well as the laws of common human decency. Frederic shoots at both as they flee and hits one. At this moment he has two different kinds of justification, but obviously he does not debate his reasons and offer explanations. Later, after his own desertion, he might. Bonello, the most brazen, cocksure, and unpatriotic of Frederic's men, administers a coup de grâce mostly for the pleasure of killing. " 'The son of a bitch,' he said. He looked toward the sergeant. 'You see me shoot him, Tenente?' " (*FA*, p. 211). Bonello and Frederic act with all "the beautiful detachment and devotion to stern justice" of the carabinieri who try to execute Henry later. But they also have a personal and particular justification. What Frederic should have done, indeed, what he would have done, about the sergeants after his own desertion, remains a point more for contemplation than solution.

After the killing of the sergeant all obligations and responsibilities to group and to military cause begin to disappear. Events make personal loyalty seem less meaningful. Before crossing a bridge, Bonello cares more for his own safety than that of the group: " 'It's probably mined,' " he says. " 'You cross first, Tenente' " (*FA*, p. 216). Faith in the general world becomes as meaningless as the words which might describe it. The loyal Aymo is shot by his own countrymen. Words and the world have failed Frederic, and about the death of Aymo he can only say, "He looked very dead. It was raining. I had liked him as well as any one I ever knew. I had his papers in my pocket and would write to his family" (*FA*, p. 222).

Bonello leaves the group because he wishes to be a prisoner. Piani stays even though he does not believe in the war. He does not wish to leave Frederic. Even before Frederic is finally convinced by the carabinieri that he should make a separate peace, the loyalty of Piani is all that is left to cling to. Personally devoted to Frederic, Piani respectfully calls him "Tenente," but the retreating troops have their own "beautiful detachment and devotion to stern justice."

Piani therefore calls his lieutenant by his first name because the men may shoot officers. At this point Frederic still feels enough loyalty to the general situation to voice to Piani his objection to the troops' throwing away their rifles.

At the end of the retreat with the army Frederic encounters the battle police. They have "all the efficiency, coldness, and command of themselves of Italians who are firing and not being fired on" (*FA*, p. 231), "That beautiful detachment and devotion to stern justice of men dealing in death without being in any danger of it" (*FA*, p. 233). They still can mouth the abstractions like *in vain*, *glory*, *courage*, and *honor*. One of them refers to "the sacred soil of the fatherland." But these men know nothing about the facts, the concrete actions which the words are supposed to describe. Of all the characters in the novel, they are the best representatives of abstraction and generality.

To escape execution by the battle police, Frederic jumps into a river and swims to safety. In words that suggest baptism Henry later reflects on his escape: "Anger was washed away in the river along with any obligation" (*FA*, p. 241). This sentence has been the delight of many critics. First was Malcolm Cowley: "When Frederick [*sic*] Henry dives into the flooded Tagliamento . . . , he is performing a rite of baptism that prepares us for the new life he is about to lead as a deserter from the Italian army; his act is emotionally significant, but it is a little unconvincing on the plane of action." [19] Acknowledging his indebtedness to Cowley, John W. Aldridge calls the escape in the river "an act of purgation symbolizing the death of the war and the beginning of a new life of love." [20] And Robert Penn Warren refers to "baptism" and "the significance of a rite." [21]

This is, however, a strange kind of baptism. Frederic's mental state does not resemble that which should accompany the Christian sacrament. In the river during his escape he thinks almost as a hunted animal. Even after he has found a hiding place in a railroad car under a canvas with guns, he does not reflect on the battle police,

19. Malcolm Cowley, "Introduction," *Hemingway*, The Viking Portable Library (New York: The Viking Press, 1944), p. xvii.

20. Aldridge, p. 9.

21. Warren, p. xxxii.

his desertion, his perilous situation, his justification. Before thinking about the general world, he ponders over the performance of his stiff knee. "The head was mine, but not to use, not to think with; only to remember and not too much remember" (*FA,* p. 240). The ceremony is an ironic parody of baptism, a travesty of the ceremony. The change and dedication that should precede baptism is a change in the appearance of the world, not in Frederic. Saint Paul's blinding light here is the threat of unjust execution. The newly baptized Christian assumes obligations; Frederic now can deny them. It is more initiation than baptism. Instead of subscribing to a new belief in the transcendent life of the spirit, Frederic uses his own personal principles to act in a new way because he has learned new things about the disorder of the world. Not only is he embarrassed at the words *sacred, sacrifice,* and *in vain,* but now he also doubts the existence of the facts that the words might describe. He had seen the sacred implicit in the names of places; but Caporetto can suggest only the profane. Whatever verities there may be exist only in the personal, in the relationship of love, in himself and Catherine.

The escape in the river does almost complete Frederic's knowledge about the war and the great world. "My life used to be full of everything," he tells Catherine. "Now if you aren't with me I haven't a thing in the world" (*FA,* p. 266). When a friendly bartender asks him why men go to war, Frederic for the first time can reply factually, although he will answer the question only for himself: "I don't know. I was a fool" (*FA,* p. 264).

The climactic escape and desertion marks a sharp change in the structure of *A Farewell to Arms.* The style and the general theme are the same but the love of Catherine and Frederic replaces the war as the vehicle of narration and meaning. Before, Frederic had to define the place of the individual in society and the world; the moment of definition came with desertion; now, he and Catherine must define the place of lovers in creation. If the individual can only try and fail to make a separate peace in a world, lovers ultimately can attain only separation and death. Disaster comes early for Catherine and Frederic, but sooner or later, they learn, it comes to all.

But before the death of Catherine and Frederic's realization of the place of love in the world, the two are almost as alone in the mountains of Switzerland as Eve and Adam were in the Garden. And as innocent. Frederic's desertion was but an early bloom on the tree of knowledge. Although *innocence* is an odd word to use in describing Catherine and Frederic, their love in a sense exists apart from the world. " 'I wish we could do something really sinful,' Catherine said. 'Everything we do seems so innocent and simple. I can't believe we do anything wrong' " (*FA,* p. 160).

The priest describes such a love as that of Catherine and Frederic in terms that are idealistic but not sexual: "When you love you wish to do things for" (*FA,* p. 75). But this sentence, concrete as it is, borders on abstraction, and the two lovers avoid such statements of what they feel. When Frederic realizes that he loves Catherine, he lets all the meanings remain in physical terms: "Everything turned over inside of me" (*FA,* p. 95). The lovers' refusal, indeed, inability, to talk about love in terms of the embarrassing words leaves much unsaid, and here may be a reason for what many regard as Hemingway's failure to characterize Catherine. John W. Aldridge, for example, regards the love affair as "strangely inadequate." "Instead of emerging as a human personality," Catherine he believes, "became merely an abstraction. . . ."[22] Hemingway had set himself a difficult task in trying to portray an individual woman who rejects all the words that the women of the world use to describe the *raison d'etre* of marriage and womanhood.

After the reality of their love has been expressed by the flesh, marriage becomes a convention, a religious or civil institution, a generalization. Catherine's friend Ferguson accuses Catherine of having no honor, but Fergy still thinks with the immoral world's embarrassing words (*FA,* p. 256). Frederic wishes marriage more than Catherine because in the priest's terms he might be doing a thing for the one he loves. In keeping with his rejection of the world, he wishes to be "married privately some way" (*FA,* p. 120), but Catherine reminds him of the meaninglessness of marriage in the moral terms of the book when she tells him that " 'There's no way to be married except by church or state" (*FA,* p. 120). And

22. Aldridge, pp. 38–39.

in a happy moment the concrete good feelings of love are so predominant that Catherine says they are already married—and given a chaotic world like that in this novel, any ceremony would be love's sacrilege.

Love therefore is a refuge from the failure of all generalities. And the world vanishes during the Edenic life in Switzerland. After Catherine and Frederic leave Italy in a small boat on a lake, the two think only of the concrete things of the sensations which they endure and enjoy. There are no thoughts of a separate peace, not even talk about the war. Switzerland is "a grand country," "a splendid country," where "The war seemed as far away as the football games of some one else's college" (*FA*, p. 301). In Switzerland they eat pretzels, drink beer, enjoy the weather, and read "about disaster" (*FA*, p. 302). The idyll which Hemingway has written about the days of Catherine and Frederic in the mountains is one of the simplest and most beautiful passages in his works.

But the world cannot be denied. In *A Farewell to Arms* it works out destinies with little or no regard for the meanings of the embarrassing words it uses. The individual is not freely given that prerogative of decision. The hard paradox is that Frederic on the one hand has every right to say farewell to arms; but the world will not let him exercise the right with impunity. Though there be chaos and evil, the individual must act in the terms of duty and honor. Already years before *For Whom the Bell Tolls* Hemingway is aware that no man can be an island. But a chaotic world still forces a man to try to be an island, and paradoxically even as he flees from evil he is wrong in his flight. Trapped in a mortal world, faced with social obligations, man must accept. There is no way to sign a separate peace with all creation and life itself. Robert Penn Warren describes well the doom of the lovers: "the attempt to find a substitute for universal meaning in the limited meaning of the personal relationship is doomed to failure."[23] Love, which helped to carry them out of the world, makes them return when Catherine goes to the hospital in Lausanne to bear her child. Always the baby reminds them that they cannot deny the press of the world. When the time of birth is near, Catherine and Frederic

23. Warren, p. xxxi.

share a "feeling as though something were hurrying us and we could not lose any time together" (*FA,* p. 321). Whether Hemingway or Henry regards the baby as the agent of the world or whether Henry's attitude is merely that of a father-to-be who does not yet know and love his child is never clear. In a sense Frederic and Catherine have even been isloated from their own unborn child. And he is so much worried about her that he has no time for concern about the baby. After Catherine and the baby die, Frederic still cannot define his role in creation. He knows that in a sense the baby also has been "biologically trapped." If he thought in Christian terms he would recognize the biological trap as mortality, the fall of man. And the trap indicates that Nature—or God if there is One—rather than man brought death into the world and all our woe. "Poor little kid. I wished the hell I had been choked like that" (*FA,* p. 338). Though he has no religion, he prays for Catherine and recognizes that the baby should be baptized.

By this time the words *glorious* and *sacred* are meaningless as well as embarrassing. The particular facts to which one may cling are that the words mean little and sometimes nothing in the world, that the individual cannot speak the words, but that he must act with sacrifice and courage and pity and pride. He must endure in a world without explanations.

In the war Frederic learns that the individual is trapped in a society that mouths words without knowing the meanings. Only the relationships between individuals in small groups can be true. In his love affair Frederic learns that he is mortal, that he is "biologically trapped." In religion he never learns anything. From the beginning to the end of the novel he yearns for a faith like that of the priest. Like the words, religion remains vague and abstract. The ultimate in Frederic's knowledge of religious things is expressed by Count Greffi, who tells him that love is a "religious feeling." But religion is too vague for Catherine, who tells Frederic that he is her religion. Hemingway's doomed lovers never know whether love is a substitute for religion because there is no God or whether it is a concrete and ideal experience which may enable them to become very devout when they are old. Even in religion they maintain a world skepticism and a personal cheeriness. Frederic's lack of faith allows him to blaspheme although he prays in moments of fear and he cannot put away religious things.

In *A Farewell to Arms,* style and the major subjects of the novel (war, love, religion) form an almost perfect harmony in the rejection of the general and vague and the acceptance only of the particular, the things of the senses, the knowable. Both style and theme reject the words which do not refer to a material thing. In historical terms *A Farewell to Arms* is very much a book of its time. The two lovers desire what Alfred North Whitehead has described as an *"Order of Nature. . . ."* "It does not matter what men say in words," Whitehead wrote in 1925, "so long as their activities are controlled by settled instincts. The words may ultimately destroy the instincts." [24] He might have been writing of Catherine and Frederic when he wrote that the "new tinge to modern minds is a vehement and passionate interest in the relation of general principles to irreducible and stubborn facts." Hemingway and Frederic and Catherine admitted the possibility of the existence of principles and mind and spirit, even with capital letters, but for author and characters the instincts could not be expressed in the embarrassing words which have been destroyed. Words change in every age; but in Hemingway's early career, he said, "words we knew were barred to us, and we had to fight for a single word. . . ." [25] In these respects *A Farewell to Arms* is one of the best manifestations of an attitude in an age, but, more significantly, Hemingway has created a novel that will be a lasting work of art. Most of Catherine's and Frederic's soul-searchings resemble those of any thinking individual in any period, and they are embodied in a vehicle so appropriate to the theme that style and subject become indistinguishable and inseparable.

24. Alfred North Whitehead, *Science and the Modern World,* Lowell Lectures, 1925 (New York: The Macmillan Company, 1925), p. 5.

25. George Plimpton, "An Interview with Ernest Hemingway," in Carlos Baker, *Hemingway and His Critics* (New York: Hill and Wang, 1961, 1963), p. 26.

9

Hemingway's First "Big Writing"

BEFORE the publication of *Death in the Afternoon* in 1932, Ernest Hemingway had written no nonfictional prose to be printed between book covers. Besides his fiction, he had published a few poems, a very few reviews, and articles in newspapers. Newspaper work had been at least in part a way to earn a living while he wrote what he wanted to write. Hemingway as a man, his own views, had not appeared naked in public; rather, they had been clothed in the requirements of journalism or in the impersonal medium of his fiction. He had written no credo, said nothing about what he believed. He had not shifted his sentence patterns nor varied his staccato style.

Hemingway, in short, had been as impersonal as the poet described by T. S. Eliot. He had written no pretty words, no generalizations, no abstractions. Throughout the first thirty years of the twentieth century, Hemingway and Faulkner had largely refused to communicate with the literary world except through the medium of art. Whatever they had had to say had been said in fiction and poetry. They had written few articles and little criticism, and they had given few interviews for quotation. Eliot, it is true, had stated his views in literary criticism; but as a critic he was formal and impersonal. Then in 1928 he affirmed his beliefs in classicism, Anglo-Catholicism, and royalty. Soon afterward Hemingway spoke out for himself in *Death in the Afternoon.*

In later years Hemingway defined journalism as "that writing of something that happens day by day, in which I was trained when young, and which is not whoring when done honestly with exact reporting. . . ." [1] As a good reporter for the Toronto *Star,* he had presented the facts of inflation, poverty, class, racism, nationalism, hate, and violence; and he usually made no personal comments and provided no solutions, no lamentations, no generalizations. Although his letters show that he could not always publish the whole truth in his newspaper articles,[2] his articles were often honest and vivid even when compared with his fiction.

Journalism, however, was never by any means a perfect vehicle for Hemingway's talents as a writer of fiction and a stylist. Either the demands of his readers and his editors or his own immaturity had been responsible for passages of embarrassing explicitness and open sentiment in his early career. In 1923, for example, he described the spirit of France with romantic analogies to sensuous experience: "There is a magic in the name of France. It is a magic like the smell of the sea or the sight of blue hills or of soldiers marching by. It is a very old magic." [3] But Hemingway's writing here would have evoked no magic for Frederic Henry or Jake Barnes. Moral terms implicit but never stated in the novels slipped into the journalism. A red-light district in Turkey was so "unspeakably horrible," Hemingway wrote, that it "festers." [4] And moral terms in the newspaper articles were sometimes applied inappropriately; he was not entirely jesting when he wrote in the Toronto *Star Weekly* in 1922 that "if you land a big tuna after a

1. Hemingway, "A Situation Report," *By-Line: Ernest Hemingway,* ed. William White (New York: Charles Scribner's Sons, 1967), pp. 471–472.

2. See Hemingway's letter to Gertrude Stein and Alice B. Toklas on Lloyd George's tour in the United States and Canada, Yale University Library.

3. Hemingway, "A Victory without Peace Forced the French to Undertake the Occupation of the Ruhr," Toronto *Daily Star,* 14 April 1923, p. 4.

4. Charles A. Fenton, *The Apprenticeship of Ernest Hemingway: The Early Years* (New York: The Viking Press, 1954), p. 177.

six-hour fight . . . you will be purified and be able to enter unabashed into the presence of the very elder gods and they will make you welcome." [5] This lack of restraint is not extraordinary for a young journalist, perhaps, but in retrospect it looks strange as the product of the pen of the author of *The Sun Also Rises* and *A Farewell to Arms.* There is no reporting by the author in Hemingway's early fiction. He disappears and leaves the characters to work out the fiction for themselves without prologue, epilogue, stage directions, and prompting. Whether or not Hemingway's fiction was factually autobiographical, as an art form it was completely independent of the personality of the author. That he would even write a book giving his personal views about death and bullfighting indicates a fundamental change. As a kind of writing, nonfictional prose rubs the personal ideas of the author against the mind of the reader—even when the author does not write a single sentence with a first-person pronoun.

In writing *Death in the Afternoon,* Hemingway became self-conscious and personal even for a writer of nonfiction; the objectivity of *The Sun Also Rises* and *A Farewell to Arms* had disappeared. In many passages in *Death in the Afternoon* and *Green Hills of Africa,* Hemingway as a writer resembles a lady who protests her virtue too much. When he announces on page one of *Death in the Afternoon,* "I must be altogether frank, or try to be," his reader remembers the frankness of Jake and Frederic, but they were honest without making claims about their own integrity. With Hemingway's reputation for hard but honest prose, he was not called upon to stoop to protest and explain. And even if the frankness survived, the reader is forced to wonder why he must bother with the claim. Paradoxically, a writer who maintains that he is not writing about himself has already committed the offense that he wishes to avoid:

> This that has been written about one person's reaction to the horses in the bull ring is not put in because of a desire of the author to write

5. Hemingway, "Tuna Fishing in Spain," *By-Line: Ernest Hemingway,* p. 17.

about himself and his own reactions, considering them as important and taking delight in them because they are his, but rather to establish the fact that the reactions were instant and unexpected.[6]

A bit later Hemingway writes a 151-word sentence (impossibly long for the style of the previous fiction) on the cowardice and "the arrogance and grace" of Cagancho and on the permanence and impermanence of the art of bullfighting (words which could be used only by sentimental and false characters in the early fiction). Then Hemingway explains and apologizes: "That is the worst sort of flowery writing, but it is necessary to try to give the feeling, and to some one who has never seen it a simple statement of the method does not convey the feeling. Any one who has seen bullfights can skip such flowerishness and read the facts which are much more difficult to isolate and state" (*DA,* p. 14).

In *The Sun Also Rises* and *A Farewell to Arms* he had not resorted to flowery writing or to abstractions in order to explain bullfighting and war for those who lacked experience and first-hand knowledge of the subject matter.

Even after the decline began for Eliot, Faulkner, and Hemingway, all of them retained for a time memories of the old rules. Hemingway in *Death in the Afternoon* states his theories which condemn his practice in the same book. "The dignity of movement of an ice-berg," he wrote, "is due to only one-eighth of it being above water" (*DA,* p. 192). And, "If a writer of prose knows enough about what he is writing about he may omit things that he knows and the reader, if the writer is writing truly enough, will have a feeling of those things as strongly as though the writer had stated them" (*DA,* p. 192). Hemingway knew what he was writing about, the arts of bullfighting and belles-lettres, but he did not any longer omit things that he knew.

If Hemingway in his nonfiction states his ideas openly in abstract words, he uses a similar method to create character: he tells what people are and gives names to their emotions. True, *Green Hills of Africa* is not fiction, but he wrote it, he said, to "compete with a

6. Hemingway, *Death in the Afternoon* (New York: Charles Scribner's Sons, 1932), p. 8. Hereafter cited in text with abbreviation *DA*.

work of the imagination." [7] But in method it does not compete. As the hero of his own book, Hemingway lacks the reticence and therefore the strength of Jake Barnes and Frederic Henry. He is excessively aware of his own emotional states: "the author repeats that he is doing what he likes most, is enjoying himself and is happy—nine times in the first seventy-two pages!—until the reader unavoidably infers that something is most certainly wrong." [8] He describes himself as "warmed with whiskey, understanding, and sentiment" (*GHA,* p. 154). The style is wrong even if there is truth in the claims. The emotions of the priest in *A Farewell to Arms* are created in the character even when he does not express them explicitly; but in *Green Hills of Africa* they are merely attributed to character: "no one can be gentler, more understanding, more self-sacrificing, than Karl. . . ." (*GHA,* p. 152). The author-character is blatantly sentimental about African savages; he refers to "that attitude that makes brothers, that unexpressed but instant and complete acceptance that you must be Masai wherever it is you come from" (*GHA,* p. 221). The love for the savage spreads out to a kind of universal world benevolence not unlike some of the B-grade sentimentality which disgusted soldiers in World War II: Hemingway thinks that "all the country in the world is the same country and all hunters are the same people" (*GHA,* p. 249).

The best art seems lifelike. Yet the reality of literature is a very difficult thing to discuss and almost impossible to prove. The best writers simply make their works seem real, as Hemingway did in his early work. But in *Death in the Afternoon* and *Green Hills of Africa* he does not create reality; he talks about it. "I must be altogether frank" on page one of *Death in the Afternoon* raises the interrogatory eyebrow, and so does the foreword of *Green Hills of Africa* when Hemingway announces his intent to write "an absolutely true book," which he hopes will be "truly presented." Such claims do not stop after the beginning: in *Death in the Afternoon* he uses *true* and its derivatives eight times; *real* and *really,* six

7. Hemingway, *Green Hills of Africa* (New York: Charles Scribner's Sons, 1935), "Foreword." Hereafter cited in text with abbreviation *GHA.*

8. Philip Young, *Ernest Hemingway,* Rinehart Critical Studies (New York: Rinehart & Company, 1952), p. 69.

times; *honest* (*honesty, honestly*), four times. Mainly, the protestations of truth create doubt, though not necessarily because the subject matter of bullfighting is foreign to the culture of the American reader. Frederic Henry's presentation of the war rings true partly because he made no claims for his own integrity. "No matter how good a phrase or a simile . . . [a writer] may have," Hemingway himself wrote in *Death in the Afternoon,* "if he puts it in where it is not absolutely necessary and irreplaceable he is spoiling his work for egotism" (*DA,* p. 191).

The words which once embarrassed Frederic Henry and which never were used in the early fiction unless spoken by some false character now appear in profusion. The explanation, according to Keneth Kinnamon, is that "Spain, as it were, had restored Hemingway's faith in the reality of the qualities that these abstract words signify. . . ." [9] But style is the question. The point is not faith or doubt, belief or disbelief; the point in the earlier fiction was that neither could be conveyed by an abstract or general word. It had to be seen or experienced concretely in the fact. And faith by this standard needs enacting as much as doubt—perhaps more. Kinnamon continues: "Hemingway is completely convinced of the reality of the quality, and he realizes the difficulty of conveying the reality to his non-Spanish audience, among whom honor is only a word. . . ." [10] Hemingway had tried to express it this way: "In Spain honor is a very real thing. Called pundonor, it means honor, probity, courage, self-respect and pride in one word. Pride is the strongest characteristic of the race and it is a matter of pundonor not to show cowardice" (*DA,* p. 91). Hemingway, as Kinnamon says, has realized the difficulty; but these further abstractions in modern English, the use of synonyms, cannot overcome it—as the concrete style in the earlier fiction.

"All our words," Hemingway wrote in *Death in the Afternoon,* "from loose using have lost their edge . . ." (*DA*, p. 71). The ones without any keenness at all according to the standards of the early

9. Keneth Kinnamon, "Hemingway, the *Corrida,* and Spain," *Texas Studies in Literature and Language,* 1 (Spring 1959), 55.

10. Kinnamon, p. 55.

fiction were the abstractions which disgusted the hero. Hemingway wrote in 1929,

The essential in big writing is to use words like the West, the East, Civilization, etc., and very often these words do not mean a damned thing but you cannot have big writing without them. My own experience has been that when you stand with your nose toward the north, if your head is held still, what is on your right will be east and what is on your left will be west and you can write very big putting those words in capitals but it is very liable not to mean anything.[11]

The statement is a good expression of the principles which made his style so effective in his early writing. It means simply that in fiction or nonfiction one may not extend his generalization beyond the individual, the group, a people to continents and global areas and civilizations. Great extension becomes abstract, pretentious, meaningless "big writing." But "big writing" occurs near the end of *Green Hills of Africa.* What Hemingway experiences in the African wilderness makes him lapse into a long diatribe on Africa, America, the frontier, modernity, progress, and the effects of civilization on the natural world:

A continent ages quickly once we come. . . . The earth gets tired of being exploited. A country wears out quickly unless man puts back in it all his residue and that of all his beasts. When he quits using beasts and uses machines, the earth defeats him quickly. The machine can't reproduce, nor does it fertilize the soil, and it eats what he cannot raise. A country was made to be as we found it. We are the intruders and after we are dead we may have ruined it but it will still be there and we don't know what the next changes are. I suppose they all end up like Mongolia.

Our people went to America because that was the place to go then. It had been a good country and we had made a bloody mess of it and I would go, now, somewhere else as we had always had the right to go somewhere else and as we had always gone. You could always come back. Let the others come to America who did not know that they

11. Hemingway, "Introduction," *Kiki's Memoirs* (Paris: Edward W. Titis, 1930), p. 10.

> had come too late. Our people had seen it at its best and fought for it when it was well worth fighting for. *(GHA,* pp. 284–285)

This is what Hemingway called "horseshit," defined in *Death in the Afternoon* as "unsoundness in an abstract conversation or, indeed, any over-metaphysical tendency in speech" (*DA,* p. 95). Whether the statement is unsound may be disputable, but Jake, Frederic, and the other characters of Hemingway's early fiction would have had no doubt that Hemingway's generalizations represented stylistically an "over-metaphysical tendency" even if they were true.

If Hemingway's manner of expressing his beliefs is stylistically inferior in his two works of nonfiction, the consistency and soundness of his morals and beliefs may also be questioned. From a "Christian point of view," he supposed, "the whole bullfight is indefensible" (*DA,* p. 1). Yet his book is a defense of bullfighting on moral and aesthetic grounds. The most frequently quoted passage in the book is about the morals of bullfighting:

> So far, about morals, I know only that what is moral is what you feel good after and what is immoral is what you feel bad after and judged by these moral standards, which I do not defend, the bullfight is very moral to me because I feel very fine while it is going on and have a feeling of life and death and mortality and immortality, and after it is over I feel very sad but very fine. (*DA,* p. 4)

Reconciling this statement with that about the "Christian point of view" results in paradoxes if not impossibilities. There are other problems. Hemingway warns the reader that he cannot make a moral judgment about bullfighting until "he, or she, has seen the things spoken of and knows truly what their reactions to them would be" (*DA,* p. 1). The same principle would prevent one from vicariously condemning adultery or murder, and one could not read *A Farewell to Arms* and condemn war unless he had spent some time on a battlefield. Of the great Spanish painters Goya, Velásquez, and El Greco, Hemingway wrote, "only Greco believed in Our Lord or took any interest in his crucifixion. You can only judge a painter by the ways he paints the things he believes in or cares for and the things he hates . . ." (*DA*, p. 203). Applied to Hemingway's early fiction, this statement reveals a wonderful consistency; applied to the abstractions of his nonfiction and to the suave and humorous treatment of values, the statement is puzzling, to say the least.

In *Death in the Afternoon* Hemingway ranges from a comic amorality to a deep appreciation of human values. He also seems to mingle piety and blasphemy. The last sentence of the following passage seems permeated with the deep piety of a true Catholic: "What it needs is a god to drive the half-gods out. But waiting for a messiah is a long business and you get many fake ones. There is no record in the Bible of the number of fake messiahs that came before Our Lord . . ." (*DA,* p. 86). But a bit later, Hemingway refers to a basic religious belief without seeming to participate in it. Writing about mercy killings, he begins a sentence by saying, "But as long as man is regarded as having an immortal soul . . ." (*DA,* p. 220). The verb is skeptical, and *as long as* perhaps suggests a coming age of enlightened disbelief.

That style which almost perfectly blends content and manner in *A Farewell to Arms* is drastically changed in Hemingway's nonfiction. The concreteness and the sensuousness remain, but they are mingled with generality and abstraction. The staccato sentence patterns have disappeared. There are long sentences with considerable subordination and complex and intellectual connectives in place of the repetitive *and*'s and the simple and compound sentences of the early fiction. Occasional sentences are unspeakably awkward: "Turning his back on a bull after he had put the sword in the bull caught him and gave him a terrific wound near the rectum that perforated the intestines" (*DA,* p. 253).

Placing one sentence from *Death in the Afternoon* beside fifteen from *A Farewell to Arms* demonstrates the indescribable change in style:

Cagancho is a gypsy, subject to fits of cowardice, altogether without integrity, who violates all the rules, written and unwritten, for the conduct of a matador but who, when he receives a bull that he has confidence in, and he has confidence in them very rarely, can do things which

I was not made to think. I was made to eat. My God, yes. Eat and drink and sleep with Catherine. To-night maybe. No that was impossible. But to-morrow night, and a good meal and all bullfighters do in a way they have never been done before and sometimes standing absolutely straight with his feet still, planted as though he were a tree, with the arrogance and grace that gypsies have and of which all other arrogance and grace seems an imitation, moves the cape spread full as the pulling jib of a yacht before the bull's muzzle so slowly that the art of bullfighting, which is only kept from being one of the major arts because it is impermanent, in the arrogant slowness of his veronicas becomes, for the seeming minutes that they endure, permanent. (*DA,* pp. 13–14)

sheets and never going away again except together. Probably have to go damned quickly. She would go. I knew she would go. When would we go? That was something to think about. It was getting dark. I lay and thought where we would go. There were many places. (*FA,* p. 242)

To measure *Death in the Afternoon* and *Green Hills of Africa* by Hemingway's own accomplishments in his earlier fiction is to compare unlike forms and to exaggerate Hemingway's development or degeneration. On the other hand, regardless of form, the blunt fact is that Hemingway's attainment was not great in his two books of nonfiction of the early thirties. A run-of-the-mill essayist might have prided himself on the achievement, but Hemingway had not been run-of-the-mill. The falling off at this time is significant also because it anticipates a fundamental change in the fiction. The two books look forward to the themes and the methods of *To Have and Have Not* and *For Whom the Bell Tolls.*

10

Garrulous Patriot

IF *The Sun Also Rises* and *A Farewell to Arms* in art and meaning were taken from the same quarry and sculptured in the same way, *To Have and Have Not* is a new sort of statuary. Finished eight years after *A Farewell to Arms* and only three before *For Whom the Bell Tolls,* it is more remarkable as an indication of what Hemingway had been and of what he would become than it is as a good book in itself. Instead of the familiar and well-disciplined first-person point of view, the narrative perspective shifts chaotically from first to third person and from one character to another. The wobbly technical point of view and the alternation of short scenes in the manner of naturalistic novelists developing social contrasts allow Hemingway to indulge a new whimsy for social commentary. Vignettes and essays at various times treat communism, social and economic contrasts in class, the depression, crime, gang violence, the old theme of the wasted land, war and the rights of veterans, and solitude versus the brotherhood of man. One nameless grain broker has no function in the novel except to portray the times and to serve as a contrast to the hero, Harry Morgan, who doesn't even know him. Thematically, the character serves the purpose of a sort of essay, and he is created with an abstract vocabulary which

Hemingway had never before used in fiction.[1] Although the hero of the novel does have a successful sex life and although he does arrive at a foggy and rudimentary understanding of his need for some kind of good relationship with other men, he is a criminal who stoops to the cruelty of the lawless gangster.

Three years later in *For Whom the Bell Tolls* Hemingway was excessively concerned with the brotherhood of men. During one of many sustained meditations, Robert Jordan, the hero of *For Whom the Bell Tolls* and a fighter for the Loyalist cause in the Spanish Civil War, remembers how he and his fellows in the Sierras "had fought there with the true comradeship of the revolution." [2] But all had not fought; some had run. They were shot. "It had seemed just and right and necessary," Jordan reflects, "that the men who ran were shot. There was nothing wrong about it. Their running was a selfishness" (*FWBT,* p. 236). The retreat, the desertion, the shooting here are exactly the same as in the episode of the shooting of the sergeants during the retreat from Caporetto in *A Farewell to Arms.* The cause is different. The sergeants placed self above the welfare of a small group who were helping them to escape from the enemy. The later soldiers place self above the patriotic cause. If the executioners of the sergeants, Frederic Henry and Bonello, thought in terms of the larger cause, they did not verbalize their thinking. Any concept of martial justice proved false in the mind of Henry a little later in the retreat when he made a separate peace rather than face his own would-be executioners. *A Farewell to Arms* presents an episode and leaves the complexities unresolved. With a technique much different from that of the early novels, *For Whom the Bell Tolls* presents a meditation on love of country and justice. There is but one issue—self vs. patriotism—and but one approved moral attitude toward that issue—the patriotic. The soldiers of the later novel, furthermore, are only remembered by the hero; they are not present in the enaction of a crucial event of the novel.

1. Hemingway, *To Have and Have Not* (New York: Charles Scribner's Sons, 1937), pp. 235–236.

2. Hemingway, *For Whom the Bell Tolls* (New York: Charles Scribner's Sons, 1940), p. 235. Hereafter cited in text with abbreviation *FWBT.*

The "whirr of wings" of sage hens "moves you suddenly more than any love of country," Hemingway said in an article on shooting birds in *Esquire* in 1935.[3] Less than two years before the beginning of the Civil War in Spain and only about five years before the publication of *For Whom the Bell Tolls,* he still valued sensuous experience more than love of country. Like Frederic Henry, he regarded patriotic causes as so false that he might make a separate peace rather than sacrifice himself in the manner of Robert Jordan. Between the middle 1930s and the early 1940s, Hemingway moved from one extreme to another, from national and personal isolationism to personal involvement in what he regarded as the cause of freedom in the world. The process of change and development was rapid but steady. In 1934 he wrote that Americans *"must keep out"* of the next European war although "There will be plenty of good reasons" for becoming involved.[4] In direct contradiction to the implications of John Donne's passage which served as an epigraph for the *Bell,* Hemingway in 1935 wrote that "no country but one's own is worth fighting for."[5] Beginning definitions of a worthy cause first began appearing in Hemingway's observations of the conflict between Italy and Ethiopia. Early in 1936 he noted that "Mussolini's sons are in the air where there are no enemy planes to shoot them down. But poor men's sons . . . are foot soldiers. . . . I wish they could learn who is their enemy—and why."[6] Here is at least a suggestion of the crusading of Hemingway during the Spanish Civil War, but even in 1936 he still spoke more frequently from the perspective of the hunter and the alienated Frederic Henry than from that of the champion of democracy and freedom. In a fishing story in *Esquire* he wrote of war in terms of the pleasure of hunting: "Certainly there is no hunting like the hunting of man and those who have hunted armed men long enough and liked it,

3. Hemingway, "Remembering Shooting-Flying: A Key West Letter," *By-Line: Ernest Hemingway,* ed. William White (New York: Charles Scribner's Sons, 1967), p. 191.

4. Hemingway, "A Paris Letter," *By-Line,* p. 158.

5. Hemingway, "Notes on the Next War: A Serious Topical Letter," *Esquire,* 4 (September 1935), p. 19.

6. Hemingway, "Wings Always over Africa: An Ornithological Letter," *By-Line,* p. 235.

never really care for anything else thereafter." [7] In 1937 when Hemingway began reporting on the war in Spain for the North American Newspaper Alliance, his dispatches from the first were exuberant with enthusiasm for the Loyalist cause. He described "a people united in its fury against foreign invasion," "a wave of enthusiasm . . . sweeping over the population." [8] By the spring of 1938 he was already writing with the universal democratic idealism characteristic of *For Whom the Bell Tolls*. The defenders of Spain, he wrote in *Ken,* "die knowing why they die; they die fighting for *you* now; knowing that unless they beat the fascists now *you* will have to fight them later." [9] Within the short period of three or four years Hemingway had reversed his position from advocating an isolationist separate peace to defending the cause of the universal brotherhood of all good democratic men. What was the effect of the new belief on his art?

From the statement in the epigraph that "any mans *death* diminishes *me,* because I am involved in *Mankinde*" to the deserter Pablo's return to his group because he does "not like to be alone" (*FWBT,* p. 391) to Robert Jordan's death stand against the Fascists while his cohorts retreat, *For Whom the Bell Tolls* is one of the most explicit statements in American fiction of how the universal communal good must prevail over the rights and indeed the life of the individual, no matter how worthy. From novels in which the individual and his personal relationships were the sole values to be verified, Hemingway has turned to the romantic theme which Robert Penn Warren's cynical Jack Burden calls "The flower-in-the-crannied-wall theory." [10] All of the good people of the world are as inter-dependent as if they were spliced together with the monkey-rope in *Moby-Dick*, "this Siamese connexion with a plurality of other mortals." [11] Or, in the words of Burden again, Robert

7. Hemingway, "On the Blue Water: A Gulf Stream Letter," *By-Line,* p. 236.

8. Hemingway, "Hemingway Reports Spain," *The New Republic,* 90 (May 5, 1937), p. 377.

9. Hemingway, "Dying, Well or Badly," *Ken,* 1 (April 21, 1938), 68.

10. Robert Penn Warren, *All the King's Men,* The Modern Library (New York: Random House, 1946, 1953), p. 234.

11. Herman Melville, *Moby-Dick: Or, The Whale,* ed. Luther S. Mans-

Jordan eats "a persimmon and the teeth of a tinker in Tibet are put on edge." [12] Hemingway, then, attempts to base his novel on "a tremendous sense of man's dignity and worth, an urgent awareness of the necessity of man's freedom, a nearly poetic realization of man's *collective* virtues." [13]

A Farewell to Arms had denied collective virtues. The marvel of Hemingway's first novels was the perfect blend of style and theme, the denial of abstract belief of any kind in favor of the concreteness of the single person, the denial of any words of truth in favor of concrete images of experience. With the change in theme in the *Bell,* the artistic problem became the finding of a style in which to embody the theme of universal brotherhood and of the supremacy of mankind over the individual—the same point Faulkner was soon to develop in *Go Down, Moses.* If Hemingway in the later novel had simply reversed his style as he did reverse his theme, if he had tried to assert his meanings in general and didactic language, he would have contradicted every principle and practice in his early style. Obviously, *For Whom the Bell Tolls* is not a simple reversal, but it is a most uneven performance. It is at times concrete and restrained and at other times as didactic as William Cullen Bryant; it is tough, and it is sentimental; it is oversimplified, and it is complex; it is a magnificent effort to express a noble theme, but it is often undisciplined art.

In parts, aspects, and episodes, *For Whom the Bell Tolls* contains some of Hemingway's greatest work. In some ways, the last stand of El Sordo on his mountaintop is as effectively created as the retreat from Caporetto in *A Farewell to Arms.* Pablo's taking of the Fascist town mingles stark simplicity of style and complexity of subject matter in the manner of the best in Hemingway's short stories. The humanity of certain Fascists (Lieutenant Berrendo and the young cavalryman whom Robert Jordan kills when he happens to ride into Pablo's camp) and the inhumanity of some of the Loyalists (Comrade Marty and Pablo) not only prevent the

field and Howard P. Vincent (New York: Hendricks House, 1952), p. 318.

12. Warren, p. 234.

13. Mark Schorer, "The Background of a Style," *The Kenyon Review,* 3 (Winter 1941), 103.

oversimplification of propaganda but also create a complexity of the characters which reflects some of the old techniques in *The Sun Also Rises* and *A Farewell to Arms.*

Despite the reversal of theme in the *Bell,* Hemingway's accomplishments come from the portrayal of the individual. As a patriot meditating on the cause for which he fights, Robert Jordan is never so real as he is when he is distracted from the danger and the issues while in the midst of a small battle he wires grenades and dynamite onto a bridge:

> Suddenly he was working only with the noise of the stream. He looked down and saw it boiling up white below him through the boulders and then dropping down to a clear pebbled pool where one of the wedges he had dropped swung around in the current. As he looked a trout rose for some insect and made a circle on the surface close to where the chip was turning. As he twisted the wire tight with the pliers that held these two grenades in place, he saw through the metal of the bridge, the sunlight on the green slope of the mountain. It was brown three days ago, he thought. (*FWBT,* p. 438)

Jordan's patriotism and his individuality are both more credible because of the beauty of the trout, because of his distraction from the suspense of the moment and from the belief for which he undergoes danger. His ability to recognize the eternity of his relationship to the normal processes of nature even during this moment adds to his identity as a person and to the intensity of the moment. Paradoxically, the refusal to confront the momentous questions of danger and the cause for which he works results in emphasis rather than distraction.

Jordan's observing the trout and forgetting what cannot really be stated fully are representative of Hemingway's major accomplishments in the novel. Part of the iceberg here is hidden. The best things in Hemingway still cannot be said. General Golz cannot say them, and therefore he resembles Count Mippipopolous's personal vitality and oral reticence when the Count could only say, "all I want out of wines is to enjoy them." [14] After Robert Jordan answers

14. Hemingway, *The Sun Also Rises* (New York: Charles Scribner's Sons, 1926, 1928), p. 62. Hereafter cited in text with abbreviation *SAR.*

that he knows the one thing he must know about the bridge, Golz replies: " 'I believe you do,' Golz said. 'I will not make you any little speech. Let us now have a drink' " (*FWBT,* p. 7). And the speech by implication has been made, though neither characters nor reader knows what could be said. Character and situation exist here without the words, just as the words existed removed from character and situation in Jordan's meditation on the soldiers who were shot because they ran. Maria's mother has a personal identity although she is not given political allegiance. She "was not a Republican," Maria says. Whether she has no political views according to the old-fashioned traditions of subservient womanhood or whether her views contradict those of her husband—these are not really the question. Her strength is apparent only in the love for her husband. As she sees him shot she says, "Long live my husband who is Mayor of this village" (*FWBT,* p. 351). The present tense of the verb may communicate personal shock or perhaps defiance of tragedy. Her words are as concrete as Frederic Henry's taking food to his men because they were hungry even though he had to risk his life during bombardment.

The restrained art of hinting at what the characters feel but cannot say and the complexity of patterns of characters (good people fighting for a bad cause, bad people fighting for a good cause) are reflected by contradictions between motivations and acts. "What we did. Not what the others did to us" (*FWBT,* p. 134), Robert Jordan thinks after Pilar tells of the killing of the Fascists. And the violent massacre in the name of the Loyalist cause begins from a personal grudge: The first blow is struck by a malcontent tenant. In his actions before the blow, Pilar sees his personal emotions: "his face was working and he was biting his lips and his hands were white on his flail" (*FWBT,* p. 108). The beauty of a town square in the morning and the simplicity of the men who are laying the dust with water and preparing to massacre the Fascists cause an apparent incongruency like that in Robert Jordan's awareness of the trout under the bridge: "the hose sweeping in wide arcs and the water glistening in the sun and the men leaning on their flails or the clubs or the white wood pitchforks and watching the sweep of the stream of water" (*FWBT,* p. 107). A similar contradiction in Pablo's reaction to the death of the priest reveals the depth of human nature. A disbeliever, a violent man, a Loyalist, later a coward, Pablo is disillusioned by the priest's lack of dignity in the moment of death.

> ". . . But a priest. He has an example to set."
> "I thought you hated priests."
> "Yes," said Pablo and cut some more bread. "But a *Spanish* priest. A *Spanish* priest should die very well."

Without questioning the excellence of the story of the killing of the Fascists as a separate episode, W. M. Frohock regards it as a digression, "particularly shocking violence for its own sake. . . ." [15] El Sordo's last stand against Fascist troops and planes is no digression; all in miniature, it represents the predicament of the good people in the novel. The brusque and wily old Spaniard and his band are sacrificed for the general patriotic cause; personal feelings dictate that Pablo's band and Robert Jordan should try to help, but to assist Sordo would jeopardize the Loyalist cause probably without saving him.

Hemingway's style in the story of Sordo, however, reflects some of the worst aspects of his technique in the novel. The technical point of view, which follows Robert Jordan as a narrative center throughout most of the novel, switches in this event from Jordan in Pilar's camp to Sordo's hill, "shaped like a chancre" (p. 311). Then it alternates from the besieged Loyalists to the attacking Fascists. For the sake of suspense and contrast Hemingway gives up some of his old discipline. A more serious problem is the violation of tone which occurs with the insertion of melodramatic and sentimental historical generalizations. Hemingway intrudes and destroys whatever objective perspective the reader has on the tough character of the Spanish guerilla.

> If he had known how many men in history have had to use a hill to die on it would not have cheered him any for, in the moment he was passing through, men are not impressed by what has happened to other

15. W. M. Frohock, *The Novel of Violence in America* (Dallas: Southern Methodist University Press, 1957), p. 191.

men in similar circumstances any more than a widow of one day is helped by the knowledge that other loved husbands have died. (*FWBT*, p. 312)

Obviously this oration at the moment of martyrdom has nothing to do with the knowledge and thoughts of Sordo. Hemingway admits the irrelevance ("If he had known . . ."). The intensity of emotion should come from the reader's awe and pity at the catastrophe of Sordo, not from a generalization about the fate of many men on hills in all time. The intrusion detracts. It accomplishes the very opposite of Hemingway's intent: instead of increasing the catharsis, it diminishes it. "Tragedy should be and always has been an individual matter," John Atkins has written. "It only exists when one is aware of the personality destroyed. But there is no personality in modern war. It is, for the most part, literally anonymous."[16] Hemingway has, however, created a personality, and the theme of *For Whom the Bell Tolls* asserts his significance. But the historical digression ignores his character, contradicts his aim, and argues for anonymity.

The Spartan Sordo accepts death, jokes about it, decides that it is "nothing," and turns to memories and definitions of life.

But living was a field of grain blowing in the wind on the side of a hill. Living was a hawk in the sky. Living was an earthen jar of water. . . . Living was a horse between your legs and a carbine under one leg and a hill and a valley and a stream with trees along it and the far side of the valley and the hills beyond. (*FWBT*, p. 313)

Shades of the worst of Whitman and Wolfe! And of the sentimental patriotic radio drama in the days of the beginning of World War II. The images to which living is equated are more rhetorical than particular and relevant. The grain, the hawks, and the jar are not associated with place, event, and time in Sordo's life. Here the heroic character is thinking abstractly rather than living concretely as Frederic Henry did with Catherine in the Alps or as he did in his imagined sojourn in the Abruzzi. The pointing and repeated gerunditive subjects ("Living was . . .") are a cheap stylistic trick;

16. John Atkins, *The Art of Ernest Hemingway: His Work and Personality* (London: Spring Books, 1952, 1964), p. 126.

no image after such an abstract phrase could appeal to a reader disciplined by the hard images of Hemingway's early prose. There is no iceberg in this style, because almost nothing is left under water.

The further the novel goes, the looser the point of view becomes. Hemingway reports the conversation of the Fascist guards at the bridge. The internal thoughts of Joaquín are recorded literally until his consciousness disappears into "the red black roar" of the bombs which cause his death. Toward the end of the novel Robert Jordan learns that the Fascists have gained enough information to prepare for the attack of the Loyalists and that the attack is likely to fail. He dispatches Andrés as a messenger so that General Golz will know to call off the attack. The life of Robert Jordan and the success of the Loyalist forces depend upon the success of Andrés's mission. To create suspense and to intensify the reader's concern with the thematic issues, Hemingway in this section makes use of the device of alternating scenes in the manner of *To Have and Have Not* and of the omniscient novels of the naturalists, such as Frank Norris's *The Octopus* and Dreiser's *Sister Carrie.* Traditionally in such novels the social issues are of overwhelming significance, and the characters largely exemplify a theme or a cause. For eleven chapters (33 to 43) every chapter switches the setting from the mission of Andrés to the scene in Pablo's cave, except that chapters 37–39 all are set in the cave with the carrying of the message treated in 36 and 40. An alternative method would have been to keep the focus upon Jordan and to allow the reader to remain in ignorance with him of the fate of the message. Then only the course of the battle and the flights of attacking Loyalist planes (or the lack of them) might reveal the fate of the message. Hemingway chose to give the panoramic view. Even if this is not an inferior technique, it is altogether different from his earlier methods. The choice allows the novelist to contrast events, to evoke suspense, and to universalize meanings. He rejected the restricted manner of the hard-disciplined style of the early novels which so powerfully portrayed character and psychology and the small individual in the grip of forces too vast in scope for him to comprehend.

As Hemingway expanded his technical point of view in *For Whom the Bell Tolls,* he also strayed away from his images and added statements of meaning. Formerly he had practiced omission, knowing that "you still have [the thing omitted] in the writing and its quality will show." [17] Now Hemingway seems to distrust his audience, to assume that the reader cannot respond unless the author dictates the response. He writes with an eye too much on the unresponsive reader. After the relationship between Anselmo and Robert Jordan is well established, for example, Hemingway still writes as if he cannot expect the reader to work within the given context. " 'You have killed?' Robert Jordan asked in the intimacy of the dark and of their day together" (*FWBT,* p. 41). If the intimacy is not obvious enough for the conversation to seem plausible on the basis of their relationship, authorial assertion cannot create it. In the very paragraph which introduces the name of Robert Jordan, Hemingway writes, "He was often hungry but he was not usually worried because he did not give any importance to what happened to himself . . ." (*FWBT*, p. 4). Clearly this statement is intended to suggest the magnanimity and self-denial of the hero. To the extent that the point of view is a reflection of his thoughts, the remark exposes a sort of martyr complex bordering on a too conscious patriotic self-righteousness. To the extent that it is a statement by the author, it is an assertion of principle that would be more effective if embodied in a scene or a deed. It is almost as if Hemingway seems not to trust his reader to make inferences or himself to imply. Or perhaps he is so much concerned with message that he does not take the time to embody it in art.

Just as Hemingway stated abstractions, he also made anticlimactic if not ludicrous statements about actions in which the emotion and the meaning had already become perfectly apparent. When Maria tells Robert Jordan about being raped by the Fascist soldiers, the simplicity of her account is exceeded only by the generality of Robert Jordan's reaction: " 'My rabbit,' Robert Jordan said and held her as close and as gently as he could. But he was as full of hate as any man could be" (*FWBT,* p. 353). In *The Sun Also Rises* Hemingway had been able to create a similar intensity of

17. George Plimpton, "An Interview with Ernest Hemingway," in Carlos Baker, *Hemingway and His Critics: An International Anthology* (New York: Hill and Wang, fifth printing, 1963), p. 28.

love for one person and hate for another group without such authorial intrusion. Mike Campbell, the fiancé of Brett Ashley, told how Robert Cohn out of jealousy fought the bull-fighter Romero after he found Brett in his room. Cohn "massacred the poor, bloody bull-fighter" and then wept with remorse.

> "It seems the bull-fighter chap was sitting on the floor. He was waiting to get strength enough to get up and hit Cohn again. Brett wasn't having any shaking hands, and Cohn was crying and telling her how much he loved her, and she was telling him not to be a ruddy ass. Then Cohn leaned down to shake hands with the bull-fighter fellow. No hard feelings, you know. All for forgiveness. And the bull-fighter hit him in the face again." (*SAR*, p. 202)

This is the art of dialogue and restraint which becomes tarnished (in *For Whom the Bell Tolls*) when Hemingway succumbs to words and omits deeds.

The patterns of didacticism and sentimentality in a writer of some diminished talent usually begin with an image or scene somewhat satisfactory in its concreteness but end with a general or a hortatory statement. One lyrical section of the *Bell* consists of Robert Jordan's reflections on a coming storm which may bring snow and reveal the tracks and sanctuaries of his allies. The hero meditates on the adversities of the snow:

> In the snowstorm you came close to wild animals and they were not afraid. They travelled across country not knowing where they were and the deer stood sometimes in the lee of the cabin. In a snowstorm you rode up to a moose and he mistook your horse for another moose and trotted forward to meet you. (*FWBT*, p. 182)

The reader at this point has ample information to conclude that snowstorms cause adversities and that old hostilities may be forgotten in a new friendship. This sort of sentiment is so inherent in the situation that a direct statement even in the explicit prose of criticism is both too obvious and too emotional. But the artist should never become his own interpreter as Hemingway does in the next sentence: "In a snowstorm it always seemed, for a time, as though there were no enemies." The thought of the passage is

Robert Jordan's. But since Hemingway is characterizing him as a strong man and a tragic hero, the author himself as well as Robert Jordan reveals a flawed sensibility in this emotional generalization.

Hemingway's critical theories and his early practice of his art are directly applicable to *For Whom the Bell Tolls*, especially to the generality, the obviousness, and the lack of restraint in the character of Robert Jordan and in the meditations of many of the characters. One significant factor in the later novel, however, is such a new phenomenon that the older standards may not apply; this element is the polysyllabic speech of the primitive Spaniards. Monosyllabic Anglo-Saxon words are peculiarly appropriate to the psychological inhibitions of the modern American heroes of Hemingway's works. Even some uneducated American rural folk, on the other hand, find that long words have a peculiarly pleasant savor. The primitive Spaniard, speaker of a Romance tongue derived from Latin origins, finds an extraordinary pleasure in "conscious latinity." [18] Or at least he does in Hemingway's works. And whether or not the generalization is true of actual Spaniards, the dialogue makes such language seem credible and colorful to ears accustomed to English words. Hemingway and his characters often express their consciousness of the peculiar qualities of the Spanish idiom. Robert Jordan "felt a little theatrical" after a speech, "but it sounded well in Spanish" (*FWBT*, p. 43). Anselmo spoke "honestly and clearly and with no pose, neither the English pose of understatement nor any Latin bravado . . ." (*FWBT*, p. 43). Speech in Spanish is pleasurable, formal, "shorter and simpler," vile (*FWBT*, pp. 91, 181, 318). The paradoxical combination of formality and familiarity of second-person singular pronouns, *thee*'s and *thou*'s, adds to the strangeness of this literally translated Romance language. Echoes of the Biblical language of the King James version help the polysyllabic words to make abstraction at times more acceptable than it could be in the worlds of *The Sun Also Rises* and *A Farewell to Arms.*

The Spanish dialogue is more successful than euphemisms used for obscenities. And the occasional introspection of Hemingway's

18. John Crowe Ransom, "On Shakespeare's Language," *The Sewanee Review*, 55 (April–June 1947), 182.

Spaniards is less oonvincing than their talk. The worst failures, however, occur in the meditations of Robert Jordan. Often Hemingway seems to become conscious of the esthetic problem and to provide explanations through the sensibility of his hero, who is aware of the failures of language but who continues to use the very inadequate words he despises. Robert Jordan feels that he is "taking part in a crusade. That was the only word for it although it was a word that had been so worn and abused that it no longer gave its true meaning" (*FWBT*, p. 235). But *crusade* is not the only inadequate word here. In the same passage his thoughts proceed to "the oppressed of the world which would be . . . difficult and embarrassing to speak about," "absolute brotherhood," "the performance of your duty," and "true comradeship." If Pilar does deny the possibility of words in the manner of Jake Barnes ("In war one cannot say what one feels"), all too often the characters think what they feel, and the communication falls flat and trite into the mind of the reader despite all the self-conscious explanations of the hero. Robert Jordan's mind uses "clichés . . . without criticism" (*FWBT*, p. 164), but Hemingway had trained his reader to be more critical than his latest hero.

The religious language of the Spanish characters is one of the minor triumphs of the novel. The Loyalists of Pablo's band have lost most of their belief in the Christian religion, but they still retain the need for the ritual, the confession, and the words of belief. Thus Pilar reveals her loss of faith and her great need for it when she remembers how a bull's head "was shrouded in a purple cloth as the images of the saints are covered in church during the week of the passion of our former Lord" (*FWBT*, p. 185). Even Anselmo's declarations of disbelief are repeated in something of the language of the creed: " 'Since we do not have God here any more, neither His Son nor the Holy Ghost, who forgives?' " (*FWBT*, p. 41).

For Whom the Bell Tolls is not sentimental and weak and inadequate because the emotion is too great for the occasion. Hemingway commanded a plot, a theme, and a cause of great and tragic potentiality. The novel fails in part because the style and the language are not great enough to indicate the depth of the theme and the tragedy. The book is often sentimental and shallow in its failure to find images and language for its great themes. Like Faulkner's "The Bear," published two years later, *For Whom the Bell Tolls* is a crusading promotion of "the communal anonymity of brotherhood." Hemingway simply was not able to adapt his old style to a novel about great social, political, and democratic causes. And when he wrote in a new style, he used the words that once would have been embarrassing.

11

The Iceberg and the Cardboard Box

HEMINGWAY'S last novel, *The Old Man and the Sea,* is the single exception in his general decline. In many ways it turns back toward the older manner of the nineteen twenties. It is certainly more restrained than its predecessor, *Across the River and into the Trees,* even more than *For Whom the Bell Tolls. The River* is ruined by the hero's sentimental meditations on events of the past; *The Sun Also Rises* and *A Farewell to Arms* were books of acts; *The Old Man and the Sea* falls somewhere between the two. The old man struggles with the fish, but also he thinks a great deal, perhaps too much. The code of the good characters of *The Sun Also Rises* was to have personal values, to see them in the facts and the deeds, but not to state them. Colonel Cantwell in *Across the River and into the Trees* dwells on old events and deeds, talks about them in order to see universal meanings. "The dignity of movement of an ice-berg . . . , due to only one-eighth of it being above water," is lost. The style in *The River* is as clumsy as a canoe maneuvered by the inept. In the early works Hemingway had cut out "damned good stuff," [1] but in *The River* and to a lesser extent in *The Old Man and the Sea*

1. Hemingway, "He Who Gets Slap Happy: a Bimini Letter," *Esquire,* 4 (August 1935), 19.

he left in damned bad stuff. Emotion had been conveyed only through the concrete; now through Colonel Cantwell's memory, sentimentality is more apparent than the concrete thing which causes the emotion. The trouble is that the author and the character refuse to trust themselves and the reader to be moved by moving things; they must state the emotion, revel in it, relish it. And all thus become sentimental. The part of the iceberg which should be hidden shows through the water when the Colonel reflects that "This country meant very much to him, more than he could, or would ever tell anyone. . . ." [2] But together author and character have told the reader and become more sentimental than genuine.

In *The Old Man and the Sea* the concrete object reappears in Hemingway's fiction, but it is still treated sentimentally at times. In some ways this novelette returns to his early manner. It is difficult to ascertain the exact time of composition of Hemingway's last two novels. He conceived the plan of *The Old Man and the Sea* in 1936, and as late as the year before publication it was part four of a work regarded as his "sea book." [3] The time of composition of *Across the River and into the Trees* is also problematical. It derived in part from an abortive and unpublished long novel, *The Garden of Eden*, begun early in 1946.[4] Time of composition, Hemingway's development as a writer in his older years, the simplicity of his story of the fisherman, the use of autobiography in the story of the general, the temptation to sentimentality and garrulity in the talk of an old general and his young mistress—many factors possibly affected Hemingway's style and made his last novel better than the previous one.

The assumption of much of the literature of the early twentieth century is that language and truth may not correspond, indeed, usually do not. Using the medium of language, the writer somehow had to convey the truth in the fact, not in statement. When the truth was not embodied in fact, it was not there; statement insured false-

2. Hemingway, *Across the River and into the Trees* (New York: Charles Scribner's Sons, 1950), p. 33. Hereafter cited in the text with abbreviation *ART*.

3. Carlos Baker, *Ernest Hemingway: A Life Story* (New York: Charles Scribner's Sons, 1969), pp. 339, 493.

4. Baker, pp. 454, 540.

ness. "The greatest difficulty," Hemingway wrote in *Death in the Afternoon* (p. 2), "aside from knowing truly what you really felt, rather than what you were supposed to feel, and had been taught to feel, was to put down what really happened in action. . . ." [5] Like Faulkner's *Old Man* and *The Bear*, Hemingway's *The Old Man and the Sea* begins like a fable: "He was an old man who fished alone in a skiff in the Gulf Stream and he had gone eighty-four days now without taking a fish." [6] Mostly this is a sentence of fact, but the explicit suggestion of truth is stronger here than in the beginnings of Hemingway's earlier work. The simple naming of occupation, the solitude, the elemental need, the specific number of days of hard luck, and the continuation of heroic effort—these cause the reader to fall into step with the suggestion of parable or fable, and he recognizes the tone of a story which begins, "Once upon a time there was an old man. . . ."

The first paragraph ends with a simile comparing concrete image to an abstraction. Every day the old man comes home and carries his sail to his cabin. "The sail was patched with flour sacks and, furled, *it looked like the flag of permanent defeat*" (italics mine; *OMS*, p. 9). Defeat is apparent in the events, in another day with no fish, and in the patching of the sail with a material which costs nothing. It is "what really happened," or "what really is." But the image of the flag is more than visual; it is not what "really happened"; it is an abstraction.

The Old Man and the Sea thus begins as fiction of creation and of statement. One who is cheerful may smile or say something cheerful or wink; and the cheer is created. He may act or speak in a way to show that he is undefeated. But when the author says, "his eyes . . . were cheerful and undefeated" (*OMS*, p. 10), he is not creating but asserting. And each of the first three paragraphs of the short novel ends with a statement slightly removed from the concreteness of the individuality of Santiago. The boy, Manolin, volunteers to go fishing with him. Then Hemingway says, "The old man had

5. Hemingway, *Death in the Afternoon* (New York: Charles Scribner's Sons, 1932), p. 2. Hereafter cited in the text with abbreviation *DA*.

6. Hemingway, *The Old Man and the Sea* (New York: Charles Scribner's Sons, 1952), p. 9. Hereafter cited in the text with abbreviation *OMS*.

taught the boy to fish and the boy loved him." The love is apparent in the offer to fish with him despite his hard luck, but Hemingway nevertheless adds the gratuitous. The iceberg is topheavy, so much out of water that it has lost a little of the dignity of its movement. In a way, this is nitpicking criticism. The elaboration of the problem makes it more serious than it is. On the other hand, it is a necessary critical point of view—because it is precisely by the omission of statements of this kind that the early Hemingway had created wonder in his early novels.

The characters tell each other what they obviously know and interpret for each other. The old man tells the boy that they have much faith. In Hemingway's better works the character showed his faith or his love without stating it. In this novel the man who returns to the sea after not having caught a fish the day before is demonstrating faith and perseverance. Here the good characters have the same strength as the older heroes. But either they show emotional weakness by feeling that the faith must be said, or the author may feel that he cannot indicate a character's feelings without statement. It is as if the author is telling the reader that the characters have faith. When explicit statements occurred in the early fiction, they were attributed to false characters like Robert Cohn and the patriot Gino, who used the words of belief and faith because they did not know the reality.

Even when the character has sufficient restraint and refuses to contemplate the general truth, the author may fail to live up to the strength of his character: "The thousand times that he had proved it meant nothing. Now he was proving it again. Each time was a new time and he never thought about the past when he was doing it" (*OMS*, p. 73). Santiago's strength enables him to ignore the past; the author does not share his strength. He moralizes and generalizes. Similarly, Hemingway writes that "many of the fishermen made fun of the old man and he was not angry" (*OMS*, p. 11). Not bad. "Others, of the older fishermen, looked at him and were sad. But they did not show it and they spoke politely about the current and the depths they had drifted their lines at and the steady good weather and of what they had seen" (*OMS*, p. 11). Better. Politeness of speech alone is enough to show kindness and consideration.

Their speech about weather and current and depths, their failure to mention their catches, the omission of the topic of the old man's streak of bad luck—these create their sadness. Here *The Old Man and the Sea* is rather like a fable or parable because the dialogue is not rendered; but the summary of the topics of conversation is better than the reporting of the general attitudes of those who "made fun of the old man." How did they?

At times Hemingway creates the dignity and mystery of the iceberg in *The Old Man and the Sea.* That same sail which had been "the flag of permanent defeat" is treated simply and truly a little later in the novel. The old man's shirt "had been patched so many times that it was like the sail and the patches were faded to many different shades by the sun" (*OMS*, p. 20). The poverty, endurance, self-reliance, and persistence are shown by the shirt, not asserted about it. Similarly, Santiago's shack is "made of the tough bud-shields of the royal palm which are called guano" (*OMS,* p. 16), and the simplicity of its furnishings reveals more than a comment could. It contains pictures of the Sacred Heart of Jesus and of the Virgin of Cobre, "relics of his wife" (*OMS*, p. 16), which suggest the faith and love of Santiago. No essay is needed to reveal his love and grief when Hemingway merely indicates that he had removed her tinted photograph.

In complete solitude except for the company of the creatures of the sea, Santiago is less of an island than any of Hemingway's other protagonists. Jake Barnes is surrounded by revelers throughout most of *The Sun Also Rises*, but his occasional intimate relationships with Brett and with those who are aficionado result in no enduring communication. At the end of *A Farewell to Arms* Frederic Henry is left in solitude to puzzle out the meanings of an enigmatic universe without his lover, Catherine, and his military comrades. Harry Morgan is left alone at his death, commenting that "a man alone ain't got no bloody fucking chance." [7] Robert Jordan and Colonel Cantwell die without even the solace of the companionship of their lovers. Santiago seems to be more alone than any other hero. But because of the nature of the society of *The Old Man and*

7. Hemingway, *To Have and Have Not* (New York: Charles Scribner's Sons, 1937), p. 225.

the Sea and because of the hero's strength, Santiago alone on the sea is more closely related to the natural world and human society than any other hero in Hemingway. He has fewer antagonists. Manolin is with him at the beginning and the end of his odyssey, and he is always with him in spirit. Patrol boats search for him; and the good wishes of other fishermen go with him. The fish is his brother, and he communes with the birds and other natural creatures. If *The Old Man and the Sea* superficially looks like a study of the solitary individual, some critics have overemphasized the isolation of man.[8] Actually this book depicts social man as favorably as any major work of the twentieth century. Manolin and Santiago's relationship at the first of the novel is oversentimental. Man seems to be so good that the novel partakes of a few of the weaknesses of the sentimental local colorists of the late nineteenth century. Santiago is physically alone but spiritually surrounded by those he loves—Manolin, his wife, his fellow fishermen, the creatures of the sea, even the creature he slays. The sections that reveal the old man fishing are among the most optimistic passages written by Eliot, Faulkner, or Hemingway. And at times it is by far the most concrete and restrained work created by any of these writers after the nineteen thirties. With lapses, it almost succeeds in proving that good as well as evil can be embodied in image.

Hemingway attains his old stylistic form best in the descriptions of the old man on the sea catching his fish and fighting the sharks. The sentences are shorter than they have been since before *For Whom the Bell Tolls*, and the shortness is appropriate to the character of the hero and to his actions. The staccato style represents not only the frantic actions of the fish and the reactions of the fisherman but also the old man's thoughts as he prepares his strategies.

> He is hitting the wire leader with his spear, he thought. That was bound to come. He had to do that. It may make him jump though and I would rather he stayed circling now. The jumps were necessary for him to take air. But after that each one can widen the opening of the hook wound and he can throw the hook. *(OMS,* p. 97)

8. Lois L. Barnes, "The Helpless Hero of Ernest Hemingway," *Science & Society,* 17 (Winter 1953), 5–6.

At last, if only occasionally, the simple words and the simple sentences are as appropriate to heroism and virtue as they had been to disbelief and anti-intellectualism. Even when the sentences are occasionally long, they are usually simple in structure. Units which have a dependent grammatical structure usually break apart easily into separate thoughts.

Even the tough dialogue, which once had proved only the endurance of the crusty hero in a world where there was no reason for endurance except personal integrity, now proves a moral order. Facing the final defeat, the destruction of his fish which he had brought to the gaff, Santiago does not puzzle over meanings or the absence of them. A great confidence arises in the old man and even in the reader at his defiant and final confrontation of the destructive sharks: "He spat into the ocean and said, 'Eat that, *Galanos.* And make a dream you've killed a man' " (*OMS*, p. 131). The sentence does not add that no victorious sharks can ever kill a man.

There are many lapses from this simplicity even when the old man is alone on the sea. At times he is a little too virtuous and self-conscious in his awareness of his manhood. Mark Schorer has rightly objected to the generalization in Santiago's reminder to himself that "pain does not matter to a man" and praised a similar passage which "does not tell us at all" ("If he [his hand] cramps again let the line cut him off").[9] When Santiago hits a tuna "on the head for kindness," benevolence shows a little too obviously (*OMS*, p. 42). The old fisherman's love for the sea is apparent without Hemingway's long comment on the subject (*OMS*, p. 32). And the deception of the Portuguese men of war and the old man's hatred of the poison in their beauty is apparent without the reminder that they are "the falsest thing in the sea" (*OMS*, p. 40). But these flaws on the whole are minor. Seldom is it that "the old fisherman sounds a little like Col. Cantwell. . . ."[10]

The basic problem in *Across the River and into the Trees* is that

9. Mark Schorer, "With Grace Under Pressure," *New Republic,* 127 (October 6, 1952), 19.

10. Philip Young, *Ernest Hemingway,* Rinehart Critical Studies (New York: Rinehart & Company, Inc., 1952), p. 97.

Hemingway attempted to make his protagonist a modern thinker, and he has never been able to present meditation so well as action. The past of *The River* is almost as remote from the present events of the novel as the silent past is remote from Quentin and Shreve in *Absalom, Absalom!* Colonel Cantwell resembles Prufrock and the old man in "Gerontion" more than he does Hemingway's heroes; and the difference is that the author seems no longer to recognize the flaws of his introspective hero. The Colonel is a meditative and aged Robert Jordan who ladles out his life in coffee spoons and shot glasses. Once he faced situations like those of the killing of the Fascists and the last stand of El Sordo on his hilltop, but now he can only think about them. The memory of the hero and the imagination of the author fail to evoke the incidents and details which could give validity to the events.

Across the River and into the Trees is in some ways an enacting of the adage about the thousand deaths of the coward, and the Colonel meditates on many before he comes to the experience. On his trip to visit his lover, Renata, in Venice, the Colonel thinks of the "great villas" of the Brenta, "with their lawns and their gardens and the plane trees and the cypresses" (*ART*, p. 34). There he would like to be buried. And perhaps the list of concrete images might justify a love of place which would avert morbid self-pity. But the emotion here is a fear of death rather than a love of place of burial. What would be a weakness, a moral sickness, for Barnes and Henry becomes apparent in the Colonel's rambling thoughts on the decay of his own body: "The stinking, putrefying part doesn't last very long, really, he thought, and anyway you are just a sort of mulch, and even the bones will be of some use finally" (*ART*, p. 35). The Colonel's thoughts of death are not unlike Quentin's vision of his drowning, but Quentin's self-pity is known to be a mental sickness; the Colonel's is viewed as a kind of courage throughout the novel.

Sensation contained its own thought in the early novels, and the character violated his integrity when he interpreted the facts and made them an abstraction. But Cantwell thinks too much, even during sexual intercourse. Earlier, love had meant doing things for, according to the definition of the priest; now, love means thinking about oneself. Colonel Cantwell knows that "it is only what man does for woman that he retains, except what he does for his fatherland or his motherland . . ." (*ART*, p. 153). Thus "The emotion which it used to be death to utter . . . ," says John W. Aldridge, "has been diluted and sentimentalized into . . . querulous self-pity. . . ." [11] The Colonel is a sentimentally portrayed autobiographical likeness of the author; and with much justification Philip Young argues that "Hemingway has realized, in fiction, a wish—has quite patently envisaged a dream of how he himself would like to die." [12]

The world pessimism and personal cheeriness of the major in *A Farewell to Arms* constitute the stance of the individual who confronts a sick world. If the theme of war most clearly reveals the over-all design of the earlier novel, in *Across the River and into the Trees* the same theme provides only an opportunity for garrulous bragging. Frederic Henry lives through a war and a terrible retreat; the Colonel lies in bed with his girl friend and thinks about and talks about war. Every facet of the Colonel's war is a memory and a concept and a psychological scar. War in *A Farewell to Arms* was blood dripping from the wounded soldier riding in an ambulance stretcher above Henry in his stretcher; retreat was Bonello's killing of the sergeant; and death was the death of Henry's friend Piani. Now there are no significant characters except the Colonel; his relationships with other soldiers do not exist except in abstract discussions of his misfortunes and the vagaries of the high command.

The Colonel has too little memory and character to re-create his life concretely. Instead of writing about a soldier enduring the hardships of warfare, Hemingway now uses his Colonel as a mouthpiece for society-column opinions and essays and gossip. Once he had called himself "Ernie Hemorrhoid, the Poor Man's Pyle," [13] and the wit was worthy of Henry and Barnes. In *The River* he was more like a worn-out Hedda Hopper. The acquiescent nearly-eighteen-year-old Italian aristocratic mistress is an audience which would suffice to get his views into the paper. Hemingway had forgotten the hero who suffers and lives only by means of a reservoir of per-

11. John W. Aldridge, *In Search of Heresy: American Literature in an Age of Conformity* (Port Washington: Kennikat Press, Inc., 1967), p. 164.
12. Young, p. 90.
13. Cowley, p. 41.

sonal integrity, and he flaunted obscene and hostile opinions of the high and mighty. Personal defeat is not the confrontation of actual carabinieri at the bridge over the Tagliamento River; now personal defeat is the memory of a ruined career and a newspaper-like reportage of a smoke line which the wind blew from the German lines to the American so that American planes bombed their own troops. This event ends not with a jump into the river and a personal separate peace, but with a meditation on the morality of air-power (*ART*, p. 224) and a request for a glass of Valpolicella. The point of view of the memory of the ex-General is of the general battle, not of the individual. Hemingway does not see the battle from the perspective of the single soldier, a Henry Fleming or a Frederic Henry.

Among glasses of wine, affirmations of love, and general descriptions of warfare to a mistress who cannot understand warfare except in general terms, there are essays on government by haberdashers (like Harry Truman), political generals like Walter Bedell Smith, good and bad war correspondents, and the excellence of Moors as soldiers. The deaths of his men have hardly impressed the ex-General individually; what he remembers is the general impression of his own defeat. He is as detached as were the carabinieri. The old code of the hero has become self-pity. The Colonel cannot forget his weak heart and the place where he wishes to be buried. The personal cheeriness of the good doctor who operated on Henry in *A Farewell to Arms* contrasts to the Colonel's rancid discussion of his own career as a "spare-parts Colonel," and this term provokes a column on the duties and fates of that kind of officer.

A Farewell to Arms and *For Whom the Bell Tolls* were good war novels when they created the details of the life of the individual in battle. One who reads about the retreat from Caporetto and the killing of the Fascists knows little about the policies and strategies of war. Instead, he has lived through his own little corner of the war. One who hears the Colonel's confession to Renata knows about warfare, but recalls nothing of his own battle. The carabinieri "had that beautiful detachment and devotion to stern justice of men dealing in death without being in any danger of it." [14] This is character-

14. Hemingway, *A Farewell to Arms,* Modern Standard Authors (New York: Charles Scribner's Sons, 1953), p. 233.

ization: the antagonists of the hero are not truly involved in warfare. Now the hero himself is like the carabinieri, detached, uninvolved; and he describes his personal defeat in a passage like a journalistic column on how orders are given to a defeated general:

> The phone rings and somebody calls from Corps who has his orders from Army or maybe Army Group or maybe even SHAEF, because they read the name of the town in a newspaper, possibly sent in from Spa, by a correspondent, and the order is to take it by assault. It's important because it got into the newspapers. You have to take it. (*ART*, p. 233)

Here Hemingway's protagonist has become a part of an impersonal system, and the fiction suffers because it states an opinion about commanding without creating a particular soldier in battle.

Details and good sensuous images are scarce in *Across the River and into the Trees*. The minute particulars of Robert Jordan's blowing of the bridge and of Santiago's catching the fish are given even if Hemingway does moralize about them. Hemingway and his Colonel are general and abstract. The Colonel himself states the stylistic problem: "I'm just telling you about things in a general way. It is better not to be specific . . ." (*ART*, p. 234). Later he says, " 'I will skip the detailed part . . .' " (*ART*, p. 247). He relates the story of the capturing of Paris as if he were writing a gossip column about Field Marshal Montgomery and Elsa Maxwell's butler (*ART*, pp. 134–135). As mouthpiece for the author, he recognizes the poor stylistic quality of the narrative when he comments on his own narrative technique to Renata: "later I will put in the sounds and smells and anecdotes about who was killed when and where if you want them" (*ART*, p. 245). But he never puts in these sense impressions.

Style, not situation, is the difference between the good novels and the bad ones, the early and the late. Superficially, the worlds confronted by Henry, Barnes, Jordan, and the Colonel are all much alike. Two lovers are biologically trapped in a mortal world with little or no solace from religious belief to enable them to confront war, its consequences, and death. Because of abstraction and generality, nothing ever happens in *Across the River*. The only effective parts of the novel are the creations of the hunting at the beginning and the end of the novel and the death of the Colonel. In between, the Colonel goes to Venice, eats, rides in a gondola, makes love, suffers alone, and tells war stories. He and Renata spend forty-two pages at dinner (*ART*, pp. 107–148). The paucity of events is reflected in the absence of significant minor characters. In *A Farewell to Arms* the silhouette maker, the inept physicians, Gino, the unknown waiter who lent money to Frederic, and many others reinforced the definition of the world order as it governed the lives of the central characters. Those who supposedly are initiated in *Across the River* are really sentimental, soft, and weepy; and the bad are hard—a complete about-face since *A Farewell to Arms.* Even the best minor characters in *Across the River* are created with sentimental assertion rather than in restrained action and dialogue. Hemingway gives the interpretation of a character's face rather than the features which the reader might interpret for himself. The Grand Master, now a head waiter, on his first appearance is "truly handsome . . . from the inside out, so that his smile starts from his heart . . . and comes frankly and beautifully to the surface. . . ." His face is "fine"; his eyes are "kind, gay, truthful"; his hair is "honorable white"; his nose is "long, straight." Hemingway tells what his face means, but not how it looks except that the nose is long and straight and the hair is white. In the next paragraph (55) Hemingway does create his hand, which is "big, long, strong, spatular fingered" (*ART*, p. 55). Rather a melodramatic sentimental assertion. Even here the adjectives are a kind of abstraction; in the earlier novels the hand would have engaged in an action which could be accomplished only by that kind of hand. Hemingway does not create the walk of the advancing Grand Master; he tells its sentimental meaning: "He advanced smiling, lovingly, and yet conspiratorially . . ." (*ART*, p. 55). Their friendship is asserted, not presented in fact and event: "Thus contact was made between two old inhabitants of the Veneto, both men, and brothers in their membership in the human race, the only club that either one paid dues to, and brothers, too, in their love of an old country . . ." (*ART*, p. 55). Likewise, the Baron Alvarito has "the strange, rare smile which rises from the deep, dark pit, deeper than a well, deep as a deep mine, that is within them" (*ART,* p. 129). Even if the relationships between the Colonel and his friends could support such an excess of sentimentality, there are worse passages which cannot be justified. A motor boat comes up "gallantly," and Cantwell's own morbid self-consciousness, along with the author's, shows through a paragraph-long digression on the gallantry of an "aging machine" (*ART,* p. 52).

The omniscience of the author in *Across the River* allows sloppy technique. Author intrudes to tell reader what he does not trust him to see: The Colonel, for example, "did not know, among other things, that the girl loved him because he had never been sad one waking morning of his life . . ." (*ART,* p. 289). Dialogue, even between the two lovers, cannot carry the weight of the fiction as it had in Hemingway's earlier work. In "The Killers" Hemingway knew that it was unnecessary to tell who said a speech or how he said it. In *Across the River* the author melodramatically describes the Colonel's manner of speaking: " '*Have to*?' the Colonel said and the cruelty and resolution showed in his strange eyes as clearly as when the hooded muzzle of the gun of a tank swings toward you" (*ART,* p. 143).

The most effective writing by Hemingway occurs when a character loses himself completely in the sensuousness of the moment, without much contemplation of the future and no meditations on the past. The account of the fishing trip in the mountains in *The Sun Also Rises* is just such an episode. In only one section of *Across the River* does this excellence occur—the description of going out to the blind for a duck hunt at the first of the novel. Here the verbs and the verbals are active, and the sense of immediacy and reality is broken by no meditation, no self-consciousness.

> From behind him, he heard the incoming whisper of wings and he crouched, took hold of his right hand gun with his right hand as he looked up from under the rim of the barrel, then stood to shoot at the two ducks that were dropping down, their wings set to brake, coming down dark in the gray dim sky, slanting toward the decoys. (*ART,* p. 5)

At the beginning of the novel the Colonel goes out to the hunting blind; after the first chapter, the next thirty-eight chapters recount in flashback the Colonel's week-end in Venice with Renata, and the fortieth chapter resumes the story of the duck hunt. But the end does not compare favorably with the beginning, because now the reader too knows Renata, and the Colonel can reminisce on his love and on his military past. The Colonel as hunter has all the strength and integrity of the earlier protagonists; the Colonel as meditator on the past is sentimental, abstract—a pathetic old man sorry for himself. The last chapters of the novel are uneven, alternating between the sensuous wonders of a duck hunt and morbid musings over emotions which such a good hunter in Hemingway should be able to suppress. The old man can still hunt without getting morbidly sentimental even if he cannot love without doing so.

From novel to novel throughout Hemingway's career the basic subject matter never changes. The hero faces life in war, religion, and love. Love is possible to all; trial by international warfare is necessary for all except Santiago and Harry Morgan, and these two must confront a conflict with nature or with outlaws; religion is ever longed for, never wholly accepted. Substantially, then, the nature of the world of the hero never changes; Hemingway's literary development is largely a matter of technique and of style—the strength, restraint, and objectivity of the hero in the best works reflect the strength, restraint, and objectivity of the novelist as he creates the conflicts. The more Hemingway loses his touch, the falser his hero.

In the better fiction the hero lives in a sensuous world as he can; when he encounters institutionalism and abstraction of any kind, he is confronting evil. To the extent that the hero makes his own institutions and arrives at abstractions which he can support, he is himself becoming false.

Hemingway's late career is a decline and fall and a rise again in *The Old Man and the Sea* if that book is the last fiction he wrote. Compared with the art of his own early fiction, he falls and rises not only from book to book but even in the smaller parts, from sentence to sentence. The standard of Hemingway's early works in perhaps stricter than is justifiable in absolute critical terms. But Hemingway and Eliot, more than any others, established the standards of the twentieth century and made them valid, a reflection of the taste of our age and controlling factors in the creation and criticism of literature. The chief reason for evaluating the late works in such strict terms is that the failures of the late works also help to prove the few successes of the late ones and the greatness of the works of the second two decades of the century. If the criticism and the practice of Eliot and Hemingway measure their successes, they also establish standards by which the critic may determine what is great and what is only fairly good.

WILLIAM FAULKNER

12

The Unbearable and Unknowable Truth in Faulkner's First Three Novels

WILLIAM Faulkner's first three novels (*Soldiers' Pay*, 1926; *Mosquitoes*, 1927; *Sartoris*, 1929)[1] commingle a youthful, brittle cynicism and suggestions of Faulkner's mature views of the nature of man. Silly characters indulging themselves in artistic chitchat ask profound questions: " 'What is there worth the effort and despair of writing about,' " Mrs. Wiseman asks in *Mosquitoes*, " 'except love and death?' " [2] At the end of *Soldiers' Pay* a skeptical Episcopal priest says that "all truth is unbearable." [3] In these early novels truth seems almost unbearable to Faulkner himself, but despite his skepticism and his presentation of several kinds of waste lands he uses a vocabulary of the words of truth more in his early novels than he did in the great works of his middle years. Faulkner himself does much of the talking in *Soldiers' Pay*, *Mosquitoes*, and *Sartoris*. Not before *The Sound and the Fury* did he remove himself from the novel and let the characters present themselves in the depths and

1. *Sartoris* was published after *The Sound and the Fury* but written before it.

2. Faulkner, *Mosquitoes: A Novel* (New York: Liveright Publishing Corporation, 1927), p. 247. Hereafter cited in text with abbreviation *M*.

3. Faulkner's *Soldiers' Pay* (New York: Horace Liveright, 1926), p. 318. Hereafter cited in text with abbreviation *SP*.

the despair and the words of their own minds. He thinks for his characters instead of letting them think for themselves. In his early career he was omniscient, intrusive, and talky.

Faulkner's characters in *Mosquitoes* come and go talking of words, trying to answer overwhelming questions, but merely talking of words. Dawson Fairchild (a satirical portrait of Sherwood Anderson) divides the life of man into stages, and his analysis anticipates Faulkner's life-long interest in the contrast between the actor and the talker, between the deed and the word. " 'You become conscious of thinking, and then you start right off to think in words. And first thing you know, you don't have thoughts in your mind at all: you just have words in it. But when you are young, you just be. Then you reach a stage where you do. Then a stage where you think, and last of all, where you remember. Or try to' " (*M*, p. 231). Again, Fairchild distinguishes between words and deeds. Words are " 'a kind of sterility,' " substituted " 'for things and deeds' " (*M*, p. 210). Although the statement here expresses a principle which is of supreme importance in the literature of the 1920s, the speaker is foolishly inconsistent. A moment later he talks himself into an acceptance of words. " 'Words,' " he opines, " 'are like acorns, you know. Every one of 'em won't make a tree, but if you just have enough of 'em, you're bound to get a tree sooner or later' " (*M*, p. 210). Out of the words the deeds may grow, and Faulkner as well as Fairchild seems to have contradicted himself. In creating a character of mere words, the novelist has become a writer of excessive verbiage. Though he despises the talk of his characters, he himself as author talks as he rails at their talk. "Talk, talk, talk: the utter and heartbreaking stupidity of words" (*M*, p. 186).[4] But in this railery Faulkner is in the strange position of a novelist abstractly talking against the word and talking against his own novel—almost reviewing his own book. He writes against the word with " 'a kind of childlike faith in the efficacy of words' " (*M*, p. 249).

Faulkner's Prufrock-like man in this novel, the sterile, empty, and romantic Talliaferro, equates love and words and sex. Although

4. See also Faulkner's comments on money and "solid business men" (*Soldiers' Pay*, pp. 31, 187, 149) and on Woodrow Wilson and the Ku Klux Klan (*Soldiers' Pay*, pp. 149, 281).

one of his friends tells him that women " 'don't care anything about words except as little things to pass the time with' " and that they are only " 'interested in what you're going to do' " (*M*, p. 112), Talliaferro remains committed to words so much that they are his only tactic in his schemes to seduce. He must still ask " 'What must I do to be bold?' " (*M*, p. 112) in futile echo of the Biblical question about salvation. Mr. Talliaferro interprets art in the same way. He explains a statue: " 'Do you see what he has caught?' he bugled melodiously. 'Do you see? The spirit of youth, of something fine and hard and clean in the world; something we all desire until our mouths are stopped with dust?' " But when the gushy Mrs. Maurier asks " 'What does it signify?' " she is answered by a character of fewer words, " 'Nothing. . . . It doesn't have to' " (*M*, p. 26). The bores talk of " 'creating—creating things. Beautiful things. Beauty, you know' " (*M*, p. 16) and of art and souls and religion. And a minister exclaims that there is " 'nothing better on God's green earth than Rotary' " (*M*, p. 37).

One of Faulkner's "basic attitudes," Olga Vickery writes, is "that language and logic act to obscure truth rather than to reveal it. . . . barrenness . . . attends all discussion." Mrs. Vickery groups the characters in *Mosquitoes* "according to their attitude toward 'talk.' " [5] Faulkner's theme was timely and provocative, but not all critics agree with Mrs. Vickery about the conscious use of the theme. Hyatt Waggoner and Irving Howe protest that "There is far more talk than action" and that *Mosquitoes* exemplifies the "radical disparity between words and action" even if it "hardly embodies this idea." [6] Frederick Hoffman believes that the "basic separation of words and deeds" is in "this very weak novel a commonplace" and that Faulkner in 1927 did not intend to examine "the failure of

5. Olga W. Vickery, *The Novels of William Faulkner* (Baton Rouge: Louisiana State University Press, 1959, 1961), pp. 8–10. See also Michael Millgate, *The Achievement of William Faulkner* (New York: Random House, 1966), p. 72, and Richard P. Adams, *Faulkner: Myth and Motion* (Princeton: Princeton University Press, 1968), pp. 41–43.

6. Hyatt H. Waggoner, *William Faulkner: From Jefferson to the World* (Lexington: University of Kentucky Press, 1959), p. 9. Irving Howe, *William Faulkner: A Critical Study*, Second Edition (New York: Vintage Books, 1962), pp. 19–20.

language to realize truth." [7] The theme, I believe, is as consciously intended in *Mosquitoes* as in *As I Lay Dying*; but Faulkner was not able to treat the subject effectively. Michael Millgate puts the point well: "Faulkner fails to solve the old problem of how to present boring characters without boring the reader." [8]

The good characters, those who understand or suffer, are people of few words. They speak little, and many of them are ironic. Genuine sentiments are hidden behind gruffness. The only possible genuine artist among the numerous phonies is Gordon, who says so little that he is enigmatic.[9] Two passages in the novel (*M*, pp. 47 and 335ff.) anticipate the concreteness, the sensuousness, and the stream of consciousness of Faulkner's later work, and both of these passages represent the mental processes of the artist Gordon. The good people in Faulkner's early works cannot say what they mean. Aunt Jenny Du Pre, whose love and irony will make her the most dependable person in *Sartoris,* speaks harsh words in any moment of sincerity and emotion. When she receives a telegram announcing the death of Bayard Sartoris in a plane crash, she says to Dr. Peabody, " 'Thank God that's the last one. For a while, anyway. Home, Simon.' " [10] The MacCallums, one of the must admirable families in Yoknapatawpha County, talk little and live in a masculine world of deeds. What Bayard Sartoris feels he never says; indeed, he is a puzzling character because he refuses to think as well as to talk. The motivations of his violence are obscure because he tries to hide them from himself. Again and again he sadly rehearses to himself the details of his twin brother's death in the war, but he curses "his dead brother savagely" (*Sar*, p. 123). He is aware of principles and values that he refuses to articulate. "His violence," Hyatt Waggoner has written, "is his way of forcing out of consciouness what he can-

7. Frederick J. Hoffman, *William Faulkner,* Twayne's United States Authors Series, Second Edition (New York: Twayne Publishers, Inc., 1966), pp. 43–44.

8. Michael Millgate, *William Faulkner,* Evergreen Pilot Books (New York: Grove Press, 1961), p. 21.

9. Millgate, p. 21. And see Joyce W. Warren, "Faulkner's 'Portrait of the Artist,' " *Mississippi Quarterly,* 19 (Summer 1966), 123.

10. Faulkner, *Sartoris* (New York: Random House, 1929, 1951), p. 369. Hereafter cited in text with abbreviation *Sar.*

not allow himself to think about. . . . he contrives ways to keep from thinking; when the contrivance fails, his thoughts are more than he can bear." [11]

Truth in Faulkner's first three novels is not only unbearable[12] but also unknowable. If "literature is not philosophical knowledge translated into imagery and verse," if it does express "a general attitude toward life," [13] Faulkner was not capable of expressing a general and consistent attitude in these novels. The problem lies not in variation from novel to novel but in vagueness, elusiveness, inconsistency in meaning within each novel. First, style and meaning do not always blend. Faulkner himself is talky while he damns the talkative. It is almost as if he used the words of truth but did not believe them. Or he used them although the most he could do was to wish that they were true. The reader encounters abstract words not only without moralizing and didacticism but almost without significant meaning. In this respect, Faulkner passed through a confused and confusing apprenticeship. For example, of the first three novels, *Mosquitoes* talks most about the verities which Faulkner listed years later in his speech accepting the Nobel Prize. But it says the least about them. Thus George Marion O'Donnell regarded Faulkner as a "traditional moralist" in all his books,[14] and Maxwell Geismar may also argue that *Soldiers' Pay* contains "no valid appraisement either as to the causes of the First World War or the solutions of the Armistice. The single heritage of the war is futility, the only response of the post-war protagonist is alcoholic." [15]

The most apparent general attitude in *Soldier's Pay*, *Mosquitoes*, and *Sartoris* is that Faulkner is against something—perhaps sin, perhaps conventional views of righteousness. The world of the first works gives Bayard Sartoris a "vision of nothingness," [16] and even

11. Waggoner, p. 21.

12. See *Soldiers' Pay*, pp. 39–40.

13. René Wellek and Austin Warren, *Theory of Literature* (New York: Harcourt, Brace and Company, 1949), p. 113.

14. George Marion O'Donnell, "Faulkner's Mythology," *The Kenyon Review*, 1 (Summer 1939), 285.

15. Maxwell Geismar, *Writers in Crisis: The American Novel Between Two Wars* (Boston: Houghton Mifflin Company, 1942), p. 146.

16. Waggoner, p. 23.

if Bayard is in many ways a fool, his confusion is still a product of his time. Donald Mahon, Faulkner's first creation who is a victim of war, knows "Time as only something which was taking from him a world he did not particularly mind losing . . ." (*SP*, p. 152). In *Mosquitoes* Faulkner satirizes not only the empty world of the characters but also their shallow and empty lives. Even the spiritual yearnings of the Waste Landers are shockingly isolated and brittle. Mr. Talliaferro, for example, muses "with regret on the degree of intimacy he might have established with his artistic acquaintances had he but acquired the habit of masturbation in his youth" (*M*, p. 10). Only Mr. Talliaferro might say how this limited accomplishment would have such a beneficial effect. His desire for immorality seems as pointless as the puritanism and prudishness in a course in literature in a denominational college which "whittled Shakespeare down because he wrote about whores without pointing a moral . . ." (*M*, p. 116). And conventions preserve sterility. Dawson Fairchild states that "only men hold to conventions for moral reasons," and the Semitic man adds, "Or from habit" (*M*, p. 222).

Faulkner's view of the world in these novels conforms in general to the over-all attitude of the Lost Generation and the Waste Landers. His characters and the situations he created would not be much out of place in the fiction of Hemingway or Fitzgerald or in Eliot's *The Waste Land*. Particular parallels to contemporary works are not of real importance except perhaps in pointing out Faulkner's derivativeness. What is important is the general similarity, the sterility and futility characteristic of the period. Some of the brittle talk of *Mosquitoes* and *Soldiers' Pay* would be appropriate to the characters of a novel by Aldous Huxley or to Fitzgerald's Daisy Buchanan. " 'What can equal a mother's love?' " asks a drunken soldier. " 'Except a good drink of whiskey. Where's that bottle' " (*SP*, p. 24). That Faulkner rather self-consciously has one eye cocked on the milieu of his age is revealed in his own comments: he refers to the period before World War I as a time "long ago, before the world went crazy" (*SP*, p. 171). He describes a typical mood of the period in his intrusive comments on Mr. Talliaferro, who has "amid his other chaotic emotions . . . a harried despair of futility and an implacable passing of opportunity" (*M*, p. 128). There are many abstract generalizations about the time. Gilligan and Cadet Lowe, for example, share "the comradeship of those whose lives had become pointless through the sheer equivocation of events, of the sorry jade, Circumstance" (*SP*, p. 30). The sirens of *Soldier's Pay* and *Mosquitoes* are boy-like (*M*, p. 240); the flat-breasted girls are masculine; they have boyish bodies. "This was the day of the Boy," Faulkner writes, "male and female" (*SP*, p. 196). Love is never fulfillment. The men on the yacht in *Mosquitoes* stay apart from the ladies and drink in sexual segregation. Only the sterile make propositions or proposals, and they attempt to seduce with words and out of despair and frustration. The only love affairs which might end in fruition in *Soldiers' Pay* and *Mosquitoes* (those of Gilligan and Mrs. Powers, and Jenny and the steward, David) end in miserable separations, and Faulkner provides as little motivation for the separations as he does for the love. Mrs. Powers says that either she is "cold by nature" or that she has spent all her "emotional coppers" (*SP*, p. 39).

Donald Mahon is the most lifeless of the doomed; he stares "with detachment, impersonal as God . . ." (*SP*, p. 45). Detachment in Faulkner's wasted land or in Eliot's is more terrible than evil; it may result from innocence or isolation or impotence. Whereas wickedness and malevolence might lead to repentance and identity, those who are aloof remain in limbo. Donald Mahon, ruined by the war, "remembers nothing. . . . He doesn't seem to care where he is nor what he does" (*SP*, p. 118). Mahon is not much more wounded and incapacitated mentally than Bayard Sartoris, who dwells in his own private waste land in Yoknapatawpha County after his return from the war. Faulkner uses his grandest rhetoric to describe Bayard's uninvolvement. He voyages "alone in the bleak and barren regions of his despair" (*Sar*, p. 218). And he remembers a life when he had hoped for more significance, "a life peopled by young men like fallen angels, and of a meteoric violence like that of fallen angels, beyond heaven or hell and partaking of both: doomed immortality and immortal doom" (*Sar*, p. 126).

Throughout *Soldier's Pay* and *Mosquitoes* Faulkner works deliberately within the terms of the Waste Land and uses Eliot's phrases and characters, even his situations and themes,[17] but he makes little significant contribution to the techniques or the themes of the period. Images of nature emphasize the frustration and depletion; the moon is old and tired in *Mosquitoes*. Lush descriptions of a fertile and rife natural world are ironic. The sun is most golden after the doctor in *Soldiers' Pay* predicts Donald's death (*SP*, p. 155). April comes like a "heedless idiot into a world that had forgotten Spring" (*SP*, p. 37). And like heedless idiots, the characters ignore the natural world around them.

Generally, Faulkner's first three novels treat the same subjects which appealed to the young Hemingway—war, religion, and love. But Faulkner's work is ambivalent. His vagueness of attitude and his search for meaning are most apparent in his puzzling presentation of war, especially in the contrast between World War I and the Civil War in *Sartoris*. In this first novel in the Yoknapatawpha cycle, Faulkner apparently accepts the romantic traditions of the Civil War. The spirit of John Sartoris on the first page is "far more palpable than the two old men" now alive, John Sartoris's son Bayard and old man Falls, a veteran of the Civil War. In beautiful language Faulkner waxes nostalgic about the peaceful and restful and romantic heroism of the older war: "Away in the darkness horses moved invisibly with restful sounds, and bivouac fires sank to glowing points like spent fireflies, and somewhere neither near nor far, the General's body servant touched a guitar in lingering, random chords. Thus they sat in the poignance of spring and youth's immemorial sadness, forgetting travail and glory . . ." (*Sar*, p. 11). Faulkner treats the Civil War as chivalric; he never applies to it the realistic imagery or the polysyllabic vocabulary of an empty doom which he uses about World War I. When he writes of a "jocund forest" (*Sar*, p. 14) in the Civil War, he gives no clues that we are to take the term as satirical or playful rather than serious. When the first Bayard Sartoris gallops back to a Yankee camp and almost certain death in his gallant attempt to steal anchovies, a captive Northern

17. See Frederick L. Gwynn, "Faulkner's Prufrock—and Other Observations," *The Journal of English and Germanic Philology*, 52 (January 1953), 65 ff.

major exclaims, " 'What is one man to a renewed belief in mankind?' " (*Sar*, p. 17). Olga Vickery has contended that "Faulkner is unimplicated in the romanticism of young Bayard." [18] But his treatment of the War, his imagery, his vocabulary, and his characters make his implication rather complete. Irving Howe interprets the daring ride for anchovies as "an effort to vindicate a principle through a willed gesture," and the first Bayard's death has a "chosen, personal quality." [19]

On the other hand, Faulkner inconsistently denies a romantic view of the Civil War in several ways in *Sartoris*. Absurdity rather than glory is the point when he describes Aunt Sally, who "lived much in the past, shutting her mind with a bland finality to anything which had occurred since 1901" (*Sar*, pp. 174–175). After old man Falls tells of Colonel John Sartoris's most glorious raid during the Civil War, old Bayard asks:

> "Will," he said, "what the devil were you folks fighting about, anyhow?" "Bayard," old man Falls answered, "be damned ef I ever did know." (*Sar*, p. 227)

Aunt Jenny, who tells of the first Bayard's death with more and more exaggeration, regards the soldiers of the first World War as silly and foolish. What can one conclude here—that bravado was meaningful in the Civil War and senseless in the later war? What Faulkner really means by his denial of values in World War I and his inconsistent attitude in *Sartoris* toward the Civil War is never clear. The most we can conclude perhaps is that there was a place for the individual in the Civil War, but that individuality in World War I had become meaningless. Yet there are contradictions even to this. Buddy MacCallum's medal, won in World War I, was meaningful, and his experiences contrast with Bayard's. Buddy survives and endures. And in *Soldiers' Pay* Joe Gilligan returns from the war with his identity and integrity intact.

Uncertainty, ambivalence, vagueness control the prominent religious themes in Faulkner's first three novels. A few passages sug-

18. Vickery, p. 16.
19. Howe, p. 37.

gest the modern theme of the death of God in the Waste Land. One of the boyish females in *Mosquitoes* reminds a friend that "The only man who could walk on water is dead" (*M*, p. 137). In the same novel Fairchild and the Semitic man bitterly attack American Protestantism: "Other nations," Fairchild says, "seem to be able to entertain the possibility that God may not be a Rotarian or an Elk or a Boy Scout after all" (*M*, p. 40). And the Semitic man: "For some reason one can be a Catholic or a Jew and be religious at home. But a Protestant at home is only a Protestant. It seems to me that the Protestant faith was invented for the sole purpose of filling our jails and morgues and houses of detention" (*M,* p. 42). But the most enigmatic religious figure in the first three novels is the minister in *Soldiers' Pay*, who has been interpreted as a man of faith and as a man of strength without faith. "The rector's faith," says Frederick Hoffman, "is firmly grounded in an acceptance which is vaguely similar to the endurance and basic integrity of Dilsey." [20] Olga Vickery understands him as balanced and sane: "The source of his calmness is his acceptance of the inevitability of all experience and the necessity of change." [21] But for Hyatt Waggoner he is "unhappy" and "unbelieving." [22] And despite his priesthood there is good evidence for his religious skepticism. He tells Joe Gilligan that "God is circumstance. . . . God is in this life. We know nothing about the next" (*SP*, p. 317). But the presence of God in the world does not make life meaningful to the minister. He tells the lecher Januarius Jones that "we learn nothing whatever which can ever help us or be of any particular benefit to us, even" (*M*, p. 69). And at times he is pompous in his language and affected as well as shallow: "But one of my cloth is prone to allow his own soul to atrophy in his zeal for the welfare of other souls that—" (*SP*, p. 57). Compared to the genuine and selfless Joe Gilligan, the minister is a lost soul.

The themes of love and the family, always of basic significance in Faulkner's works, seem brittle and unresolved in the first three novels. He is cynical not only in regard to the particular time and his particular characters but also generally. Mr. Talliaferro in *Mos-*

20. Hoffman, p. 42.
21. Vickery, p. 6.
22. Waggoner, p. 7.

quitoes is "the final result of some rather casual biological research conducted by two people who, *like the great majority* [italics mine], had no business producing children at all" (*M*, pp. 31–32). Faulkner's intrusive comment is an observation about life in general rather than a part of his fiction, and it seems to apply to love as well as to the conception of children. Most of the relationships between the sexes are as casual as were the parents of Mr. Talliaferro and the gossips who sit in a pub and talk of abortion in *The Waste Land*. Cecily Sanders, betrothed to the returned veteran in *Soldiers' Pay*, cannot bear the sight of her beloved after he is wounded. Still engaged, she gives herself to George Farr. Mrs. Powers is the only really admirable woman who is marriageable and seducible in the first three novels. She is always efficiently sympathetic and humane, but she is no longer capable of deep passion and romance. Joe Gilligan knows "that she would go through with all physical intimacies, that she would undress to a lover (?) with this same impersonal efficiency" (*SP*, p. 151). The affair between Horace Benbow and Belle Mitchell and their marriage in *Sartoris* lead to Horace's disillusionment. Even though his sister, Narcissa, is somewhat attractive and admirable in her courtship with Bayard Sartoris and their marriage, the seeds of her shallow concern with mere appearance and reputation (later developed almost to caricature in *Sanctuary*) are at times apparent. She almost treasures the obscene propositions of Byron Snopes, which already point to her loss of virtue in "There Was a Queen."

But there are many admirable persons in the first three novels and at least the appearance of the support of the values named in the famous Nobel Prize Speech. What Faulkner himself admires is not defined, but the basic goodness of Gilligan in *Soldier's Pay* and the MacCallums is so simple that it just exists without the need of comment or definition. The Negro church service at the end of *Soldier's Pay* anticipates the one which Dilsey attends in *The Sound and the Fury*: "It was nothing, it was everything; then it swelled to an ecstasy, taking the white man's words as readily as it took his remote God and made a personal Father of Him" (*SP*, p. 319). And Donald Mahon's old Negro nurse genuinely and naturally welcomes him home. She alone puts her hands on his scarred face without repulsion, and she exclaims, " 'Lawd, de white folks done ruint you . . ." (*M*, p. 170). Aunt Jenny, old Bayard, old man Falls, Dr. Peabody—several characters in *Sartoris* have escaped the frustration and the nothingness of Faulkner's moderns.

The ornate rhetoric and the abstract words which name truths and principles are often applied to objects that could not in any sense deserve the vocabulary. A cow chews with "slow dejection" (*Sar*, p. 137). Old plows are "skeletons of labor healed over by the earth they were to have violated, kinder than they" (*Sar*, p. 137). Faulkner lavishes words on the mule, which was "steadfast to the land when all else faltered before the hopeless juggernaut of circumstances, impervious to conditions that broke men's hearts . . ." (*Sar*, p. 278). Even chickens have "predatory, importunate eyes" (*Sar*, p. 107), and a jug of moonshine sits "rotund and benignant" (*Sar*, p. 139). To write about the trivial with "flaming verbal wings" (*Sar*, p. 172) is to be meaninglessly enigmatic or sentimental or both.

In Faulkner's first three novels he intrudes and talks a great deal about his meanings, but he never makes a significant thematic point which is sustained throughout any one work. He loves words, but misapplies them and also distrusts their applications.

13

The Word and the Deed in Faulkner's First Great Novels

LYING on her deathbed and listening to the shallow moralizings of her neighbor Cora Tull, Addie Bundren in William Faulkner's *As I Lay Dying* thinks "how words go straight up in a thin line, quick and harmless, and how terribly doing goes along the earth, clinging to it, so that after a while the two lines are too far apart for the same person to straddle from one to the other; and that sin and love and fear are just sounds that people who never sinned nor loved nor feared have for what they never had and cannot have until they forget the words." [1] Those who can, Addie says, love and act; those who cannot, talk and speak the words of truth.

Sometimes the mere articulation of a thought may prove its falsity, as when Dewey Dell talks about her communication with Darl: "He said he knew without words . . . and I knew he knew because if he had said he knew with the words I would not have believed that he had been there and saw us" (*AILD*, p. 26). And Caddy asks Quentin, "*do you think that if I say it it won't be.*" [2] Along with Frederic

1. Faulkner, *As I Lay Dying,* The Modern Library (New York: Random House, 1930, 1964), pp. 165–166. Hereafter cited in text with abbreviation *AILD*.

2. Faulkner, *The Sound and the Fury* (New York: Jonathan Cape and Harrison Smith, 1929), p. 151. Hereafter cited in text with abbreviation *SF*.

Henry's statement about the obscenity of such words as *glory*, *honor*, *courage*, *hallow*, *sacred*, and *sacrifice*, Addie's speech is one of the most effective rejections of abstraction written in the early twentieth century. Her denial of the efficacy of a moral vocabulary and her reliance on concrete image, fact, and action are reflections of the best aesthetic principles of Eliot, Faulkner, and Hemingway early in their careers. As a standard of criticism, Addie's view provides a sound perspective from which to view the works of these four writers, and it is an especially good clue to Faulkner's themes and techniques in *The Sound and the Fury*, *As I Lay Dying*, and *Sanctuary*.

Apparently Addie and Frederic would have regarded Faulkner's own Nobel Prize Speech as embarrassing and obscene because it contains the words "that go straight up in a thin line, quick and harmless." In 1950, twenty years after the creation of Addie, he wrote that it is the writer's duty to remind man "of the courage and honor and hope and pride and compassion and pity and sacrifice which have been the glory of his past." The early Faulkner did not remind his reader, who had to find the moral principles in the work if he could. Later, Faulkner seldom missed an opportunity to walk around his characters and discuss all the ramifications of their meanings. *The Sound and the Fury*, *As I Lay Dying*, and *Sanctuary*, however, are conspicuously alike in the extreme indirection of the way in which they remind the reader of the "old verities and truths of the human heart."

These three novels are amazingly similar in a number of ways. Each treats the theme of love and the family. Love between the sexes, the lack (or need) of such love, and the perversions of it are significant aspects of the life of almost every mature character. Addie and Anse Bundren, Mr. and Mrs. Compson, Horace and Belle Benbow—a tortured and confused marital relationship is significant in each. The young women in the novels are as confused as the parents—Dewey Bell Bundren and Caddy Compson conceive illegitimate children; Temple Drake and Little Belle Benbow are not pregnant probably because of better luck or more careful precautions. Caddy's fatherless daughter promises to drop a child by the roadside. The nearest thing to a normal and happy family presented in any of the novels is the relationship between Ruby Lamar and Lee Goodwin, a prostitute and a bootlegger. Even their union is cursed with an unhealthy baby. It has "lead-colored eyelids" and a "putty-colored face." [3] "It lies in drugged apathy," and it moves "now and then in frail, galvanic jerks, whimpering" (*S*, p. 123). Darl Bundren and Benjy Compson are committed to the insane asylum at Jackson. Faulkner's treatment of families with insufficient love indicates his anxiety about the problems of the family in the modern world.

Point of view, the author's way of presenting his material, varies a great deal in these three novels. *As I Lay Dying* and *The Sound and the Fury* contain Faulkner's only extended ventures into the technique of stream of consciousness. In *Sanctuary* and the last section of *The Sound and the Fury* Faulkner tells the story himself. But whether the character thinks or the author tells, Faulkner keeps his own views completely out of the fiction except by implication and indirectness. It is easier to tell what he thinks from the talk of his characters than it is from his objective writing in his own person. He either completely reveals the mental processes of a character or refuses to give any glimpse into a mind. In each novel there is a blank mind or an idiot or a confused child: Lee Goodwin's deaf and dumb and blind father (who is so isolated that he has only "one pleasure" and "one sense"—taste—left), Benjy, the insane Darl, and the child Vardaman (troubled by his first encounter with death). At the center of each novel is an ineffectual character with an abstract, intellectual sensibility—Darl, Quentin, and Horace. In all three novels incapacitated females symbolize the weaknesses and failures of the person and the family: Mrs. Compson on her sick bed, Addie on her deathbed, and Temple languishing on her bed in Miss Reba's whorehouse.

At one time, Faulkner refused to acknowledge any relationship between *As I Lay Dying* and *The Sound and the Fury* beyond the fact that the two "together made exactly enough pages to make a

3. Faulkner, *Sanctuary* (New York: Random House, 1931, 1958), pp. 54, 60. Hereafter cited in text with abbreviation *S*.

proper-sized book that the publisher could charge the regulation price on." [4] But on a different occasion when he was asked whether "Darl is the Quentin of the Bundrens and . . . Cash is the Jason of the Bundrens," he enigmatically agreed that his questioner could say that "if that is any pleasure to you" (*UNIV*, p. 121). And again he admitted a similarity "due to the fact that in each one of them there was a sister surrounded by a gang of brothers" (*UNIV*, p. 207). This is still not an extensive concession, but Faulkner's testimony years after publication is made questionable by forgetfulness as well perhaps as an author's seemly reluctance. Without being particularly conscious of similarities, furthermore, a creative mind may develop significant parallels in different works of art written in a short period of time.

Many minor features reflect the major points of similarities in *The Sound and the Fury*, *As I Lay Dying*, and *Sanctuary*. A key phrase repeated in *The Sound and the Fury* and *As I Lay Dying* indicates a significant similarity in character relationships. Jewel, Addie says, "is my cross and he will be my salvation" (*AILD*, p. 160). Jason for his mother is "my joy and my salvation" (*SF*, p. 127). Both Quentin and Horace Benbow are haunted again and again by thoughts of the surfeiting odor of honeysuckle, which they associate with the sexual promiscuity of Caddy and Little Belle (*S*, pp. 198, 215). Quentin, Horace, and Darl are all excessively sensitive souls. Not one of them can deal with life in a manly way. If Quentin and Horace share the obsession of honeysuckle, Horace and Darl think of isolation and their longings for an ideal or eternity in terms of the sound of rain. Darl thinks, "How often have I lain beneath rain on a strange roof, thinking of home," (*AILD*, p. 76). Horace thinks "of a gentle dark wind blowing in the long corridors of sleep; of lying beneath a low cozy roof under the long sound of the rain: the evil, the injustice, the tears" (*S*, p. 214). The tortured minds of Quentin and Darl use the same image to reveal their poetic and distorted impressions of reality: Quentin sees "A gull on an

4. Faulkner, *Faulkner in the Univeresity: Class Conferences at the University of Virginia 1957–1958*, ed. Frederick L. Gwynn and Joseph L. Blotner (Charlottesville: The University of Virginia Press, 1959), p. 109. Hereafter cited in text with abbreviation *UNIV*.

invisible wire attached through space dragged" (*SF*, p. 129). Darl watches "cane and saplings lean as before a little gale, swaying without reflections as though suspended on invisible wires from the branches overhead" (*AILD*, pp. 134–135). Loneliness and desire for love in the family are suggested in beautiful images in the thoughts of Addie and Quentin. Quentin remembers a picture in a book: "a dark place into which a single weak ray of light came slanting upon two faces lifted out of the shadow" (*SF*, p. 215). Addie thinks of a similar terrifying image, and, like Quentin, she remembers children isolated from parents: "the cries of the geese out of the wild darkness in the old terrible nights, fumbling at the deeds like orphans to whom are pointed out in a crowd two faces and told, 'That is your father, your mother' " (*AILD*, p. 166).

In each, Faulkner is concerned primarily with the character's ability or inability to communicate love in language. In general those characters who use the words of love are those who have not loved. And those who do not talk of love usually have had profound experiences which, they know, cannot be communicated in language. Olga Vickery has written that "each of the first three sections [of *The Sound and the Fury*] presents a version of the same facts which is at once the truth and a complete distortion of the truth." [5] The theme of the novel, she suggests, "is the relation between the act and man's apprehension of the act, between the event and the interpretation." [6] This statement also describes the theme of *As I Lay Dying*. There is, however, an additional similarity and complexity in the three novels. Those who articulate their interpretations of acts use meaningless words. Those who know and understand do not speak the words. Most of them remain silent in the novel, and emotion and truth are apparent in their deeds. Some reject empty words so much that they not only refuse to speak them but also reject them even in their internal monologues, their stream of thought. To know Faulkner's themes, his meanings, his characters, therefore, one must recognize the difference between truth and statement in each of the characters. Faulkner's techniques enable

5. Olga W. Vickery, *The Novels of William Faulkner: A Critical Interpretation* (Baton Rouge: Louisiana State University Press, 1959, 1961), p. 29.
6. Vickery, p. 29.

him to treat each character's relationship to love, fact, deed, and abstract word. The failure of language and the meaning of object and act are keys to the most important ironies and meanings.

The plots of all three novels turn upon the silent woman at the center of the work—Caddy Compson, Addie Bundren, and Temple Drake. In each book the other characters are defined (and they define themselves) by the way in which they are related to these strange women. Caddy is perhaps the most admirable of the three. She may seem to be merely a slut whose maidenhead, Faulkner has said, was "the frail physical stricture which to her was no more than a hangnail would have been." [7] Actually, she is the heroine and the central figure of the novel. In Faulkner's later years he called Caddy "my heart's darling" (*UNIV*, p. 6), complimented her courage, and especially praised her selfless love.[8] In the appendix first written seventeen years after the publication of the novel, he explicitly stated for the first time his admiration of Caddy. Four times in one sentence he wrote that she loved her brother Quentin, even loved him because he "was incapable of love." [9] In an excellent study, Lawrence E. Bowling has stated that Caddy, unlike the idiotic Benjy, acquires knowledge, but she acquires, he says, "no spiritual depth or worthwhile knowledge." "Because of her moral transgression, Caddy may appear to be active, but she is really passive, for she does not truly act, but only allows herself to be acted upon." [10] This view excessively damns her for sexual promiscuity and ignores her very real virtues.

Caddy only acts. She is the one child of the Compsons who does not talk, who does not tell a section of the novel. She does not use the words, Faulkner has explained, because she is "too beautiful and too moving to reduce her to telling what was going on, that it would be more passionate to see her through somebody else's eyes . . ."

7. Faulkner, "Appendix," *The Sound and the Fury,* The Modern Library (New York: Random House, 1946), p. 10.

8. See Catherine B. Baum, " 'The Beautiful One': Caddy Compson as Heroine of *The Sound and the Fury," Modern Fiction Studies,* 13 (Spring 1967), 33–44.

9. *The Sound and the Fury,* The Modern Library, p. 10.

10. Lawrence E. Bowling, "Faulkner and the Theme of Innocence," *The Kenyon Review*, 20 (Summer 1958), 476, 479.

(*UNIV*, p. 1). And if she were to speak, her genuine love would sound like only empty and embarrassing words. Indeed, she lies when the facts are unimportant and refuses to speak at all when it is possible to communicate without words. The puritanical Quentin despises disorder. Literally and symbolically, he is shocked when Caddy gets her dress wet playing in the branch. But she says her dress is not wet, because in play its wetness is simply unimportant, just as in love a maidenhead becomes no more significant than a hangnail. People and genuine feelings and needs are all that matter to her. If Frederic Henry gives up words because they obscure the truth, Caddy gives them up for the sake of a greater truth. While Benjy howls his protest, Charlie attempts to make love to Caddy.

> "He cant talk." Charlie said. "Caddy."
> "Are you crazy." Caddy said. . . . "He can see. Dont. Dont." (*SF*, p. 57)

Caddy does not care for reputation or virtue or herself. She cares only for Benjy and Quentin and her father. And after this scene she promises, purely for the love of Benjy, that she won't "anymore, ever" (*SF*, p. 58).

When Quentin demands that Caddy tell him in words that she loves her seducer, Caddy assumes that words cannot convince him. Twice Quentin asks, and each time Caddy puts his hand against her throat or her heart so that he can feel the fact instead of hearing the word. Quentin feels the "surge of blood . . . in strong accelerating beats" (*SF,* pp. 187, 203). But even the beat of the pulse is empty like words to Quentin, because he can know only the words—never the love itself. In contrast, the Negroes who hear Brother Shegog's sermon can transubstantiate words into love and reality. Their hearts speak "to one another in chanting measures beyond the need for words . . ." (*SF*, p. 367).

The deeds of the selfless Caddy are Faulkner's triumph in *The Sound and the Fury.* Benjy cannot use a word even so simple and abstract as love unless he hears someone say it. But he remembers Caddy's acts. Three times he remembers how she was kind to him on a cold day. *"Keep your hands in your pockets, Caddy said. Or they'll get froze"* (*SF,* p. 3). No one else is concerned about his cold hands. Caddy's acts show that she actually likes to care for her idiot brother. She feeds him, carries him about, gives him his beloved cushion, defends him from the cruel Jason and his self-pitying mother. When Mrs. Compson weeps over him, Caddy says, "Hush, Mother. . . . You go upstairs and lay down, so you can be sick . . ." (*SF*, p. 78). "I'll feed him tonight." Caddy said. "Sometimes he cries when Versh feeds him" (*SF,* p. 86). But her own daughter, Quentin, asks, *" 'Why dont you feed him in the kitchen. It's like eating with a pig'* " (*SF,* p. 86). After Caddy submits to a dishonorable marriage, she no longer has an opportunity to care for others in the family. Time and again, however, she forgets her own despair and asks her brother Quentin to do what needs to be done.

Are you going to look after Benjy and Father. . . .
Promise. . . .
Promise I'm sick you'll have to promise. . . . (*SF*, p. 131)

But Quentin never promises.

Caddy's loss of virginity and her love affairs apparently are not shoddy like the lust of her daughter, Quentin, with the carnival man. Caddy's heartbeat should prove her love for Dalton Ames, and that Dalton is not a mere mustachioed seducer in a sentimental melodrama is shown in his own concern for Caddy's welfare when Quentin comes to him as an outraged brother: "did she send you to me"; "I want to know if shes all right have they been bothering her up there" (*SF,* p. 198).

In utter selflessness Caddy comforts the stricken Quentin on the night when she is first seduced—a rather curious reversal of the usual roles of brother and sister in such a situation. Her sympathy goes out to anyone in need of understanding. When she believes that her lover Dalton has hurt Quentin, she tells him never to speak to her again. Later, when she learns that he did not hurt Quentin, she wishes to ask his pardon. She stops dressing for a date to lie down with Benjy to get him to sleep. She is willing to commit incest with Quentin, although she never indicates any lustful feelings for him. Her reasoning is never explained, but possibly she sees that such an evil would lead to his self-knowledge and then salvation instead of madness and suicide. Pregnant and unmarried, she marries a man she does not love apparently for the sake of the family's honor, loses her husband, is separated from those she loves (Benjy, Quentin, and her father), and finally gives up her illegitimate daughter to her family in the hope that they will bring up the child in the way she should go. She sends the daughter money, attends her father's funeral wearing a veil so that the family will not be shamed, apologizes to Jason because her divorce from her husband prevented his getting a job in a bank. She visits Jefferson and her daughter once or twice a year.

Caddy has every virtue except wisdom and chastity. Mrs. Compson's only virtue is chastity. Caddy allows an unloving family to rear her daughter, Quentin, who would be better off reared in a bawdyhouse. Jason wishes to keep Quentin so that he can steal the money her mother sends; so he suggests to Caddy that, living with her, Quentin would grow up a loose woman. Jason has touched a nerve and defined Caddy's real fears: " 'Oh, I'm crazy,' she says, 'I'm insane. I can't take her. Keep her. What am I thinking of' " (*SF,* p. 260). Ironically, Caddy, who placed no value at all on her own virginity, puts too high a value on the chastity of her daughter. And also ironically, Quentin becomes even less chaste than Caddy. But the greatest tragedy of Caddy and of *The Sound and the Fury* is that Caddy and her capacity for love are lost. She loved most of all; she expressed her love in action rather than in word. Two of her brothers mourned her fall for selfish reasons. She falls more than any of the Compsons; the fault is her own; but Faulkner seems to suggest that the Compsons had too little regard for Caddy herself and her love and too much respect for the conventions and proprieties. Only Benjy loves her enough. When he goes to sleep after the long day of regrets for Caddy on April 7, 1928—eighteen years after Caddy has gone—"the Dark," he says, "began to go in smooth, bright shapes, like it always does, even when Caddy says I have been asleep" (*SF,* p. 92). In his limited mind, Caddy still exists in the present tense. The tragedy of the Compsons is that only an idiot remembers the character Faulkner referred to as "my heart's darling."

Caddy does not talk in abstractions. Addie Bundren in *As I Lay Dying* talks not at all except when others quote her and when she makes her one long speech in the novel. Within the "dark voicelessness" of her long monlogue however, she condemns abstract words but uses them to describe the facts of her own sin and salvation. Outside the monologue she speaks abstractly only when she is provoked to reply to the sanctimonious preachments of Cora Tull. Addie's philosophy of words and deeds raises immediate questions. Why do her own words not "go straight up in a thin line"? Addie's husband, Anse, is a man of words. "He had a word, too. Love, he called it. But I had been used to words for a long time. I knew that that word was like the others: just a shape to fill a lack; that when the right time came, you wouldn't need a word for that anymore than for pride or fear" (*AILD,* p. 164). Addie herself speaks the words she condemns. In one paragraph of her soliloquy, she mentions *sin* eight times. She discusses *hate, fear, pride, love,* and *duty.* Faulkner seems aware that he and Addie in this speech need to stretch the framework of language and the novel. On the other hand, Addie's interior monologue is hypothetical; these are the words she might have thought. She never says them. The artist formulates the words for us, and Faulkner and Addie explain how she may speak the words which she damns others for using. Addie hears "the dark land talking the voiceless speech." In "dark voicelessness" the "words are the deeds" rather than words (*AILD,* pp. 166–167). Olga Vickery resolves the difficulty by stating that words are not empty if they are based on "non-verbal experience." [11] Perhaps we should add that they must not be spoken aloud. Only in this voiceless sort of language, apparently, may one whose doing goes terribly along the earth express his beliefs.

The meaning of Addie's life is the search for the fact of love. First as a sadistic school teacher she cruelly whips her pupils so that she can make them aware of her: "Now you are aware of me!

11. Vickery, p. 246. See also Richard P. Adams, *Faulkner: Myth and Motion* (Princeton: Princeton University Press, 1968), p. 106.

Now I am something in your secret and selfish life, who have marked your blood with my own for ever and ever" (*AILD,* p. 162). For the same reason she marries Anse after a strange and brief courtship. An affectionate courtship would violate the mores of these hill people, and Addie searches for love. So her premarital love-making with Anse consists of her asking him if he has any "womenfolks" to make him cut his hair and hold his shoulders up. Addie never discusses her connubial bliss or the lack of it in the early days of the marriage. But her sex life apparently did not bring the experience of love, for only when she becomes pregnant with Cash does she realize "that living was terrible and that this was the answer to it" (*AILD,* p. 163). But after the birth of Cash, Anse dies; that is, he becomes merely a word because love for him becomes "a shape to fill a lack." The conception of Darl, Addie thinks, is an accident, as though Anse had tricked her, "hidden within a word like within a paper screen"; she has "been tricked by words older than Anse or love . . ." (*AILD*, p. 164). After love between Addie and Anse becomes meaningless, she turns to sin in search of reality. She hopes that adultery with Preacher Whitfield will destroy her aloneness "and coerce the terrible blood to the forlorn echo of the dead word high in the air" (*AILD*, p. 167). But this affair destroys her isolation only by presenting her with an illegitimate son whom she loves. This son, Jewel, can love his mother, but their love remains as incommunicable in words as any other. After the birth of Jewel, Addie tries to expiate her sin: "I gave Anse Dewey Dell to negative Jewel. Then I gave him Vardaman to replace the child I had robbed him of. And now he has three children that are his and not mine. And then I could get ready to die" (*AILD,* p. 168).

Addie is enigmatic; she seems to be a good mother to Cash and Jewel, but her other children—Darl, Dewey Dell, and Vardaman—suffer from the lack of mother love. Yet even the unloved Darl recognizes his mother's virtues and admires her integrity. He remembers her trying "to teach us that deceit was such that, in a world where it was, nothing else could be very bad or very important, not even poverty" (*AILD,* p. 123). But when he sees his mother weeping by Jewel's bed and intuits the secret of Jewel's birth, he suggests that "she felt the same way about tears she did about deceit, hating herself for doing it, hating him because she had to."

The plot situation in *As I Lay Dying* derives from Addie's making Anse promise that he will bury her with her family in Jefferson. She is not as much interested in being buried by her relatives as she is in what happens to her immediate family while they take her corpse on the long wagon journey to the cemetery. She arranges the odyssey just after the birth of her second child: "I asked Anse to promise to take me back to Jefferson when I died, because I knew that father had been right, even when he couldn't have known he was right anymore than I could have known I was wrong" (*AILD,* pp. 164–165). Her father had said "that the reason for living was to get ready to stay dead a long time" (*AILD,* p. 161). What Addie means in this mysterious clause remains enigmatic: one may achieve immortality by impressing his will on others so much that he continues longer after death to affect the living; or death is oblivion and therefore all definition of the self must come before the eternity of the grave; or life is a constant process of preparation for death and the immortality of the soul. Faulkner does not, I believe, give a basis for choice of a single meaning.

When Addie after the death of her second child gets "ready to stay dead a long time," she extracts Anse's promise to take her corpse to Jefferson; her revenge, she says, "would be that he would never know I was taking revenge." Now there is no question that Addie is bitterly resentful toward Anse, the man of words which "go straight up in a thin line, quick and harmless." Her promise commits him for once in his life to doing which goes terribly "along the earth." The meaning of *As I Lay Dying* hinges on Addie's motive. Does she disrupt Anse's entire philosophy out of pure revenge? Are her motives admirable because she wishes to involve him in life in spite of himself? Does love outweigh revenge? Does Anse transcend himself on the journey and, little as he does, become committed and involved? Or does his selfish motive of buying false teeth in town prevail? Critics take all these views, and evidence may be found for all. Probably *As I Lay Dying* must remain a tantalizing enigma because Faulkner does not seem to have provided enough evidence for resolution.

Hyatt Waggoner has concluded that "unlike Cora . . . , Addie has no faith." [12] But one should not be certain of this. Cora declares her faith again and again in empty words, and Addie has some sort of unorthodox belief. She hears the dark land "talking of God's love and His beauty and His sin"—whatever the sin of God may be and mean. J. L. Roberts maintains that the Bundren family is "doomed by the nihilistic philosophy of an egocentric and selfish mother." [13] Carvel Collins regards Addie as "a failure as a wife and mother, especially in her relations with Darl." [14] The novel itself provides some evidence of love. Human beings must use words, yet words paradoxically betray. Addie's error in part is her inability to voice her love. Certainly motherhood is an admirable virtue even to her. Motherhood, she says, "was invented by someone who had to have a word for it because the ones that had the children didn't care whether there was a word for it or not" (*AILD,* p. 163). She says that she knew this after the birth of Cash. Is it conceivable that she can be as conscious as she is of her duty to Anse and not be aware of her duty to her children? Her last thought before death seems to be a dying mother's concern for the youngest child: "She looks at Vardaman; her eyes, the life in them, rushing suddenly upon them; the two flames glare up for a steady instant" (*AILD,* p. 47). And at this moment of death her great concern is for a child she had spoken of as Anse's and not hers.

Addie and Caddy are profoundly acquainted with the mysteries of life. Addie's monologue reveals an ignorant country mother grasping for meaning; Caddy needs no monologue because her love needs no voice. But Temple Drake can neither think nor feel. She is silent because she never thinks anything worth saying. At times she talks in the garrulous chatter of a teen-ager playing at life, just as Ruby

12. Hyatt H. Waggoner, *William Faulkner: From Jefferson to the World* (Lexington: University of Kentucky Press, 1959), p. 68.

13. J. L. Roberts, "The Individual and the Family: Faulkner's *As I Lay Dying,*" *Arizona Quarterly,* 16 (Spring 1960), 38.

14. Carvel Collins, "The Pairing of *The Sound and the Fury* and *As I Lay Dying,*" *The Princeton University Library Chronicle,* 18 (Spring 1957), 121.

Lamar accuses her of playing at sex. She tries to pray, "But she could not think of a single designation for the heavenly father, so she began to say 'My father's a judge; my father's a judge' over and over" (*S,* p. 50). Words and deeds of love are rare in *Sanctuary.* The focal episode, Popeye's raping of Temple with a corncob, is a meaningless event in the lives of meaningless characters. Only Horace speaks of truth, and he is weak and the forces of evil are so formidable that he cannot make the truth prevail. One of Faulkner's favorite words, *pride,* appears once in the novel, and significantly it is spoken by the shallow Temple. When Horace visits her in Miss Reba's whorehouse, Temple tells about her experience "with actual pride, a sort of naïve and impersonal vanity" (*S,* p. 209). That Temple should take this attitude toward her deflowering is appropriate in the world of this novel, Faulkner's most pessimistic treatment of the modern Waste Land. If anyone in *Sanctuary* knows love and acts accordingly, it is Ruby Lamar, the commonlaw wife of Lee Goodwin. She has prostituted herself for her lover, and she offers to do so again. She loves; she is capable of courageous sacrifice. She has every virtue on Faulkner's list, but like Caddy, she has the appearance of none.

Darl and Quentin and Horace are insane, mentally disturbed, or simply ineffectual in dealing with the realities of a world of good and evil. Darl is the strangest case of the three. Obsessed by a terrible need for love, he is so clairvoyant that he lays bare the souls and reads the minds of the members of his family. Thus he learns of Dewey Dell's illicit pregnancy and Jewel's repressed love for his mother. Apparently his clairvoyance is a violation of the secrets of the human heart. He learns the things which torture others, but he cannot clairvoyantly see others' thoughts about him. For example, he does not know that Jewel and Dewey Dell plan to send him to the insane asylum in Jackson until they move to capture him. His goading and his secret knowledge make his brother and sister wild with anger. He is a man of the word who never acts except to separate Jewel and Addie or to try to stop the Bundrens' journey to the cemetery with the rotting corpse. Yet Faulkner has made him a lovable character. His monologues, his sensitiveness and his language, Irving Howe has written, reveal Faulkner's "implicit belief that the spiritual life of a Darl Bundren can be . . . important." [15]

Darl's sanity is a question difficult to settle. In 1957 Faulkner said that Darl

> was mad from the first. He got progressively madder because he didn't have the capacity—not so much of sanity but of inertness to resist all the catastrophes that happened to the family. Jewel resisted because he was sane and he was the toughest. The others resisted through probably simple inertia, but Darl couldn't resist it and so he went completely off his rocker. But he was mad all the time. (*UNIV*, p. 110)

To Irving Howe, Darl's "sudden crackup comes too much as a surprise." [16] But J. L. Roberts describes Darl as "the sane and sensible individual pitted against a world of backwoods, confused, violent, and shiftless Bundrens." [17] Darl is likeable enough for all who read his monologues to wish he were sane. But his isolation from his family and from life is great enough to cause derangement. He lives without identity and outside any moral order.

Reading the dialogue in *As I Lay Dying* and ignoring all the thoughts of the characters produces startling results. Darl seldom speaks to anyone except his brothers; even his manner of speech is abstract and impersonal—the very opposite of his thoughts. Armstid describes the way he says a sentence: "He said it just like he was reading it outen the paper" (*AILD,* p. 181). He refuses to answer many questions, and he goads and taunts almost everyone to whom he speaks except Cash and Vardaman.

> "It's not your horse that's dead, Jewel," I say. . . . "But it's not your horse that's dead."
>
> "Goddamn you," he says, "Goddamn you." (*AILD,* p. 88)

His speech reveals little or nothing of the poetry and the depth of his thought.

Darl hopes to thwart the family's commitment to complete the

15. Irving Howe, *William Faulkner: A Critical Study,* Second Edition (New York: Vintage Books, 1962), p. 189.

16. Howe, p. 185.

17. Roberts, p. 33.

journey and bury Addie in Jefferson. He hauls a load of wood, but his purpose is to separate his brother Jewel from his mother at the time of her death. He sets fire to a barn in the hope that he can destroy the stinking corpse and frustrate Addie's and the family's will. He refuses to help to save the coffin from the flooding river. "Darl jumped out of the wagon and left Cash sitting there trying to save it and the wagon turning over . . ." (*AILD,* p. 145). When Cash loses his tools in the flood, Darl goes through the motions of searching for them, but Jewel actually finds them. As the barn burns, he passively watches others save the stock. In all the novel he acts with kindness only twice: with words he stops a fight between Jewel and a man with a knife, and after Cash breaks his leg, Darl brings his tools into Armstid's house.

Darl, then, is thought. He does not speak the words of love aloud because he seeks love but cannot find it. "This world is not his world"; Cash says, "this life his life" (*AILD,* p. 250). Even when he fights Dewey Dell and Jewel to avoid going to the insane asylum in Jackson, he is distant from the action. "It was like he was outside of it too, same as you, and getting mad at it would be kind of like getting mad at a mud-puddle that splashed you when you stepped in it" (*AILD,* p. 227).

The language of Darl's monologues is so beautiful and poetic that there is little wonder that many readers do not understand how Dewey Dell and Jewel hate him. In concrete and poetic imagery Darl expresses his terrible longings for the love he cannot experience. Whatever he looks on or remembers creates an indelible image. A cedar waterbucket and Cash making his mother's coffin evoke the best of Faulkner's style and Darl's: "Standing in a litter of chips, he is fitting two of the boards together. Between the shadow spaces they are yellow as gold, like soft gold, bearing on their flanks in smooth undulations the marks of the adze blade: a good carpenter, Cash is" (*AILD,* p. 4). Darl's thought processes are also revealed in Faulkner's most exalted vocabulary of sonorous and somewhat onomatopoetic polysyllables—a style like what John Crowe Ransom has called Shakespeare's "conscious latinity." [18]

18. John Crowe Ransom, "On Shakespeare's Language," *The Sewanee Review*, 55 (April-June 1947), 182.

As the funeral procession nears the flooding river, Darl thinks,

> Before us the thick dark current runs. It talks up to us in a murmur become ceaseless and myriad, the yellow surface dimpled monstrously into fading swirls travelling along the surface for an instant, silent, impermanent and profoundly significant, as though just beneath the surface something huge and alive waked for a moment of lazy alertness out of and into light slumber again. (*AILD,* p. 134)

The comparison suggests Darl's search for love, for some larger significance in whatever he sees. He is a man of beautiful words who doubts his very existence. In "conscious latinity" and Shakespearian figures he debates whether he is: "How do our lives ravel out into the no-wind, no-sound, the weary gestures wearily recapitulant: echoes of old compulsions with no-hand on no-strings: in sunset we fall into furious attitudes, dead gestures of dolls" (*AILD,* pp. 196–197). Or in stark monosyllables he meditates on the same point: "And then I must be, or I could not empty myself for sleep in a strange room. And so if I am not emptied yet, I am *is*" (*AILD,* p. 76). And when Vardaman asks about his mother, Darl says, " 'I haven't got ere one. . . . Because if I had one, it is *was.* And if it is was, it can't be *is.* Can it?' " (*AILD,* p. 409). Darl and his beautiful words are engaged in a mad search for identity, love, and truth.

An unsatisfactory relationship with the mother also begins Quentin's problems. A fragmentary sentence suggests that sorrow and suicide might have been avoided if he had had a mother: *"My little sister had no. If I could say Mother. Mother"* (*SF,* p. 117). And again: *"if I'd just had a mother so I could say Mother Mother"* (*SF,* p. 213). And Darl thinks, "I cannot love my mother because I have no mother" (*AILD,* p. 89). The despair of Quentin reduces him to debating his existence almost in the same words which Darl uses. He thinks in confused fragments about the reality of his existence: "thinking I was I was not who was not was not who" (*SF,* p. 211); "Peacefullest words. *Non fui. Sum. Fui. Nom* [*sic;* should be *Non*] *sum.* . . . I was. I am not. . . . I am. Drink. I was not" (*SF,* p. 216). It is almost as if they exist only in the words.

Caddy loves only persons and shows her love only in deeds;

Quentin cannot think of persons and love except in terms of principles. He commits suicide because of Caddy's loss of her virginity—not because of his loss of Caddy herself. The person of Caddy hardly matters to him. He is defined by the absence of love and deep personal feeling. In the appendix to *The Sound and the Fury* Faulkner wrote that Quentin "loved not his sister's body . . . loved not the idea of incest . . . , loved death above all, . . . loved only death, loved and lived in a deliberate and almost perverted anticipation of death as a lover loves. . . ." [19]

Quentin uses the word *love* only three times, and twice it occurs when he experiences revulsion as he asks Caddy if she loved her seducers. He is more distraught than Darl. He recognizes that he has reached an abnormal moral and psychological state, that he is outside the realm of reality: "It's not when you realise that nothing can help you—religion, pride, anything—it's when you realise that you dont need any aid" (*SF,* p. 98). These are the only instances when Quentin uses abstractions. Frederic Henry and Caddy avoid speaking them because they know them without being able to say them. Quentin avoids them because the virtues to him are an abstract code—as abstract and meaningless as his feeling of duty which makes him complete the year at Harvard before he puts to death the mind that was supposed to be educated with the money derived from the sale of Benjy's pasture.

Quentin remembers well his conversations with Caddy, the many questions he asked her; and every single one is concerned with a concept of honor rather than with Caddy herself. Like Narcissa Benbow in *Sanctuary,* he is too conscious of reputation. "Why must you do like nigger women do" (*SF,* p. 113), he asks Caddy, and *"Have there been very many Caddy"* (*SF,* p. 142). He seems to wish to measure her loss of chastity quantitatively as though she could be either a little bit pregnant or a great deal. Regard for his own shame is probably the cause of Quentin's opposition to Caddy's taking off her wet dress before the children playing at the branch. He slaps her, suggesting that he loves the idea of virtue but not his sister.

19. *The Sound and the Fury,* The Modern Library, p. 9.

Quentin is like a sensitive little child hearing for the first time in some repulsive fashion how he was made, how babies are born; and all his life he lives with the child's momentary revulsion and nausea. Once Versh told him a story about a man who castrated himself. Quentin's recalling the story suggests that he has considered castration as a solution instead of suicide. But making himself a eunuch would not remove the stains of dishonor from the world, because even if all men were castrated, sex would still have existed in creation: "But that's not it. It's not not having them. It's never to have had them . . ." (*SF,* p. 143). Quentin's suicide is absurdly idealistic; it is a protest against the way the world is made.

In Quentin and Darl, Faulkner has created characters who exist and live by the empty word. Salvation lies outside the word, but each is incapable of finding the way to life. Darl yearns for love, but does not himself love. He does not act or even speak with kindness. He only thinks. Quentin presumably might define himself first by an act of evil, which would give him identity, and then by knowledge and repentance, which would enable him to accept the world as it is and go on from there—in acts rather than words.

Almost every character in *The Sound and the Fury, As I Lay Dying,* and *Sanctuary* has his own peculiar relationship to Faulkner's governing concepts of abstraction and concreteness and the deed. A great many loquacious users of the word are entirely false, and the falseness of the characters' words is perfectly obvious to everyone except the person who talks and thinks in empty terms. If anyone is worse than a hypocrite, it is the self-deluded soul who does not recognize that the sound and the fury of his own phraseology signifies nothing. Anse, Narcissa, Jason, and Mrs. Compson are evil not only because they represent evil but especially because each one of them believes he is the representative of goodness and truth. Narcissa is an evangelist of status and reputation. She does not care who committed crime nor who is punished so long as Horace does not stain the family honor. "I don't care," she tells Horace, "how many women you have nor who they are" (*S,* p. 178). But the people in Jefferson think he is having an affair with Ruby Lamar. "So it doesn't matter whether it's true or not" (*S,* p. 179). Narcissa resembles Quentin in seeming to care for love and truth, but she does not share his integrity or his longing.

Mrs. Compson makes the sounds of love. But even the idiot Benjy knows how hollow the words are:

> Caddy took me to Mother's chair and Mother took my face in her hands and then she held me against her.
>
> "My poor baby." she said. She let me go. "You and Versh take good care of him, honey."
>
> . . . .
>
> "You're not a poor baby. Are you. You've got your Caddy. Haven't you got your Caddy." *(SF,* p. 8)

Mrs. Compson's words are wrong on two counts: that she uses them at all; and that they are the wrong ones. Her sentiments are unworthy. She thinks she pities and loves, but all her pity and love are for herself.

Jason is like his mother—evil but with complete assurance of his own righteousness. His section of *The Sound and the Fury* is often called stream of consciousness;[20] but the main basis of any stream of consciousness is the irrational and poetic associations of a sensitive mind. Jason, however, is too sane and rational ever to make associations which are illogical and poetic. His actions and his words "are the result of clear, orderly thinking in terms of cause and effect. . . ." [21] Like Narcissa, he is concerned with status and reputation. He despises Miss Quentin not because of her lack of chastity but because she has "no more respect for what I try to do for her than to make her name and my name and my Mother's name a byword in the town"(*SF,* p. 291). Love is so alien to his thinking that he cannot even understand why Benjy continues to mourn for the absent Caddy (*SF,* p. 315).

The word is widely separated from the deed in Mr. Compson's talk. He uses abstractions in order to tell his son that truths do not exist: "All men," he tells Quentin, "are just accumulations dolls stuffed with sawdust swept up from the trash heaps where all previous dolls had been thrown away" (*SF,* p. 194). But Mr. Comp-

20. Vickery, p. 28. William R. Mueller, *The Prophetic Voice in Modern Fiction* (New York: Association Press, 1959), p. 111.

21. Vickery, p. 31.

son loves despite his skeptical denial of the possibility of love. He shows his love when Quentin breaks his leg: *"damn that horse damn that horse"* (*SF,* p. 132), he says in sympathetic anger. He acts with love and kindness to his contemptible wife. He is gentle to his children. His principles will not permit him to accept money from Herbert Head for Caddy's illegitimate daughter. He defends Caddy and wishes to bring her home after her disgrace. True, he drinks himself to death, but love and disappointment are among the causes of his weakness. One cannot be certain that he is so cynical as Quentin thinks he is. Part of his nihilism, perhaps, is the attempt of a worldly wise father to shock an excessively innocent son into an awareness of evil which will lead to understanding and strength.

Other characters in *The Sound and the Fury* and *As I Lay Dying* should be viewed in the same terms. Virtue to Benjy is as physical as the smell of trees. Whatever thoughts or emotions he has are smelled as immediately as the odor of a rose, and they remain just that—immediate and physical. He recognizes love but has no word for it. Words fail Vardaman. He loves his mother and grieves for her, but is too young to know the abstractions which should convey his feelings. Cash reconciles Anse's words with Addie's deeds. He is, writes Olga Vickery, "the one character in the novel who achieves his full humanity in which reason and intuition, words and action merge into a single though complex response." [22]

The word in these novels is often the lie of the mouth, and the

22. Vickery, p. 58. But there is much critical disagreement about Cash. For sympathetic readings, see Waggoner, p. 84; Michael Millgate, *William Faulkner,* Evergreen Pilot Books (New York: Grove Press, Inc., 1961), p. 37; Frederick J. Hoffman, *William Faulkner,* Twayne's United States Authors Series (New York: Twayne Publishers, Inc., 1961, 1966), p. 62; Jack Gordon Goellner, "A Closer Look at 'As I Lay Dying,' " *Perspective,* 7 (Spring 1954), 46; Joseph Warren Beach, *American Fiction 1920–1940* (New York: The Macmillan Company, 1941), p. 134. For interpretations of Cash as a Jason-like villain, see Edwin Berry Burgum, *The Novel and the World's Dilemma* (New York: Oxford University Press, 1947), p. 215; Edward Wasiolek, "*As I Lay Dying*: Distortion in the Slow Eddy of Current Opinion," *Critique* 3 (Spring-Fall 1959), 19–20. I suggest that Cash's name is not symbolic of money at all, but is a shortening of Cassius. Cassius Gudger, the prototype for a character in Thomas Wolfe's *Look Homeward, Angel,* was called Cash.

deed is the truth of the heart. Those who speak are usually false. Those who act are true. "Dilsey, almost as inarticulate as Benjy," writes Olga Vickery, "becomes through her actions alone the embodiment of the truth of the heart which is synonymous with morality." [23] Mrs. Compson believes in words so much that she changes Benjy's name when she learns that he is an idiot. And after Caddy's fall, she refuses to allow her name to be spoken. But for Dilsey words have a different power. *"My name been Dilsey since fore I could remember and it be Dilsey when they's long forgot me"* (*SF,* p. 77). The name and the word for Dilsey have a meaning which transcends the individual, the immediate, and the human. She does not talk of truth, but she knows that the words of truth, like her name, are written in the book of life. They are the facts, the truths of the heart. Long after people have ceased to know her name, she will still be Dilsey. Truth is truth even when it is not spoken and forgotten.

23. Vickery, p. 32.

14

Language of Irony: Quiet Words and Violent Acts in *Light in August*

IN many ways *Light in August* was for Faulkner a new kind of novel. He abandoned the stream-of-consciousness technique as the over-all method, the subjective point of view which he had used in *As I Lay Dying* and *The Sound and the Fury*. And he abandoned the objectivity and the restraint of *Sanctuary*. In his first three novels he was talky but hostile to the talkative; he created characters who used "language and logic . . . to obscure truth." [1] And he himself obscured truth with language and logic. In the next three novels he created two kinds of characters: those who know and can interpret but do not speak the words; and those who speak the words but cannot know and interpret. The actual relationship between the word and the truth in *Light in August,* however, cannot be stated so tersely. Almost all the characters speak the words of goodness, and Faulkner strangely applies the abstractions of righteousness to all the characters alike—both the sublimely good and the savagely evil. "The problem of evil" in *Light in August,* Frederick J. Hoffman has said, is "intricately treated." [2] The style and the diction

1. Olga W. Vickery, *The Novels of William Faulkner: A Critical Interpretation* (Baton Rouge: Louisiana State University Press, 1959, 1961), p. 8.
2. Frederick J. Hoffman, *William Faulkner,* Twayne's United States Authors Series (New York: Twayne Publishers, 1961, 1966), p. 69.

are especially intricate. Certainly the relationship between what a character is and what he says is more complex in this novel than in the earlier ones. In *The Sound and the Fury* Mrs. Compson talks of goodness, but her hypocrisy and negativeness make her a most wicked woman. No such easy summary will encompass all the confused facets of the character of Gail Hightower. Alfred Kazin has seen that the characters are driven by "murderous abstractions," and Joe Christmas "remains, as he is born, an abstraction," "only a thought in other people's minds." [3]

The plot and the theme of self-definition in *Light in August* focus upon the life and death of that bastard Joe Christmas, who may or may not be part Negro. The community of Jefferson, Mississippi, defines itself in terms of its relationship to Joe, and even those isolated souls who live in the community but have never become a part of it either know themselves or display their characters to the reader in terms of the effect of Joe upon their lives.

After Joe murders his mistress Joanna Burden, descendant of fanatic Yankee abolitionists and carpetbaggers, he flees from a posse for days and then gives himself up in Mottstown. Taken to Jefferson, he awaits his trial. "In the town on that day lived a young man named Percy Grimm," [4] a preserver of law and order, a patriot. Grimm "was a Nazi Storm Trooper" created before Faulkner had ever "heard of one," [5] but he is also almost a perfect embodiment of the emotional and abstractionist morality of World War I. Born too late to participate in the War, Grimm is the antithesis of Frederic Henry. He resembles instead the patriot Gino. Like Gino, Grimm speaks the words of patriotism, and the diction which Faulkner lavishes upon him could be torn from the pages of Wilsonian rhetoric or from the billboard slogans of the period of America's patriotic orgy.

Percy and his followers from the American Legion seem genuine

3. Alfred Kazin, "The Stillness of *Light in August,*" in Charles Shapiro, *Twelve Original Essays on Great American Novels* (Detroit: Wayne State University Press, 1958), pp. 260, 263.

4. Faulkner, *Light in August* (New York: Harrison Smith & Robert Haas, 1932), p. 425. Hereafter cited in text with abbreviation *LA*.

5. Faulkner, *Faulkner in the University,* ed. Gwynn and Blotner (Charlottesville: The University of Virginia Press, 1959), p. 41.

in their desire to avert a lynching and to let the course of the law prevail. These defenders of moral and legal order in Jefferson are a study in abstraction, in the "hysteria" (p. 394) which "passed away" in the Roaring Twenties. Then even those "who had been loudest in the hysteria" begin "to look at one another a little askance"—but not Percy. He has a "sublime and implicit faith in physical courage and blind obedience"; and he is a racist. He speaks in terms of principles: "where we stand," "where the government of the country stands" (*LA*, pp. 424–426). At one point, Faulkner quotes only abstract phrases from the speeches of Percy to his men: ". . . order . . . course of justice . . . let the people see that we have worn the uniform of the United States . . . And one thing more" (*LA*, p. 429; the ellipses are Faulkner's own). Swayed by this archaic emotionalism, the town accepts Grimm and his "vision and patriotism and pride," accepts him with "a little awe and a deal of actual faith and confidence" (*LA*, p. 432).

When Joe escapes in the mob on the square, Grimm suddenly changes from protector to pursuer. He thinks "calmly," with "quiet joy" (p. 404), and his face has "that serene, unearthly luminousness of angels in church windows" (*LA*, p. 437). He is calm and serene when he is protecting a prisoner from a mob, when he is himself leading the mob with all the self-assurance and "the implacable undeviation of Juggernaut or Fate," and even when he castrates the dying man, shouting with all the moral certainty of a god, "Now you'll let white women alone, even in hell" (*LA*, p. 439).

Percy's fanaticism, his self-deception, his pretense of virtue make him one of the most despicable characters in modern literature. But he is described in terms of principles and moralities, and in his own mind he acts in the name of truth and justice even at the very moment when he commits his most despicable crime. In many ways, furthermore, the portrait of Grimm exemplifies the diction, the style, and the method of *Light in August.* Faulkner fully displays for the first time his magnificent polysyllabic vocabulary, but the abstract and general words are as often ironic and false as they are true.

Language and even abstraction in *Light in August* function ironically and symbolically. If the good deed in *The Sound and the*

Fury may be known only by the fact, if love can be known and proved only in the rapid beat of Caddy's heart, the evil in *Light in August* may be known mainly by the words of virtue. Thus when Faulkner uses the words that can easily become didactic, the novel still moves by indirection. And good words ironically describe an evil soul. Although Faulkner filled this novel with abstractions and Hemingway shunned them in *A Farewell to Arms,* the word is essentially meaningless in both novels. Hightower puts it well when he asks, " 'Ah, Byron, Byron. What are a few mumbled words before God, before the steadfastness of a woman's nature? Before that child?' " (*LA,* p. 290). " 'Me and Lucas,' " Lena tells Mrs. Armstid, " 'dont need no word promises between us' " (*LA,* p. 17).

Mentally, many of Faulkner's characters are always able to comprehend facts and feelings even when they cannot think them in words. In "Old Man," for example, he wrote that "man always has been drawn to dwell beside water, even before he had a name for water and fire. . . ." [6] Feeling, the drawing to the water, was present before articulation. Similarly, in *Light in August*, Byron talks in a "level, restrained tone, not once at a loss for words until he came to something still too new and nebulous for him to more than feel" (*LA,* p. 297). Now the chief obligation of the reader is to distinguish between the word and the feeling. Sometimes the two (language and thought) correspond exactly; at other times, they are exactly antithetical. But the distinction may be one of the most important things in reading the novel. The question is not sincerity or hypocrisy. For the character, the difference between what is said and what is felt is so fundamental that he cannot yet even think it into words. This curious psychological phenomenon is described by Gavin Stevens in his speculation about the talk in the jail between Joe Christmas and his grandmother: "I dont think that she knew herself, planned at all what she would say, because it had already been written and worded for her on the night when she bore his mother, and that was now so long ago that she had learned it beyond all forgetting and then forgot the words" (*LA,* pp. 423–424). Mrs. Hines knows what she will say at a level more basic and true than

6. Faulkner, *The Wild Palms* (New York: Random House, 1939), p. 155.

the level of words and language. If truth exists in the mind without words, the words may of course exist without truth. Hightower reads Tennyson: "the fine galloping language, the gutless swooning full of sapless trees and dehydrated lusts begins to swim smooth and swift and peaceful. It is better than praying without having to bother to think aloud" (*LA*, p. 301). Knowledge and awareness come not in words, and words are not belief. Byron Bunch knows that Lena Grove is to have a baby and helps her to plan for its birth. But his awareness is not a reality to him until the baby is born. Experience lies outside of language. To Byron, *"It was like me, and her, and all the other folks that I had to get mixed up in it, were just a lot of words that never even stood for anything, were not even us, while all the time what was us was going on and going on without even missing the lack of words"* (*LA*, p. 380).

Words of emotions and morality and religion, explicit and abstract descriptions of characters—all appear with surprising frequency and great complexity in *Light in August*. They are written by Faulkner in his own person, and they are spoken or thought directly or indirectly by the characters. They are true at one time and ironic at another. But the most surprising revelations which would be made by a concordance of the novel would be the omnipresence of the words of peace, such as *peace* itself and its derivatives, and *serene, tranquil, quiet, calm, placid* and their derivatives. The general agreement among critics that Joe Christmas is in some way a figuring of Jesus Christ has been matched in recent years by the puzzlements about the irony of describing a violent, unloved, unloving murderer as being like Christ. Perhaps Faulkner's concern with the theme of peace helps to define the irony. The heavenly host proclaimed, "peace, good will toward men" at the birth of Christ, and peace is the theme of *Light in August* and the obsession of Joe Christmas and other characters. *Peace* and its synonyms appear in the novel at least twice as often as all the other abstract words of the Nobel Prize Speech combined. (I have counted more than 120 occurrences, but my count is probably still incomplete.)

Faulkner uses the words of peace in strange and various ways. Violence is always described in terms of peace. The novel begins when Lena Grove rides into town on a wagon and sees the smoke from the burning house of Joanna Burden. Half the novel later, Faulkner describes the crime which occurred just before the house was set afire—Joe's murdering of Joanna. The relationship between these two dissimilar souls has progressed through several stages—from an almost perverted intense sexual passion to, at last, Joanna's attempt to get Joe to repent and to make something meaningful of his life. At the end she speaks in abstractions which Faulkner quotes with ellipses, just as he had quoted the phrases of Percy Grimm elliptically: " '. . . not to school, then, if you dont want to go . . . Do without that . . . Your soul. Expiation of . . .' And he waiting, cold, still, until she had finished: '. . . hell . . . forever and ever and ever . . .' " (*LA*, p. 264). The closer the catastrophe comes, the more frequently Faulkner describes the lovers as peaceful and tranquil. Joanna listens "quietly" (p. 264); her voice is "calm" (p. 264), "calm and tranquil" (p. 265); she speaks "quietly," rises "quietly," says "quietly" (all on p. 265). Joe thinks "quietly," and "with quiet astonishment" (pp. 265–266). The very earth is "still, quiet." And at the moment of death Joanna points a pistol at Joe just before he cuts her throat with a razor. Her eyes are "calm and still as all pity and all despair and all conviction" (*LA*, p. 267).

The death of Joe Christmas at the hands of Percy Grimm and his mob is more violent than the death of Joanna; yet this scene too is described in terms of peace. Percy pursues Joe (see above) with "untroubled faith in the rightness and infallibility of his actions" (*LA*, p. 434); he thinks "calmly with . . . quiet joy"; his face has "that serene, unearthly luminousness of angels in church windows" (*LA*, p. 437). Castrated and dying, Joe looks at his murderers with "peaceful" eyes. And in the most exalted rhetoric of the novel, in language almost Biblical in its tone and rhythm, Faulkner describes the mob's future memory of the "black blast" of Joe's blood: "They are not to lose it, in whatever *peaceful* valleys, beside whatever *placid* and *reassuring* streams of old age, in the mirroring faces of whatever children they will *contemplate* old disasters and newer hopes. It will be there, *musing, quiet, steadfast,* not fading and not particularly threatful, but of itself alone *serene,* of itself alone triumphant" (*LA,* p. 440; italics mine).

Peace and violence go hand in hand throughout the novel. Stories of the Civil War bring Gail Hightower a "peaceful shuddering of delight" (*LA*, p. 452). While Joe is in jail, Faulkner lavishes the words of peace upon the town: Grimm "recrossed the empty square, the *quiet* square empty of people *peacefully* at suppertables about that *peaceful* town and that *peaceful* country" (*LA*, p. 430; italics mine). The violent religious fanatic Doc Hines sleeps "profoundly and peacefully" (*LA*, p. 375). When Byron sees Lena's ex-lover, the contemptible Lucas Burch-Joe Brown, flee from Lena for the second time, a wind "blows through him," and "It is at once violent and peaceful" (*LA*, p. 402). Even the fire truck which dashes up to Joanna's burning home to put out the fire is "serene, arrogant, and proud" (*LA*, p. 272).

Terms of peace are used straightforwardly as well as ironically. Lena Grove enjoys true peace more than any other character in *Light in August*. The words of peace which describe her fall into deliberate patterns and clusters. Again and again in the first fifty pages of the novel Faulkner describes her as "tranquil," "serene, peaceful." Then the words disappear for almost two hundred pages before Faulkner begins applying them with truth and irony, first to Joanna Burden, then, in turn, to Joe, Gail Hightower, Lena again, Byron, the town and the mob, Gail again, and finally to Lena again. In general, the true peace of Lena Grove surrounds or frames the false peace of Jefferson and other characters in the main body of the novel. At the end, as always, Lena listens "quiet," "placid and calm," and her face is "quiet and calm as it had ever been," "calm as church."

The words of peace apply to the truly peaceful as well as ironically to the most savage violence. Faulkner's design is to demonstrate the omnipresent and terrible need of peace on earth and its blessedness when it is—so rarely and simply—attained. Hyatt Waggoner has defined the two polarities of character in *Light in August* in terms which help to explain Faulkner's use of abstractions and the words of serenity: "Hope may be found in *Light in August* only by giving up the intellectual and emotional struggle for ultimate certainty embodied in Hightower and Christmas [those who lack but desire peace] and turning to the humble and unself-conscious engagement of Lena and Byron [Lena, who has peace inborn; Byron, who attains it]." [7]

The manner of Southern folk or country people is often quiet and serene. A good example is the family of Lena Grove. They live in a "hookwormridden" land devastated by a sawmill, a land where peace seems possible only to the inanimate, "a stumppocked scene of profound and peaceful desolation." But they die quietly and peacefully. The mother says only, "Take care of paw." She speaks not a word of death or of herself. The last words of Lena's father indicate that he also thinks only of others. "You go to Doane's Mill with McKinley," he tells Lena. "You get ready to go, be ready when he comes" (*LA*, p. 2). The quietness and the imperturbability of these characters on their deathbeds reveals true peace. They have the strength and the quietness of peace at the critical moment of death in an environment where peace seems impossible. Yet it is supremely important also that it is their strength that makes them die so serenely. They are a good example of how quiet and peace is a part of the manner of Southern folk or country people who endure.

Ironically and paradoxically, the desperate and the despairing always wear a peaceful demeanor. Joe Christmas himself has this manner, a "cold and quiet contempt" (*LA,* p. 28). Gail Hightower's fanatically religious father "dwelled by serene rules in a world where reality did not exist" (*LA,* p. 448). Much of the peace of the town and of the characters is merely the appearance of peace, a hypocritical facade, a symbolic abstraction. Peace and serenity of manner in this novel mean many things. The most impervious villains, such as Grimm and Doc Hines, are tranquil and calm. Puritans, Peter Swiggart maintains, "tend to express their emotions, if at all, within the framework of rigid social conventions," and the "puritan mind avoids natural expression of feelings." [8] Evil, fanaticism, self-assurance, and a restless desire for

7. Hyatt H. Waggoner, *William Faulkner: From Jefferson to the World* (Lexington: University of Kentucky Press, 1959), p. 119.

8. Peter Swiggart, *The Art of Faulkner's Novels* (Austin: University of Texas Press, 1962), p. 133.

peace—all appear under the guise of peace. Pursued by the posse, Joe hears "the peaceful and tentative waking of birds" in a natural scene of "loneliness and quiet that has never known fury or despair. 'That was all I wanted,' he thinks, in a quiet and slow amazement" (*LA*, p. 313). A few pages earlier, Hightower had heard of Joe's capture and made the same statement: " 'I just wanted peace . . .' " (*LA*, p. 293). On a previous occasion Joe had uttered the same thought after he saw four people sitting at a card table "on a lighted veranda . . . , the white faces intent and sharp in the low light, the bare arms of the women glaring smooth and white above the trivial cards. 'That's all I wanted,' he thought. 'That dont seem like a whole lot to ask' " (*LA*, p. 108). Here also peace and quiet may be only a façade, but Joe cannot know that. Joanna's peace of mind arises either from the routine of her life of assistance to Negroes (she "spent a certain portion of each day sitting tranquilly at a desk and writing tranquilly for the eyes of both youth and age the practical advice of a combined priest and banker and trained nurse" [*LA*, p. 244]) or from conviction. She offers Joe complete charge of her philanthropic enterprise, "And all the while her calm profile in the peaceful firelight was as grave and tranquil as a portrait in a frame." And when Joe tries to argue, she listens "quietly" and then talks "again in that level, cold tone as if he had never spoken" (*LA*, p. 254).

Faulkner's uses of the words of peace represent a new aspect of his technique in *Light in August*. He uses language which he and his characters had avoided in *The Sound and the Fury, As I Lay Dying,* and *Sanctuary*. The abstractions used, however, reflect directly and indirectly the mind of the character rather than Faulkner's own moral intent. The words of Protestant theology, for example, are frequent in the novel, but they are spoken by the fanatics Doc Hines, Simon McEachern, and the New England Burdens. Faulkner's familiar rhetoric on the evils of slavery appears first in *Light in August* (*curse, God, doomed, sins* [*LA*, p. 239]), but they are spoken by Joanna Burden's father entirely in a dramatic context, and no Burden's vocabulary is completely reliable and true.

Another kind of abstractions is intended to remain almost inexplicable and confusing in order to show the abstract and confused mind of Joe Christmas. When Faulkner begins to create the life of Joe at the orphanage, he writes, "Memory believes before knowing remembers. Believes longer than recollects, longer than knowing even wonders. Knows remembers believes a corridor in a big long garbled cold echoing building of dark red brick . . ." (*LA*, p. 111). Faulkner echoes these phrases approximately twenty times in the novel. They reflect glimmers of meaning, but they remain largely mysterious and unknowable; they therefore describe well Joe's groping confusion and desire. These are psychological descriptions rather than moralizings. They represent an idealistic and abstracted mind somewhat like Quentin Compson's and Darl Bundren's, but the technique is different. Quentin's revulsion at sex and menstruation is equalled only by Joe's incredulous refusal to believe that the wonders of physical love can be thwarted by the filth of menstruation. Byron's refusal to acknowledge the fact of Lena's pregnancy is a similar ideality and abstraction.

Lack of involvement, irony, and abstraction are significant in the characters, the language, and the situations of *Light in August.* The most depraved of characters sees only virtue in his own position. Justice triumphs in the shallow life of Lucas Burch when he gets no thousand-dollar reward for the betrayal of his friend, but Burch nevertheless thinks of his own virtue and speaks the words of truth. Even the fact that he is confronted with "unpredictable frustrations . . . elevates him somehow above the petty human hopes and desires which they abrogate and negative" (*LA,* p. 412). That Burch is given just punishment is perfectly apparent to every reader and to every character in the novel, but he still mouths the words of justice because he is too shallow to know his own evil: "All Lucas Burch wanted," he thinks self-righteously, "was justice. Just justice" (*LA,* p. 415). A similar sort of contradiction or irony is apparent in the religious figures in the book. Calvin Burden promises to "beat the loving God" into his children (*LA,* p. 230). Abstraction, irony, the failure to reconcile opposing principles are apparent in the life of Gail Hightower's fanatically religious father, who is patriotic enough to go to war but religious enough to refuse to carry a gun. His stand is exactly like that of Cass Mastern in Robert Penn Warren's *All the King's Men.* These inconsistencies are merely a few examples of the profundity and complexity of Faulkner's themes, his ironies, and his abstractions. They illustrate how the words function in the novel. The abstractions themselves are somewhat like concrete symbols even though they do not appear as concrete images.

In *Light in August,* Faulkner is progressing toward the overt didacticism of "The Bear" and *A Fable* and *Requiem for a Nun,* and his pattern of development corresponds to that of Hemingway, who changed his diction also in the early nineteen thirties in *Death in the Afternoon* and *The Green Hills of Africa.* But the sonorous rhetoric of *Light in August* and its complexity make the book abstract more in the fashion of the Bible or Shakespeare than in the manner of Longfellow. The use of learned polysyllables to describe simple things usually results in pomposity or affectation, or it may be a device to achieve humor. But the exalted language of *Light in August* is none of these. The effect of Faulkner's language is that he does succeed in using abstractions to persuade the reader to attribute exalted concepts and emotions to things usually regarded as trivial. The style or technique begins at the very first page of the novel, when Faulkner describes the sawmill at Doane's Mill, Alabama, and its "motionless wheels rising from mounds of brick rubble and ragged weeds with a quality profoundly astonishing." And "gutted boilers" lift "their rusting and unsmoking stacks with an air stubborn, baffled and bemused upon a stumppocked scene of profound and peaceful desolation . . ." (*LA,* p. 2). A few paragraphs later, Faulkner sets the scene, establishes a mood and an atmosphere, subtly communicates the mood of the character, and suggests an attitude for the reader in a magnificent polysyllabic description of the motion of a country wagon:

The sharp and brittle crack and clatter of its weathered and ungreased wood and metal is slow and terrific: a series of dry sluggish reports carrying for a half mile across the hot still pinewiney silence of the August afternoon. Though the mules plod in a steady and unflagging hypnosis, the vehicle does not seem to progress. It seems to hang suspended in the middle distance forever and forever, so infinitesimal is its progress, like a shabby bead upon the mild red string of road. So much is this so that in the watching of it the eye loses it as sight and sense drowsily merge and blend, like the road itself, with all the peaceful and monotonous changes between darkness and day, like already measured thread being rewound onto a spool. So that at last, as though out of some trivial and unimportant region beyond even distance, the sound of it seems to come slow and terrific and without meaning, as though it were a ghost travelling a half mile ahead of its own shape. (*LA*, pp. 5–6)

What Faulkner accomplishes here with image and abstraction can be experienced aesthetically. The stylistic devices he uses can be categorized. But exactly how he creates his effects may be, like most truly great art, beyond exact description.

The complexity, the obliqueness, the irony of *Light in August* spring as much from the use of generalization and abstraction as they do from the use of images, from the presentation of character in a wholly restrained fashion without comment, explanation, interpretation, and suggestions from the writer. "A Shakespeare or a Goethe," Herbert J. Muller, contends, may "be as simple, forthright, eloquent as he pleases." [9] That is, he may state overtly. One cannot contend flatly that all modern literature must use implicit rather than explicit language. If the critic does, he will be required to "regard as of an 'inferior' order most of the literature the world has been content to think great; for the Bible is as full of didactic heresy as Dante or Milton, and there is as little wit in the old epic or saga as in the pure song or psalm." [10]

Light in August falls considerably short of the greatness of *The Sound and the Fury* and *As I Lay Dying,* and part of the reason may be that Faulkner does intrude more, does use abstractions and generalizations more extensively and frequently. But at the same time the sonorous vocabulary of *Light in August* is effective. It is almost as if Faulkner transcends the limitations of his method as a truly great or prophetic writer may transcend the limitations of his use of the pathetic fallacy. "A poet is great," John Ruskin wrote, "first in proportion to the strength of his passion, and then, that strength being granted, in proportion to his government of it.

9. H. J. Muller, "The New Criticism in Poetry," *The Southern Review,* 6 (1941), 824.

10. Muller, p. 823.

. . ."[11] The government of art, the control of passion, in this sense is supreme in the literature of the twenties. There is a point, Ruskin also says, "beyond which it would be inhuman and monstrous if he pushed this government. . . ."[12] It is a switch in terms to apply Ruskin's statement to Faulkner's use of abstraction as contrasted to restraint and concrete images, but the principle is the same. And there is a point in *Light in August,* to use Ruskin's terms again, when all abstraction becomes, through profundity and complexity, "just and true"; and Faulkner's new language achieves magnificent effects, results in "great astonishment."[13]

11. John Ruskin, *Modern Painters, The Works of John Ruskin,* ed. E. T. Cook and Alexander Wedderburn (London: George Allen; New York: Longmans, Green, and Co., 1904), V, 215.
12. Ruskin, p. 215.
13. Ruskin, p. 215.

15

Thirteen Ways of Talking about a Blackbird

THE distinction between doing and merely talking, always significant in Faulkner's work, is central in *Absalom, Absalom!*. The silence of an active past contrasts to the logorrhea of a talkative present. Much of the narration is accomplished directly or indirectly through two mediums (Quentin Compson and his father) who try to re-create an unknown and distant past and who are also significant in the story-telling process of another novel, *The Sound and the Fury*. If Caddy, the central figure in the novel about the Compson family, is silent, is "too beautiful and too moving to reduce her to telling what was going on," [1] all the characters of the older days in *Absalom, Absalom!* are for some similar reason silent—not reduced "to telling what was going on."

The point of view in *Absalom, Absalom!* is something like a combination of the stream-of-consciousness technique and a folkish Southern conversation running interminably on. A Harvard freshman from Jefferson, Mississippi, and his Canadian roommate,

1. Faulkner, *Faulkner in the University: Class Conferences at the University of Virginia*, ed. Gwynn and Blotner (Charlottesville: The University of Virginia Press, 1959), p. 1. Hereafter cited in text with abbreviation *UNIV*.

Shrevlin McCannon, puzzle over family and community stories about the rise and fall of Thomas Sutpen and his family. Shreve often repeats to Quentin parts of the stories previously told him by Quentin, who has heard them mainly from Miss Rosa Coldfield and his father. The extent of hearsay in the novel may be illustrated by the occasion when Quentin tells Shreve that his father reported that Grandfather Compson heard Thomas Sutpen tell about the state of mind of his employer, a Haitian planter: "what he took to be the planter's gallic rage was actually fear, terror. . . ." [2] The planter's actual state of mind is five minds or steps removed from Shreve's and the reader's; and every step involves the possibility of wrong conjecture or misinformation.

Time obscures the past. In the 1830s Sutpen and his wild Negroes overran "suddenly the hundred square miles of tranquil and astonished earth and" dragged "house and formal gardens violently out of the soundless" past. As there is difference between the deed and the remote hearsays of the narrators, there is also a profound distinction between the action or deed and the language which describes it. Every one of Faulkner's narrators realizes not only that he is subject to factual error but also that he must speak with words which may be unable to communicate the experience. Mr. Compson recognizes that there is communication which is truer than words. His daughter Caddy had proved to Quentin that she was in love by letting him feel the beat of the pulse in her throat. Thomas Sutpen and his daughter Judith, moreover, are so close that they do not even need the heartbeat:

> They did not need to talk. They were too much alike. They were as two people become now and then, who seem to know one another so well or are so much alike that the power, the need, to communicate by speech atrophies from disuse and, comprehending without need of the medium of ear or intellect, they no longer understand one another's actual words. (*AA*, p. 122)

Although Mr. Compson seldom does very much besides drink and talk, he is aware that a man's bond may transcend any words,

2. Faulkner, *Absalom, Absalom!* (New York: Random House, 1936), p. 252. Hereafter cited in text with abbreviation *AA*.

and he makes that same awareness a trait of the character of Henry Sutpen. After Charles Bon has begun his courtship of Henry's sister, Judith, Mr. Compson imagines a dispute between Charles and Henry about Charles's relationship with his octoroon mistress and the ceremony making her Charles' concubine. One issue in the dispute is the significance and integrity of language as contrasted to act. Charles is a modern who believes that language may become meaningless. To him, the ceremony is a "formula, a shibboleth," partly because it is mumbled by a crone "in a tongue which not even the girls themselves understand anymore . . ." (*AA*, p. 117). Henry argues for an old-fashioned notion of the integrity and similarity of language and deed. " 'Suppose I assume an obligation to a man who cannot speak my language, the obligation stated to him in his own and I agree to it: am I any the less obligated because I did not happen to know the tongue in which he accepted me in good faith? No: the more, the more' " (*AA*, p. 118). The contract, Henry argues, is sacred—like that in "Old Man" between the convict and the Louisiana Cajun swamprat, who could not put into a single language a binding agreement about sharing alligator hides. The futility of words is again the point when Mr. Compson describes comfort as "the lame vain words, the specious and empty fallacies" (*AA*, pp. 204–205). For Grandfather Compson, words are not altogether specious and empty. Spirits come from darkness and go into oblivion, but in rare instances they may communicate through language, which Grandfather Compson calls

> that meager and fragile thread . . . by which the little surface corners and edges of men's secret and solitary lives may be joined for an instant now and then before sinking back into the darkness where the spirit cried for the first time and was not heard and will cry for the last time and will not be heard then either. . . . (*AA*, p. 251)

Even this limited affirmation is hearsay—Quentin quotes his father, who in turn quotes his father.

The instants when "solitary lives may be joined," according to Shreve, may not long endure. When there is too much talk, and especially when emotions are put into words again and again, meaning is destroyed. Shreve conjectures that Eulalia Bon, put aside as the wife of Thomas Sutpen because her small fraction of Negro blood would prevent the achievement of his design to found a dynasty, describes her hatred to her son Charles, so often that it becomes meaningless.

> Or maybe she was already telling it before he was big enough to know words and so by the time he was big enough to understand what was being told him she had told it so much and so hard that the words didn't make sense to her anymore either because they didn't have to make sense to her, and so she had got to the point where when she thought she was saying it she was quiet. . . . (AA, p. 296)

For Miss Rosa Coldfield also language may be futile: words may not communicate, and communication may be accomplished without words. Even as a child when she visited her older sister, Ellen Sutpen, and saw her niece Judith and her step half-niece-in-law, the mulatto Clytie, she realized that words could never define the confused relationships. *"Even as a child,"* she says, *"solitude . . . taught me . . . to listen before I could comprehend and to understand before I even . . . heard . . ."* (*AA*, p. 140). Later when she stays with Clytie and Judith while Sutpen has gone to war, Rosa thinks of herself and Clytie as *"speaking no language which the other understood, the very simple words with which we were forced to adjust our days to one another being even less inferential of thought or intention than the sounds which a beast and a bird might make to each other" (AA,* pp. 153–154).

These views of language, of course, are not necessarily those of the author. The characters in the novel divide easily into two kinds: those of the present, who tell; and those of the past, who are told about. Only Miss Rosa and Grandfather Compson might fall into both classes, yet they are passive story tellers. Even in the remote past, the time of despicable and herioc deeds, they were listeners rather than participants. These attitudes toward language seem to be rather incidental; even Faulkner himself may have regarded them as unimportant. On the other hand, they reflect the most important aspects of the novel: the difference between word and deed, between the past and the present, between those who talk and those who do, between those who know and those who attempt to learn by deduction and ratiocination and talk.

Absalom, Absalom! is a speculative reconstruction of history. Faulkner himself seldom tells any of the novel except when he describes the narrators who are telling the story for him. The narrators belong to the twentieth century; they live until 1910 or later; they participate in no significant actions; they talk; they seek to define themselves by defining the past. Those who are told about belonged to the nineteenth century; most of them died not long after the Civil War; they acted; they were largely unable to talk, to speculate; they defined themselves by actions which were based on principle, right or wrong; one who survived until 1910 (Henry) had years before vanished from Yoknapatawpha County and the scene of the novel, and the other (Clytie) lived a silent recluse in a decaying mansion. The people of this "dead time," Mr. Compson says, were "simpler and . . . more heroic . . . , uncomplex who had the gift of loving once or dying once. . . ." People of the present (and therefore the narrators), in contrast, are "dwarfed and involved . . . diffused and scattered creatures . . . author and victim too of a thousand homicides and a thousand copulations and divorcements" *(AA,* p. 89).

When the older characters do speak, they talk with a terrible terseness. Thomas Sutpen talks twice with Grandfather Compson. Otherwise, no character of the past speaks long with anyone. Judith Sutpen talks briefly to Grandmother Compson; the narrators conjecture one conversation she had with Charles Etienne Bon; Charles Bon wrote one letter which survived for posterity. Henry Sutpen, Clytie, Wash Jones exist only in the hearsay of brief fragments of conversations at the turning point of someone's life. All the crucial speeches of the older characters deal with only three subjects: war, death, and love or marriage. Unlike the conjectured motivations of the characters in the novel, the terse and cryptic speeches at times of disaster are based on rather direct and reliable hearsay. Quentin talks directly with Henry once; Mr. Compson himself writes to Quentin of the death of Clytie and Henry and the burning of the mansion—events which occurred in time close to the writing of the letter; Mr. Compson hears from his father the details of the deaths of Sutpen and Wash and his granddaughter (Milly) and her illegitimate child by Sutpen; and Miss Rosa witnessed Sutpen's return from the War and heard his proposal to her; and she heard all the conversations about Bon's death. Of all the talk at these vital moments, only the final words of Henry and Bon before Bon's death are pure surmise by the characters.

These terrible confrontations, then, are significant because they represent a substantial part of the facts actually known to the narrators. That they are more fact than supposition is evident from the difference between this talk and the involved musings of the narrators. Quentin, Mr. Compson, and Shreve especially are never active enough to be entangled in relationships which would result in such blunt confrontation. Even if they were so entangled, they would still be prone to engage in endless analysis and debate. Again, the older characters act and speak tersely; the moderns think and debate.

Faulkner in some ways has patterned much of the structure of the novel on these speeches. A major method he used to create suspense was to intersperse the speculations of the moderns with the outrageous and incredible talk of the actors in the drama. If the moderns talk in endless speculative sentences, their predecessors speak with an almost unbearable brevity. Henry and Judith's "short brief staccato sentences," Faulkner says, are "like slaps, as if they stood breast to breast striking one another in turn neither making any attempt to guard against the blows" (*AA*, p. 172). They slash "at one another with twelve or fourteen words and most of these the same words repeated two or three times so that when you boiled it down they did it with eight or ten" (p. 174). These constitute a drastic "change of pace," what Irving Howe could not find in the novel[3] (p. 230).

Many of Faulkner's interpreters have pointed out the significance of the symbol of the stranger knocking at the gate in *Absalom, Absalom!,* seeking acceptance, and meeting denial. Sutpen is turned away first by the Negro house servant of a plantation owner in Virginia. To gain acceptance he establishes his own plantation. Al-

3. Irving Howe, *William Faulkner: A Critical Study,* Second Edition (New York: Vintage Books, 1962), p. 230.

though in his old age he says that he would not deny admission to that boy (*AA,* p. 261), his innocence[4] or naïveté leads him or his representative to deny his son Charles Bon, Wash Jones, Wash's granddaughter, Sutpen's own daughter by Milly, and perhaps others. Almost without exception the terrible confrontations and the brief conversations also occur symbolically at a gate, a door, stairs, or some sort of threshold. Denial and outrage are predominant postures in the situations.

1. Wash Jones screams at Rosa from her gate (*AA,* pp. 87, 133), telling her to come to Sutpen's. There Henry has killed Charles Bon, who sought admission and the hand of Judith. At Sutpen's, Miss Rosa meets the silence of Judith and Clytie, and she is never permitted even to see Bon's corpse.

2. Sutpen comes home from the war to meet Judith, Rosa, and Clytie; he learns that Bon has been killed and Henry has fled (*AA,* pp. 159, 163, 277).

3. Sutpen proposes to Rosa in such a cold and matter-of-fact way that she is outraged (*AA,* p. 164).

4. Sutpen returns to war after a brief leave (*AA,* p. 276). (Of all these terrible confrontations, this is the only one not in chronological order.)

5. Rosa and Quentin go to Sutpen's Hundred to visit Henry (*AA,* pp. 369–371, 373).

6. Rosa returns to Sutpen's Hundred to take Henry to a hospital in an ambulance. Thinking Henry is to be arrested and tried for killing Bon, Clytie burns Sutpen's mansion, Henry, and herself.

7. The most extensively developed confrontation centers around the deaths of Sutpen, Wash, Milly, and Sutpen's daughter by Milly. Quentin recounts this episode twice (*AA,* pp. 185–186, 285–292). Had Faulkner chosen to delete the comments of his narrators and to render the scene dramatically as he did in *Requiem for a Nun,* the result would have been unbearably brief. The scene is given dramatically below because it is a good example of the impact of one kind of style which Faulkner uses in *Absalom, Absalom!:*

4. *Absalom, Absalom!,* p. 265. Cleanth Brooks, *William Faulkner: The Yoknapatawpha Country* (New Haven: Yale University Press, 1963, 1964), p. 297.

SCENE I

Inside Wash Jones's hut. Dawn.

SUTPEN: Penelope foaled this morning. A damned fine colt. Going to be the spit and image of his daddy when I rode him North in '61. Do you remember?

NEGRO MIDWIFE: Yes, Marster.

SUTPEN: Well? Damn your black hide: horse or mare?

NEGRO MIDWIFE: [Hit's a gal.]

SUTPEN: Well, Milly, too bad you're not a mare like Penelope. Then I could give you a decent stall in the stable.

SCENE II

Outside Wash Jones's hut. Dawn.

SUTPEN: Stand back, Wash. Don't you touch me.

WASH: I'm going to tech you, Kernel.

SUTPEN: Stand back, Wash!

(*Sutpen hits Wash with his whip, and Wash kills him with a scythe.*)

SCENE III

Outside Wash Jones's hut. Just after dark. Sutpen's body still lies in the yard.

WASH: That you, Major?

SHERIFF MAJOR DE SPAIN: [Come on out, Wash.]

WASH: In just a minute. Soon as I see about my granddaughter.

DE SPAIN: We'll see to her. You come on out.

WASH: Sho, Major. In just a minute.

GRANDDAUGHTER MILLY: Who is it? Light the lamp, Grandpaw.

WASH: Hit wont need no light, honey. Hit wont take but a minute.

DE SPAIN: You, Wash! Come out of there!

WASH: (*to granddaughter*) Wher air you?

MILLY: Right here. Where else would I be? What is------

DE SPAIN: Jones!

(*Sound of butcher knife on both neckbones. Then Wash runs with the scythe above his head, straight into the lanterns and the gun barrels, making no sound, no outcry.*)

DE SPAIN: Jones! Stop! Stop, or I'll kill you. Jones! Jones! *Jones!*

SCENE IV

At the door of Sutpen's mansion. They "fetch Sutpen home in a wagon and carry him, quiet and bloody and with his teeth still showing in his parted beard . . . in the light of the lanterns and the pine torches, up the steps where the tearless and stone-faced daughter holds the door open for him. . . ."

SCENE V

SUTPEN: What was it, Wash? Something happened. What was it?
WASH: I dont know, Kernel. Whut?
Long pause.
WASH: They mought have kilt us, but they aint whupped us yit, air they?[5]

Reducing the novel to the spoken dramatic lines in this fashion gives it the appearance of melodrama, and the condensation is unfair to Faulkner. Within the novel, the melodrama is avoided because of the extensive development of situation and character, because the intense lines are buried within the speculations of the narrators, and because the intensity of the lines is not excessive in the narrative form. This gathering of the speeches into a dramatic vehicle, however, does have a critical purpose; it demonstrates the brevity of the speeches of the older characters. In comparison, the dialogue of Hemingway's "The Killers" is verbose.

Altogether, around twenty scenes in *Absalom, Absalom!* include this kind of harsh, terse language—or action without any speech at all.[6] The bringing of Sutpen's corpse home is foreshadowed in a passage just one page before the account of his death. He is brought home drunk. This time, also, Judith opens the door without a word. Clytie walks into the office of Grandfather Compson, pays for a tombstone, and leaves without speaking. After the Civil War the Ku Klux Klan asks Sutpen for help. He refuses. Then: " *'This may be war, Sutpen.' . . . 'I am used to it'* " (*AA,* p. 162). And there is the terse interview between Sutpen and his son Henry on the battlefield. All the dialogue is reproduced below except for the use of ellipsis in one speech:

SUTPEN: *Henry. (. . . they embrace and kiss. . . .) Henry, My son.*

5. I have made a composite of the two versions of dialogue (pp. 185–186 and 285–292), used many ellipses, changed tenses in stage directions, and even given in brackets some of the dialogue which is derived from Faulkner's indirect quotation.

6. See Brooks, pp. 320–323.

(. . . they sit. . . .) You were hit at Shiloh, Colonel Willow tells me.

HENRY: *Yes, sir.*

SUTPEN: *I have seen Charles Bon, Henry. (Pause.) You are going to let him marry Judith, Henry. (Pause.) He cannot marry her, Henry.*

HENRY: *You said that before. I told you then. And now, and now it wont be much longer now and then we wont have anything left: honor nor pride nor God. . . .* [87 words omitted] *Yes. I have decided, Brother or not, I have decided. I will. I will.*

SUTPEN: *He must not marry her, Henry.*

HENRY: *Yes. I said Yes at first, but I was not decided then. I didn't let him. But now I have had four years to decide in. I will. I am going to.*

SUTPEN: *He must not marry her, Henry. His mother's father told me that her mother had been a Spanish woman. I believed him; it was not until after he was born that I found out that his mother was part negro.*

The silent embrace and kiss, the verbal restraint in this greeting during the terrors of the last days of a losing war, and the hostility of Henry's "Yes, sir"—these silences are typical of many of the characters in Faulkner's early novels, especially such central figures as Addie Bundren, Caddy Compson, and Joe Christmas. And silence is a dominant character trait of every major character in *Absalom, Absalom!* except those who tell major parts of the story. No cast of characters in any work of literature that I know is so silent as the family of Thomas Sutpen. The most silent of all is Judith. Faulkner describes the rigidity of her face and her demeanor with a refrain repeated in almost infinite variation throughout the novel. Her face, an "impenetrable mask," is cold, calm, frozen, stone-faced, absolutely serene, indifferent, like marble, tranquil. After the death of her betrothed by the hand of her brother, for example, her "serene quiet voice . . talked of plowing corn and cutting winter wood" (*AA*, p. 152). When her father lays bare his life to Grandfather Compson (the only person to whom he speaks more than a few sentences), he is "quiet and calm"; his voice is flat and final; and he sits "as if there were no haste nor urgency anywhere under the sun" (*AA*, p. 271). Clytie too is "impassive," "serene"; her voice is "deadly and cold"; and at moments of crisis she too refuses to speak. Charles Etienne Bon, who also has a quiet and docile manner, refuses to speak; he is silent, sullen, impassive, harsh; his face has "no more expression than Judith's." When Wash Jones's world crumbles about him just before his death, his voice is described in a single sentence as "quite quiet . . . too quiet, too calm . . . too quiet and calm . . . too calm and quiet" (*AA,* p. 291). When he rushes the posse come to arrest him, he makes "no sound, no outcry." Charles Etienne Bon's wife is described as having "nothing alive about her but her eyes and hands" *(AA,* p. 209).

Besides the old people, the only character described as quiet and silent is Quentin. Again and again, he answers "Oh," and "Yes" and "No'me" and "Yes" and "Yes"—one word interrupting long passages of dialogue by other narrators. Faulkner writes that "he did not answer," "did not answer," "did not answer this either." Quentin is stunned by his own story. For most of the long evening of his dialogue with Shreve, he sits without moving before "the table, the open book," and "the letter." He does not even look up. He has a "curious, repressed calm voice," a "flat, curiously dead voice."

The most striking effect of this method of characterizing the people of the older time is the contrast between them and those who talk incessantly. The silences stand in stark opposition to the polysyllabic narratives of the deducers. But the silences are much more than a stylistic technique. They are the old people's style, or manner, of confronting life. They reveal the psychological effects of disaster upon disaster. Those who endure are silent because words fail. "There are some things for which three words are three too many," Miss Rosa says, "and three thousand words that many too less" (p. 166).

The disaster-struck characters of *Absalom, Absalom!* find that silence and restraint are the only refuge. What a character expresses by word or action is no indication of what he feels and thinks. Psychologically or emotionally, all the older characters share a condition which is explained and described lyrically by Emily Dickinson:

After great pain, a formal feeling comes—
The Nerves sit ceremonious, like Tombs—
The stiff Heart questions was it He, that bore,
And Yesterday, or Centuries before?

The Feet, mechanical, go round—
Of Ground, or Air, or Ought—
A Wooden way
Regardless grown,
A Quartz contentment, like a stone—

This is the Hour of Lead—
Remembered, if outlived,
As Freezing persons, recollect the Snow—
First—Chill—then Stupor—then the letting go—[7]

Miss Dickinson's poem and Wash Jones and the Sutpen family have much in common: "great pain," a formal feeling or manners, mechanical or wooden actions, "A quartz contentment, like a stone" (compare the "stone-faced" Judith, whose face is "like marble"), and coldness (compare Miss Dickinson's "freezing," "snow," "chill" with words describing Judith: "icy calm," "cold," "frozen"). One critical explication of "After Great Pain" also may serve as an explanation of the psychological state of the character in *Absalom, Absalom!:* "externalizations did not always correspond to the internal condition but at times, in fact, represented the exact opposite. Yet . . . if such signs were completely misleading, they would obviously defeat their own purpose by communicating the wrong thing. Consequently, they must offer some oblique means for the reader to penetrate appearances to the reality beneath." [8]

Many readers of *Absalom, Absalom!,* almost completely misled by external manners, have failed "to penetrate appearances to the reality beneath." Sutpen is not only inconsiderate and cruel but also unable to communicate the kindly feelings and love he does have. Although he can never break through his restraint, his very

7. Emily Dickinson, *The Complete Poems of Emily Dickinson,* ed. Thomas H. Johnson (Boston: Little, Brown and Company, 1960), p. 162.

8. Francis Manley, "An Explication of Dickinson's 'After Great Pain,'" *Modern Language Notes,* 73 (April 1958), 260–261.

presence causes Judith to burst into tears. She has survived the murder of her betrothed, Bon, without weeping. But on the return of her father from the War, even the stoney-faced Judith does find emotional release in tears.

> *'Henry's not----?' 'No. He's not here.'----'Ah. And----?' 'Yes. Henry killed him.' And then burst into tears. Yes, burst, who had not wept yet, who had brought down the stairs that afternoon and worn ever since that cold, calm face which had stopped me in midrunning at that closed door; yes, burst, as if that entire accumulation of seven months were erupting spontaneously from every pore in one incredible evacuation. . . .* (*AA*, p. 159)

Sutpen's own brief utterances ("Henry's not—?" and "Ah, Clytie?" and "Well, Clytie, take care of Miss Judith") indicate not a lack of feeling but what Miss Dickinson terms "formal feeling." Sutpen, of course, is deficient in feeling—that is a major theme of the book; but he is even more deficient in his ability to express in language the feelings he does have. Language fails him because he is underbred and undereducated and also because he is a brave man of great strength. He does not speak because he believes that "words go straight up in a thin line, quick and harmless," as Addie Bundren puts it. In Sutpen's and Judith's "dark voicelessness . . . the words are the deeds"; or more accurately, the deeds are the only words which the character is capable of uttering.

Besides inhibitions and the inability to speak, there are other reasons for the silences of Wash Jones and the Sutpen family. The barriers between Negro and white cause silence, especially between the poor-white Sutpens and the Negroes in the Tidewater region of Virginia. During the trials of the Civil War and the deprivations of Reconstruction, there is "no time to mourn" (*AA*, p. 185). One must turn to plowing and cutting wood (*AA*, p. 152) or starve and freeze. Arrogance and self-assurance in Sutpen as well as inability to express emotions cause the silences. Wash Jones is silent partly because of his self-respect.

The silences and the abrupt confrontations of the old characters suggest a reality and an identity not possible to the modern intellectualizing narrators. It would be possible, of course, to create old characters who intellectualize about the fate of their descendants. Clytie, for example, in bare terms of plot, lives long enough to be a speculator over the later activities of Charles Etienne Bon and Quentin Compson and Miss Rosa. But the theme of Faulkner's novel stresses the reality and the action of the old and the mere intellectualization and speculation of the modern. Quentin is the only character in the novel who shares the speculation of the narrators and the silence and terse speech of the Sutpen family. He is so paralyzed emotionally and morally that he can neither act nor talk. The sections of the novel which he narrates (1) contain the most concrete imagery in the novel, (2) quote other narrators (Miss Rosa, Father, Grandfather Compson) and let them accomplish all the moralizing (see for example p. 287), and (3) generally avoid the abstractions and the moralizings and demonizings of the other narrators. Quentin remembers his talks with Miss Rosa in her parlor and with his father on the front gallery and his trips with her to Sutpen's Hundred in terms of images as concrete as those of the section which he narrates in *The Sound and the Fury* (see, for example, pp. 7–9, and 174–176). Sutpen, and perhaps Quentin, are responsible for the vividness of detail and the lack of moral speculation in the account of Sutpen's boyhood in the mountains and in Virginia. Again, Quentin views the world without moralizings, and his concrete speculations take form in a language that is strongly reminiscent of the Quentin of *The Sound and the Fury*. Musings on the interrelationships between events in *Absalom, Absalom!* appear in images which suggest Quentin's thoughts about the old trout in the river in *The Sound and the Fury:*

Maybe nothing ever happens once and is finished. Maybe happen is never once but like ripples maybe on water after the pebble sinks, the ripples moving on, spreading, the pool attached by a narrow umbilical water-cord to the next pool which the first pool feeds, has fed, did feed, let this second pool contain a different temperature of water, a different molecularity of having seen, felt, remembered, reflect in a different tone the infinite unchanging sky, it doesn't matter: that pebble's watery echo whose fall it did not even see moves across its surface too at the original ripple-space, to the old ineradicable rhythm. . . . (*AA*, p. 261)

The critical problems in connection with Quentin's narration of *Absalom, Absalom!* seem almost overwhelming. From his relationship to Caddy in *The Sound and the Fury,* it is easy to see why he is interested in the story of possible incest between Judith and Charles. And Henry's anguish and the ultimate fratricide reflect Quentin's own emotional state and his suicide. But Quentin's style of narration in *Absalom* is a more difficult problem than the pure plot and the similar human relationships in the two novels. In *The Sound and the Fury* he recognizes that he is outside the realm of reality. An intellectual, he would like to reason himself into humaneness; and he (like Darl Bundren) uses extremely concrete images in an attempt to cling to reality. A similar rationale controls his reasons for telling Shreve (and himself) the entire story of the Sutpen dynasty. Quentin is fascinated by the action and the strength of the Sutpens. The narration of Mr. Compson appeals to him because Mr. Compson and his grandfather see the saga from moral and ethical standpoints. Quentin says over and over, "Father said . . ." and "Father said Grandfather said. . . ." Quentin himself, however, never shares their ability to evaluate and judge. He puzzles over Father and Grandfather just as he puzzles over the Sutpens. There is contrast also between Miss Rosa's certainty and Quentin's lack of a view. She believes what she says even when she is inconsistent in her admiration and her hatred of Sutpen. When she makes him a demon, she at least has a perspective. Quentin's abstraction is also indicated by his very last speech: over and over he tells Shreve that he does not hate the South. But that is no positive view of any kind. How *does* he react toward the South and view the Sutpens? If he does not hate, what does he do? The point here is that he can take no positive moral, ethical, religious, philosophical view. If he is almost a perfect vehicle for the story-telling in the novel because of his curiosity and his lack of prejudice, his lack of identity makes his life a nightmare and leads to his self-destruction.

Absalom, Absalom! is a book of amazing abstraction. Faulkner seems to make use of a new vocabulary in this novel, a group of words not unlike those of the late stage of Faulkner's career, words like those he mentioned in the Nobel Prize speech and his other public addresses in the 1950s, such as *love, honor, pity, pride, endure, courage,* and *sacrifice.* These words appear more frequently, I believe, in *Absalom, Absalom!* than in *As I Lay Dying, The Sound and the Fury, Sanctuary,* and *Light in August* all combined. I have counted 231 appearances of these words in *Absalom,* and perhaps I missed many. Only a concordance to the novel (the task of compiling one might make the best of computers dizzy-headed) would accurately indicate a mathematical count of Faulkner's moral terms.

In 1955 Faulkner described a language of "babbling . . . mouthsounds; the loud and empty words which we have emasculated of all meaning whatever—freedom, democracy, patriotism. . . ." [9] He mentioned only a political vocabulary, but the language of morality and religion also became empty in the twenties. The writer found himself in the peculiar position of having to eschew much of his own language. Only the babbling and empty character might speak the "babbling . . . mouthsounds." Within twenty years, however, those who had most violently rebelled against abstraction, even Hemingway, had turned back to what had once been regarded as babbling. *Absalom, Absalom!* seems to be one of the pivotal points. If it is one of Faulkner's greatest books, if there was a validity in the attitude toward language of Hemingway, Addie Bundren, and Faulkner himself, the crucial problem takes a form something like this: how can a great book be constructed on a language that is babbling emptiness?

The answers are difficult, numerous, unsatisfactory. An empty language is altogether appropriate for the intellectualizers who tell the novel. They cannot see truth, and their language is as false as their facts.

I think that no one individual can look at truth [Faulkner said about *Absalom, Absalom!*]. It blinds you. You look at it and you see one phase of it. Someone else looks at it and sees a slightly awry phase of it. But taken all together, the truth is in what they saw though nobody saw the truth intact. So these are true as far as Miss Rosa and as Quentin saw it. Quentin's father saw what he believed was truth, but that was all he saw. But the old man was himself a little too big for people no

9. Faulkner, *Essays, Speeches and Public Letters,* ed. James B. Meriwether (New York: Random House, 1965), pp. 65–66.

greater in stature than Quentin and Miss Rosa and Mr. Compson to see all at once. It would have taken perhaps a wiser or more tolerant or more sensitive or more thoughtful person to see him as he was. It was . . . thirteen ways of looking at a blackbird. But the truth, I would like to think, comes out, that when the reader has read all these thirteen different ways of looking at a blackbird, the reader has his own fourteenth image of that blackbird which I would like to think is the truth. (*UNIV*, pp. 273–274)

The babbling words, like the views of the narrators, then, are false. Faulkner himself speaks seldom, usually avoids abstractions; the older characters avoid them; Quentin can only quote abstractions because they have no validity for him. Pitiful and inadequate as the words are, they are nevertheless the only means of self-expression available to the narrators. They are a method of searching for reality, the only method available to the kind of people who must search for meaning in an older time and in other people rather than themselves. The book gains its power partly because of the contrast between the actors and the talkers, those who say and those who do. The silence and the abrupt speech of the old people has greater impact because it is enclosed in babbling mouthsounds. The narrators and the listeners in the novel themselves experience the aesthetic effect which the reader should at last enjoy. If there is "a relative absence of physical detail," [10] the impact of the novel is that it creates in modern character and in the reader suspense in terms of a longing for detail, meaning, reality. Ultimately, the babbling mouthsounds of his narrators do not communicate fully and satisfactorily. If Faulkner "makes language transcend itself by hypersuggestion," [11] one of its transcendent meanings is that it is a noble attempt, but a babbling failure. If he "refuses to accept at face value the contemporary faith in concrete words," if he "dares to generalize, to utter judgment upon evil doing, and to evaluate an act, in words, in the larger context of man's long journey and

10. Robert H. Zoellner, "Faulkner's Prose Style in *Absalom, Absalom!*," *American Literature*, 30 (January 1959), 498–499.

11. Florence Leaver, "Faulkner: The Word as Principle and Power," in Frederick J. Hoffman and Olga W. Vickery, *William Faulkner: Three Decades of Criticism* (East Lansing: Michigan State University Press, 1960), p. 201.

destiny" [12] in *Absalom, Absalom!* he is still excruciatingly aware of the failure of all words except the concrete, of the failure of generalization and evaluation.

The reader can never know the facts, the reality, in the lives of the Sutpen family. Sutpen never had the language to communicate with his son Henry. He did not succeed in preventing fratricide and a wasted life. Quentin and Shreve cannot comprehend. Miss Rosa and Mr. Compson can only rave and puzzle. In some of his actions Mr. Compson is capable of sympathy, love, compassion; he is cynical; he talks in moral terms; he spends many hours or even days talking with his son. Yet he never himself experiences the reality for which he searches, and all his talk cannot save his son. He can never explain to Quentin well enough to prevent his suicide. One theme of *Absalom, Absalom!*, like that of Hemingway's best novels and Eliot's best poems, is the failure of language. It is a sign of the age. Language in the novel has a powerful effect, but it is as useless as the wedding gown that Rosa sews for Judith, "a garment which she [Rosa] would never wear and never remove for a man whom she was not even to see alive" (*AA*, p. 78) and a garment which Judith herself was never to wear as a wedding gown.

12. Leaver, p. 201.

16

Faulkner's Inexhaustible Voice

BETWEEN 1936 and 1942, Faulkner, as Eliot and Hemingway had before him, began to make the word the center of his fiction. In the two parts of *Wild Palms,* "Old Man" and "Wild Palms," explanation begins to play a prominent role. The author of "Old Man" asserts over and over that his character cannot explain for himself, and then he makes lengthy explanations for him. Actions are not allowed to stand in the concrete integrity of unexplanation as they do so well in *As I Lay Dying* and *The Sound and the Fury.* "Wild Palms" is based upon self-contemplation by two lovers of their own diseased love. Faulkner had begun to move away from deeds to words. More and more the protagonist becomes the talker; and in the few works in which the central figure is silent, his deeds are less concrete and talk about him predominates over his actions. Ike McCaslin in *Go Down, Moses* temporizes in his action and reveals the meanings of the novel in his meditations upon his own actions.

Before *The Unvanquished,* every one of Faulkner's major works contained objective narration by the novelist or stream of consciousness of the character. *The Unvanquished* is the first book-length work told by the character in the manner of *Huckleberry Finn* and Hemingway's early fiction. And there are some indications that this change signals the beginning of Faulkner's excessive use of talkative story-telling characters such as Gavin Stevens and the narrator of *The Reivers*. Bayard Sartoris, who tells the stories about the Civil War in *The Unvanquished,* however, is different from the garrulous narrators of the later books. At times, indeed, he is one of Faulkner's most accomplished tellers of stories. In "An Odor of Verbena" Bayard confronts a carpetbagger who, with some justification, has killed Colonel Sartoris, Bayard's father. Given to violence after his heroic escapades in the War and during the struggles of Reconstruction, the swashbuckling father renounces bloodshed before his death: when he is killed, he has his derringer with him but does not use it. The carpetbagger, Redmond, has also renounced violence after killing the Colonel, and he waits for the son to come to kill him. Required by custom to avenge his father's death but committed to peace, the son goes unarmed to a confrontation with Redmond. He expects to meet his own death. The integrity, honor, and courage of Bayard Sartoris are revealed, not by his stream of consciousness as his thoughts dwell on the principles by which he acts, but by remarkably concrete imagery which in some almost inexplicable way reveals his strength and agitation by seeming irrelevance The inevitability of the meeting and the seeming necessity of Bayard's approaching death hover above his relentless movement toward Redmond's office and his sensitive awareness of everything he passes: "the remote still eyes [of the watchers], . . . just stopped . . . , waiting," "the small faded sign nailed to the brick *B. J. Redmond. Atty at Law,*" "the stairs, the wooden steps scuffed by the heavy bewildered boots of countrymen approaching litigation." Redmond, "freshly shaven and with fresh linen," and Bayard, walking "in a dreamlike state in which there was neither time nor distance," confront each other formally and wordlessly like two members of the silent Sutpen family. What they have to communicate cannot be put into words: "We didn't speak. It was as if we both knew what the passage of words would be and the futility of it. . . .[1] Deliberately, Bayard strides toward Redmond and his gun; Redmond shoots twice and deliberately misses Bayard. Each

1. Faulkner, *The Unvanquished* (New York: Random House, 1938), pp. 285–286. Hereafter cited in the text with the abbreviation *Uv.*

acts according to the prevailing code of honor but refuses to kill. Redmond's pistol descends "to the desk in short jerks." Every action reveals Bayard's awareness of Redmond's emotional state. Then Redmond walks out of the office and past Bayard's friends and the Colonel's "old troop . . . , saying no word, staring straight ahead and with his back to them, on to the station, . . . and [he] went away from Jefferson and from Mississippi and never came back" (*Uv,* pp. 287–288). Thus with never a word spoken Bayard and Redmond set Yoknapatawpha County on a road away from the violence of Reconstruction and toward peace. Faulkner made no statements about his meanings; the images and action conveyed all he needed to say.

Both Bayard and Redmond are men of deeds. At one point Bayard thinks that "those who can, do, those who cannot and suffer enough because they can't, write about it" (*Uv,* p. 262). This distinction is a significant clue to the interpretation of *The Unvanquished.* The strong and the good are silent. Simon mourns his master, the Colonel, by saying nothing, "not weeping the facile tears which are the white man's futile trait and which Negroes know nothing about but just sitting there, motionless . . ."(*Uv,* p. 277). A "big preacher refugeeing from Memphis or somewhere" (*Uv,* p. 178) tries to preach an elaborate sermon for the funeral of Granny Rosa Millard, but Brother Fortinbride leans on his shovel above the grave, says a few words, and sends the people home: " 'And what do you reckon Rosa Millard would say about you all standing around here, keeping old folks and children out here in the rain?' " (*Uv,* p. 180). A sermon is what one does, not what is said above the dead. The greatest accomplishments in *The Unvanquished* occur when Faulkner precisely describes actions which reveal unusual psychological states of persons in extreme social stress: the confrontation of Redmond and Bayard, the blank stares and the sounds and the movements of the mob of freed Negroes who believe they are marching to the river Jordan and freedom, the terror and the determination of the youths Bayard and Ringo as they pursue the bushwhacker Grumby to avenge the death of Granny Millard.

More than in any previous books, Faulkner in *The Unvanquished* begins to intrude into his fiction to express his own opinions, to interpret his own work and moralize about it. Although Bayard is presumably the narrator of the entire work, some of the statements which ostensibly belong to him actually cannot be his. Faulkner now shifts his tone and diction for the sake of the issue, the truth, his meaning. He moves from a child's wish to see the wonders of war to his own adult oratory about the War. In "Raid," the boys Ringo and Bayard long for martial glory; yet the furor of war is reduced to "the fading fury of the smoke and the puny yelling, and . . . the sorry business which had dragged on for three years . . ." (*Uv,* p. 109). The adjectives *fading* and *puny* and *sorry* are extraneous to the boys' point of view. Presumably the pejorative terms might be appropriate to the reminiscences of an older Bayard telling the story years afterward, but that is not the point of view of the story. Comments on Southern history are alien to the character of the boy Bayard, perhaps alien to the man. In an essay on the two locomotives, the Texas and the General, Faulkner intrudes to comment upon the course of Southern history: "Only not gone or vanished either, so long as there should be defeated or the descendants of defeated to tell it or listen to the telling" (*Uv,* p. 112).

In *The Sound and the Fury,* Faulkner had not been able to reduce Caddy to the telling, but in *The Unvanquished* he does reduce Drusilla, who makes a long statement about the domesticity of peace and the destruction of war. Often Faulkner comments upon a character's consciousness instead of creating it: "There is a limit to what a child can accept, assimilate; not to what it can believe because a child can believe anything, given time, but to what it can accept, a limit in time, in the very time which nourishes the believing of the incredible" (*Uv,* p. 75). Where mental process is the point of the entire work, as in *Absalom, Absalom!,* this sort of comment would be appropriate; in *The Unvanquished* it is largely extraneous.

"Old Man" strangely looks backward to Faulkner's older techniques and forward to his late preachments. The unnamed convict is silent and active and committed to the task assigned him by penal authorities. A rescue worker in the great flood of 1927, he is given a boat and told to save a woman from a cypress snag and a fellow from a cotton house. In the weeks that follow he paddles a boat in violent flooding waters, picks up the pregnant woman on the snag, does his best to find a place for her to have her baby, helps her deliver the baby with only a tin can to cut the umbilical cord and shoe laces to tie it, makes a living by killing alligators with his bare hands and a knife, and after incredible effort and devotion to duty returns the boat to the guards and the woman to whatever life she will be able to establish. His reward is an additional ten years added to his sentence by bureaucrats because, they say, he escaped. But the convict's action and heroism do not represent real commitment and involvement. His selflessness, his trying to do what is best for the pregnant woman "in the right way, not for himself, but for her," remains only a duty, an imposed obligation. In their primitive fashion and with their improvised means they establish a sort of domesticity and live as man and wife but without the sexual privileges thereunto appertaining. Years later, Faulkner described the novelette as "the story of a man who got his love and spent the rest of the book fleeing from it, even to the extent of voluntarily going back to jail where he would be safe." [2] The convict, then, acts and lives in the world of deeds as completely as Caddy and Addie, but he is not merely one of the silent good. He is the first character in Faulkner's works to be physically active in the world and spiritually uninvolved. He is isolated like Quentin, Darl, and even the lazy Anse Bundren.

Gesture means more than statement to the convict as it does to Caddy. The social contract which joins him and a Cajun together in mutual enterprise to kill alligators is more binding because it is neither written nor said: "two people who could not even talk to one another made an agreement which both not only understood but which each knew the other would hold true and protect (perhaps for this reason) better than any written and witnessed contract." [3] At this point Faulkner's hero has retreated, in language at least, almost to the animal, to that "dimly lit period between higher animal and lower man [when], sounds made merely from

2. Interview, *Writers at Work: The* Paris Review *Interviews,* ed. Malcolm Cowley (New York: The Viking Press, 1958), p. 133.

3. Faulkner, *The Wild Palms* (New York: Random House, 1939), p. 260. Hereafter cited in text with abbreviation *WP.*

impulse came to be associated with things experienced at the time, and hence to be used as signs of them."[4] This transitional state between language and growl (for Faulkner is reversing the process) produces more fidelity and constancy than civilized seals on documents.

Unable to speak the Cajun's language, the convict trusts the facts of companionship (sharing a hut, lending and borrowing a pair of trousers) more than his creator, Faulkner, does as author. Faulkner beautifully embodies the convict's heroism in deeds, but the stream of consciousness of the earlier characters and their restraint and wordlessness have given way to intrusive explanations of the author. Faulkner's handling of the point of view is a new method in his career: he explains the convict's deeds with words, articulates for him, and points out his inability to articulate himself. The necessity of stating for him poses several problems and, indeed, may be a flaw in the fiction. At first there are explanations of man's general capacity to feel what he cannot say: "man always has been drawn to dwell beside water, even before he had a name for water and fire, drawn to the living water . . ." (*WP,* p. 155). Later in the novelette the primitive feeling evolves into incapacity as Faulkner describes the convict's inability to tell his fellows about many things in his odyssey. A thought (if that is what it is) exists in "a flash," which the convict "could not have expressed . . . , and hence did not even know that he had ever thought it . . ." (*WP,* p. 266). Again he is unable "to phrase it, think it instead of merely knowing it" (*WP,* p. 266). He knows a thing though he does "not think this in actual words" (*WP,* p. 271).

Explanation can become an art of its own, as it does in *Moby-Dick.* It is more artful when it is a poetry of detail and of learning (or even antiquarianism) and when a humorous or philosophical and omniscient narrator is deliberately making his own thinking and personality a part of his work. But explanation may also be patronizing statements of incapacity of character. In "Old Man," theories about mental processes and consciousness at times almost obscure the character's deeds. The convict was obviously doomed

4. Brand Blanshard, *The Nature of Thought,* Library of Philosophy (New York: The Macmillan Company, 1940), I, 538.

by the burden of the pregnant woman, and Faulkner did not need to comment that he had assumed his obligation "unwitting and without choice" (*WP,* p. 177). Such reminders do not well pinpoint the drama of the situation. The convict hears a sound of flooding waters: "he had never heard it before and he would never be expected to hear such again since it is not given to every man to hear such at all and to none to hear it more than once in his life" (*WP,* p. 156). Faulkner here has written a brief essay on rarity, but it has made the sound no more realizable.

Intrusion of author to comment on character's mind is not the only change in "Old Man." More than ever before Faulkner calls attention to his own myth-making in inflated historical allusions (*WP,* p. 29), makes semididactic statements about morals which his characters only half realize (*WP,* p. 30), keeps his eye on social situations and systems and generalizes about themes which his characters are not aware of (*WP,* pp. 66–67, 70–71), points out the obliviousness of characters to experiences which are significant to the author, uses figures alien to the subject matter and to the character (the flooding water "sounded like a subway train far beneath the street"), and even in self-explanation adds that none of the convicts "could have made the comparison" (*WP,* p. 62). Vocabulary and figures outside the ken of the characters appeared in the earlier and better novels, as in the monologues of Darl Bundren; but Faulkner before "Old Man" used them mainly to reveal the sensibility of a sensitive character; in "Old Man," despite Faulkner's admiration for his hero, he uses them to reveal his own thoughts to the reader and to point out the limitations of the character.

"Wild Palms," the companion piece of "Old Man," treats cosmopolitan and sophisticated characters in inflated rhetoric and polysyllables. Neither of the lovers, who sacrifice career and life and family for their lustful relationship, is a person of the deed. Charlotte is a woman of abstraction and of the word. She speaks in terms of "comfortable safe peaceful purgatory . . . good behavior . . . forbearance . . . shame . . . repentance" (*WP,* p. 83). And her lover, himself a thinker who indulges in polysyllabic monologues on sin and love, defines her abstraction: "So it's not me you believe in, put trust in; it's love. . . . Not just me; any man" (*WP,* p. 83). Like Charlotte and her lover, Faulkner himself occasionally uses an exalted style and abstractions for unworthy subjects; he orates about a doctor and his wife who like their seafood straight from cans, "the tuna, the salmon, the sardines bought in cans, immolated and embalmed three thousand miles away in the oil of machinery and commerce" (*WP,* p. 10). And a clock becomes "the ubiquitous and synchronised face, oracular admonitory and unsentient" (*WP,* p. 131). At this point in his career he was relying more and more on a sonorous and latinate vocabulary and sometimes applying it to an unworthy subject matter.

After *Absalom, Absalom!* Faulkner wrote many books which are not sufficiently unified to be termed one novel nor diverse enough to be regarded as separate short stories. *The Unvanquished* consists of stories that can be read independently but which also have most of the progression and development of time and character usually associated with a novel. The counterpoint of *Wild Palms* is followed by *The Hamlet,* which is itself a part of *Snopes,* written over a period of decades. *The Hamlet* contains revisions of five stories published over a period of several years in periodicals. *Knight's Gambit* is a gathering of short stories held together by the brilliant, ratiocinative, and deductive crime detection of Gavin Stevens. And *Requiem for a Nun* is half-history, half-play. Within any one of these books, Faulkner establishes a kind of interrelated fiction which in microcosm somewhat resembles his grander creation of the whole saga of Yoknapatawpha County.

Go Down, Moses (1942) is Faulkner's most widely known and most successful collection of related works. The three and six generations of two different branches of the white McCaslin family and the seven generations of the Negro and mulatto Beauchamp family (related to the McCaslins) span most of the history of Yoknapatawpha County and north Mississippi. The McCaslins and their kin and neighbors build a plantation, hunt communally in the wilderness, start the curses of bondage and miscegenation, witness the destruction of the wilderness, and at least begin their penance and atonement for the curse of bondage. *Go Down, Moses* as a whole and "The Bear" as the most substantial and accomplished part suffer from a weakness similar to that in "Old Man": Faulkner wavers from superb embodiment of fiction in fact and event and character to a moralizing garrulity more notable for sentiment and meaning than for artistic accomplishment. "The Bear," Cleanth Brooks has written, is "perhaps Faulkner's masterpiece." [5] It has the grand design and scale (though not the scope and size) of *Absalom, Absalom!*; it is Faulkner's best treatment of the natural world of forest and animals; and it contains his grandest vision of the history of America and of man. But the mastery of "The Bear" comes in fits and starts. One wishes that Faulkner had been able to embody his greatest preachments in his greatest art. But, in part, he failed. "The Bear" is a lesser work than *As I Lay Dying*, and certainly less than the greatest novels Faulkner wrote in the late 1920s and 1930s.

"Except for rare moments," Murray Baumgarten has written of "The Bear," "it never, as does the language of Yeats and Vaughan, *becomes* the rose at the center of the world. It always remains an instrument which manipulates us into feeling the presence of the rose: it does not present it." [6] And, on the other hand, Andrew Nelson Lytle contends that "The shock of meaning in terms of mystery he handled superbly well in *The Bear*. The concrete footprint disappearing before the boy's eyes made present the invisible bear, evoking the awe of the immortal in the mortal beast." [7] When the bear looks at the boy from the cover of the trees, a bird grows silent, and the "sudden cessation of sound produces the silence because it affects the boy. The very fact that it is a bird which in no way can be harmed by the bear makes the ominous quality of the danger immediate." [8] In other words, Faulkner fails to embody his thought concretely, and he succeeds at the same task. And both critical observations are correct. Faulkner

5. Cleanth Brooks, *William Faulkner: The Yoknapatawpha Country* (New Haven: Yale University Press, 1963, 1964), p. 244.

6. Murray Baumgarten, "The Language of Faulkner's *The Bear*," *Western Humanities Review*, 15 (Spring 1961), 182.

7. Andrew Nelson Lytle, "The Son of Man: He Will Prevail," *The Sewanee Review*, 63 (1955), 127.

8. Lytle, p. 127.

never fails utterly, but he never again rises to the concreteness of the greater and early works.

The decline of artistic genius which leads to unevenness within the same work and to unnecessary moral preachment may also be accompanied by superficiality and shallowness. Faulkner begins to oversimplify issues even in the old complexity of his style. Parts of "The Bear" are a sensitive representation of the race issue in the South and in America, but other parts of *Go Down, Moses* treat Negro and white relationships with incredible naïveté. Faulkner idealizes the Negro race in "Pantaloon in Black" and attacks the whites so that doctrine triumphs over art. What seems to be a simple and straightforward account of the death of a Negro wife, her husband's grief, his insane rage and violence, and his lynching becomes a fable of Negro goodness and white depravity. The only flaw of the Negro protagonist, Rider, is violence which is attributable to grief. In every instance when Faulkner describes the same aspect of the lives of Negroes and whites, the Negroes are idealized and the whites are belittled. Rider is a marvel of physical perfection: he is clean and wears clean clothes until his wife dies; he moves "almost as fast as a horse"; [9] he has strength to handle alone logs "which ordinarily two men would have handled with canthooks . . ." (*GDM,* p. 137). His wife, Mannie, is physically dainty. Her bare feet leave "narrow, splay-toed prints" (*GDM*, p. 137) in the dust. Her back and haunches and hands are all "narrow." Fewer physical details are given about the whites, but every single one is uncomplimentary. A bootlegger is unshaven; the wife of a deputy sheriff who allows Rider to be taken by lynchers is stout and her grossness is revealed by "a neck definitely too short." Mannie cooks for Rider in love, with one "hand shielding her face from the blaze over which the other hand held the skillet" (*GDM,* p. 140). Her kitchen table is "scrubbed." The "choleric" wife of the deputy speaks "harshly" and prepares dinner in annoyance: "The deputy snatched his feet rapidly out of the way as she passed him, passed almost over him, and went into the dining room" (*GDM*, p. 155).

Negroes are peaceful; whites are violent. Rider is kind to

9. Faulkner, *Go Down, Moses and Other Stories* (New York: Random House, 1942), p. 142. Hereafter cited in the text with abbreviation *GDM.*

animals; he resorts to violence only after a white man cheats him in a dice game and threatens him with a pistol. After killing the cheater, Rider is found asleep, not as expected, waiting with shotgun and open razor. When grief makes him insanely tear up his jail cell, he promises not to hurt his aunt, who is in the cell with him; and he reassures the jailer over and over that he is not trying to escape. Except for the uncharacterized white foreman of the sawmill, all the whites in the story are closely linked with violence and weapons. A shotgun stands by the side of the bootlegger; a heavy pistol is conspicuous in the hip pocket of a white nightwatchman, and he draws a pistol when Rider proves he is cheating. The white jailer kicks other Negro prisoners and beats them with the flat of a pistol until they subdue Rider for him. All Negroes in "Pantaloon in Black" are moral and virtuous and truthful. Twice Faulkner writes about Rider's instantaneous change from a dissolute life to unwavering fidelity and love when he really sees Mannie for the first time. Even when drunken and crazy with grief, Rider refuses to tell his first lie to the aunt who raised him. Money associated with Rider and Mannie is a "bright cascade of silver dollars" (*GDM,* p. 138) and the loving young couple are frugal; each week they bank what is left over from Rider's pay. The money in the gambling game run by a white man is a heap of coins and worn bills; the white man cheats in gambling; the deputy sheriff did not resist Rider's lynchers because they represented forty-two active votes; and at the rook party attended by the deputy's wife a recount of the scores results in "the ultimate throwing out of one entire game" (*GDM,* p. 155). The most scathing attack on the whites occurs in the last sentence of the story. After hearing the deputy's vivid but insensitive account of Rider's anguish and his lynching, the shrewish white wife expresses no sympathy, not even interest. When her husband asks what she thinks about Rider's weeping and saying that he can't stop thinking, she replies: " 'I think if you eat any supper in this house you'll do it in the next five minutes. . . . I'm going to clear this table then and I'm going to the picture show" (*GDM,* p. 159).

Obviously, when two groups are in conflict, as Negro and white are in "Pantaloon in Black," one group may be better than the other in morality, virtue, and humanity. But history and life do not provide many instances when right is wholly on one side and when all peripheral details are wholly complimentary to one side and unfavorable to the other. The artist who idealizes one side and castigates the other is treating an issue more than creating art. He is indulging himself in sentimentality and propaganda. Faulkner's "Pantaloon in Black" resembles *Uncle Tom's Cabin,* the worst of Erskine Caldwell's stories about racism in the South, the oversimplifications of Harper Lee and the late work of Carson McCullers. This story is a prime example of how Faulkner at times after 1940 begins to let meaning and message control his art.

"The Bear," a much greater work than "Pantaloon in Black," treats and tries to pull together two great themes: man's loss of Eden and the wilderness, and man's abuse of his fellows. Faulkner succeeds in part and fails in part with both themes. The treatment of the wilderness is more concrete than the treatment of the race question, but it too has its own abstractions. The characterization of Sam Fathers is a remarkable accomplishment, and the terse and illiterate entries about transactions involving slaves in the McCaslin plantation ledgers embody the whole race problem of American history. But Faulkner and Ike McCaslin moralize too much on the subjects, and the attempted fusion of the themes of wilderness or land with the theme of the abuse of a race remains nebulously abstract and difficult. "The Bear," then, is both a didactic documentary and a remarkable creation of American and human history in fiction.

Melville's whale, Hemingway's marlin, and Faulkner's bear are mythically just a little lower than God, but they are at the same time a little more and a great deal less than man. As creatures in literature, each must be completely animal. No matter how much each participates in the author's myth-making and no matter to what extremes the novelist attempts to "manhandle" his creation and to explore "the minutest seminal germs of his blood, . . . and the uttermost coil of his bowels," [10] the animal must be purely a natural creature during the hours of the chase and the moment of

10. Herman Melville, *Moby-Dick: Or, The Whale,* ed. Luther S. Mansfield and Howard P. Vincent (New York: Hendricks House, 1952), p. 452.

the kill. As an animal, Old Ben is more completely realized than either the marlin or the whale despite all Melville's anatomical dissectings and the immediate feel of the tugging rope which pulls Santiago over the sea. Of the three, Old Ben is more knowable because, in part, he is a creature of the mysterious land and forest rather than the unknown sea. Faulkner's imagery of the wilderness and its creatures is some of the best he ever created. He had to reveal in sensuous object the unseen presence of the bear. Ike sees the "crooked print" of Old Ben's injured foot and imagines the "shaggy, tremendous, red-eyed" "phantom" of the bear (*GDM,* p. 193). The dogs bark in "no ringing chorus strong and fast on a free scent but [in] a moiling yapping an octave too high" (*GDM,* p. 197). And even the lack of a visual image of Old Ben is created in visual terms; there is "no sense of a fleeing unseen smoke-colored shape" (*GDM,* p. 197) of the deer that usually runs before the dogs. The doghood of the dogs—the pack, the little fyce, and Lion—helps to make the bear a bear. Old Ben's forest habitat seems natural because of the clattering of "the big woodpecker called Lord-to-God by negroes" and also supernatural because the noise of the bird stops "short off" *(GDM,* pp. 202–203) in the presence of Ben even though Isaac cannot see him. When Ike does see him first, Faulkner creates him in physical motion but provides no interpretation. Old Ben moves across "the glade without haste, walking for an instant into the sun's full glare and out of it, and stopped again and looked back at him across one shoulder" (*GDM,* p. 209). And when he vanishes, Faulkner again refuses the temptation to interpret. Instead he emphasizes the bear's naturalness—and his longevity, suggesting immortality—by describing an old fish similar to the one seen by Quentin in *The Sound and the Fury:* Ike remembers that he has "watched a fish, a huge old bass, sink back into the dark depths of its pool and vanish without even any movement of its fins" (*GDM,* p. 209). When Ike and the fyce at last see the bear, he turns at bay "against the trunk of a big cypress" and the fyce charges so close that Ike can smell him "strong hot and rank."

The second book of "The Bear" creates the mysterious but real character of the dog which will trail and help to kill Old Ben. When Lion, Ben, and Boon Hogganbeck finally come together at the end of the chase and at the moment of the kill, stillness and movement create the scene. Lion clings to the throat of the bear; Old Ben, "rising and rising as though it would never stop," stands and begins "to rake at Lion's belly with its forepaws." Boon flings "himself astride the bear" and his gleaming knife rises and falls. For a moment before the fall they "almost resembled a piece of statuary"; together they fall; the bear surges erect, takes "two or three steps toward the woods on its hind feet," then falls "all of a piece, as a tree falls, so that all three of them, man dog and bear, seemed to bounce once" (*GDM,* p. 241).

After the kill, Faulkner emphasizes the living reality of those in the death scene: the wounds and physical mortality of the injured Boon (a shredded left ear and "bright blood" which "thinned in the thin rain down his leg and hand and arm and down the side of his face"); the dying Lion ("his goddamn guts . . . all out of him"); the stricken Sam ("his eyes were open. . . . But he couldn't move" [*GDM,* pp. 241–243], and after he is undressed for examination by the doctor, they see his "copper-brown, almost hairless body" [*GDM,* p. 246]); and finally the dead bear ("with his eyes open too and his lips snarled back from his worn teeth and his mutilated foot and the little hard lumps under his skin" of the fifty-two "buckshot rifle and ball" and "the single almost invisible slit under his left shoulder where Boon's blade had finally found his life" [*GDM,* p. 247]). The greatest accomplishments of "The Bear" are two clusters of images: those about the wilderness and the hunt, and those in the misspelled and illiterate entries of Uncle Buck and Uncle Buddy in their plantation ledgers. From these Faulkner draws his myths, and before there can be myth either of bear or of the Eden-like wilderness and its later devastation, mortal bear and men and wilderness must live in the flesh and die of fleshly wounds.

In the much more difficult task of creating the immortality of these mortal things, Faulkner fails. Again in fiction the frailty of the flesh is mysteriously more realizable than the immortality of the spirit. Faulkner's pompous and abstract interpretations of the immortality of the creatures of the hunt are "allegorical" [11] and "somewhat sentimental in spots." [12] He "plants, if anything, too many clues to his wider ranges of meaning." [13] When he attempts to tie together his theme of the wilderness and the land which man must use in "the communal anonymity of brotherhood" and the theme of freedom of man versus the bondage and the curse of slavery, he mainly asserts. Only vaguely does he create in plot, action, drama. The bear of course runs in the freedom of the wilderness, but he cannot be made to run in the freedom of social issues without a forcing of the vehicle of the story into an artificial pattern to fit the meaning. Old Ben becomes more myth and abstraction than bear in Ike's meditations, more supernatural than natural. Faulkner calls him "fierce . . . ruthless . . . ruthless with the fierce pride of liberty and freedom, jealous and proud enough of liberty and freedom" (*GDM,* p. 295). Abstractions like this run on through the descriptions of Sam Fathers and the deliberations of Ike McCaslin. Characters in Faulkner's early novels acted; these think about themselves and truth. After all, Old Ben is more of a meditator and an intellectual than Caddy Compson. Although Faulkner admits that Sam "could not have defined" humility and pride, "The Bear" does become a literature of statement, and the arguments and associations become rather far-fetched.

The controversial and didactic fourth book of "The Bear" is not the only abstract part of the work. Faulkner is moralistic about myth and hunting and property at the beginning. The prologue fails to bring together the issues of wilderness and freedom in the dramatic unfolding of the actions of the book. Here in the beginning he is forced to assert that "only Sam and Old Ben and the mongrel Lion were taintless and incorruptible" (*GDM,* p. 191). He faced a difficult task in transferring the concrete virtues of the hunt to the social problems of servitude and racism.

11. Lynn Alternbernd, "A Suspended Moment: The Irony of History in William Faulkner's 'The Bear,'" *Modern Language Notes,* 75 (November 1960), 572.

12. Harry Modean Campbell and Ruel E. Foster, *William Faulkner: A Critical Appraisal* (Norman: University of Oklahoma Press, 1951), p. 158.

13. R. W. B. Lewis, "The Hero in the New World: William Faulkner's *The Kenyon Review,* 13 (Autumn 1951), 656.

For years Faulkner tinkered with the materials of "The Bear" before he finally published it as a part of *Go Down, Moses.* Seven years before the publication of the book of related stories, the story "Lion" appeared in *Harper's,* [14] and in the same month when the book was released, the story "The Bear" was published in *The Saturday Evening Post.* [15] The revisions of "Lion" are much more extensive than those of the first version of "The Bear"—probably an indication that the development in Faulkner's mind was a long and slow process. Stylistically in both stories the general development is from the concrete to the abstract, although the sureness of the hand of even the older Faulkner is indicated by frequent reversals of the tendency and excellent additions of poetic detail. The point of view changes from a first-person story by Quentin Compson in "Lion" to a third-person, internal account of the mind of Ike in "The Bear" of *Go Down, Moses.* The third-person allowed Faulkner more freedom to propound his didactic and intrusive abstractions. But in the final version of the story Quentin became Ike, and Quentin's father was changed to Ike's cousin McCaslin. The Compsons would have been a poor vehicle for Faulkner's treatment of the race question. Quentin could never have become a prophet like Ike; he has the necessary sensitivity but not the wisdom and experience.

In the short story "Lion" there is no Sam Fathers, and even the death of Old Ben, reported to the boy Quentin, is witnessed only by Boon and the cook, Ash. In "The Bear" in *Go Down, Moses,* Ike and Sam Fathers and others witness the killing. Sam's mixed racial heritage brings overtones of the racial question to the fiction and enables Faulkner to attempt to weld together his thematic interests in land and race. Sam is added, and Old Ben is more idealized. In the first version he steals shoats and calves, but his moral violation of one of the ten commandments is omitted when he merely kills—rather than steals—thc animals in the revised version. He has a bad name in the short story, though "everyone knew

14. Faulkner, "Lion," *Harper's,* 172 (December 1935), 67–77.

15. James B. Meriwether, *The Literary Career of William Faulkner: A Bibliographical Study* (Princeton: Princeton University Library, 1961), pp. 30–31.

that he deserved a better name." In *Go Down, Moses* he has earned a better name, one that "a human man could have worn and not been sorry." He has been transsubstantiated from a hunted animal to a mythical being. A change in racial views may also be apparent in Faulkner's account of Boon's gunfight with a Negro in the two versions of the story of Lion. In the earlier one the Negro (called a "nigger" by the narrator) shoots first at Boon—with no given reason. In the later account the white man, Boon, shoots five times before the Negro returns the fire.

The two versions of the story of Lion are so different that it is rather difficult to compare them stylistically. But only two days passed between publication of the two versions of "The Bear." Significant variations in style may indicate a considerable period of time between the writing of the two. Again and again in the version in *Go Down, Moses,* Faulkner has added elements which universalize the significance of the events of the hunt. Many of the additions emphasize Ike's role as prophet. His hunting for the bear has much greater mythical import when Faulkner adds abstract statements about his apprenticeship to Sam and the wilderness. Only in the book does Ike witness "his own birth," enter his "novitiate . . . his apprenticeship in miniature to manhood" (*GDM,* p. 195), and attempt "to earn for himself from the wilderness the name and state of hunter provided he in his turn were humble and enduring enough" *(GDM,* p. 192). In the short story the verities stand mainly embodied in the deeds of Ike's hunting. In the book Faulkner interprets over and over. He adds such terms as "humility," "patience," "patience and humility," "immortal." He adds exalted statements about man's relationship with the wilderness (fields are "the last trace of man's puny gnawing at the immemorial flank"); homeric or epic similes; personifications of the consciousness of the wilderness; statements about the bear's high position in a supernatural hierarchy (Sam calls him "the head bear. He's the man"); comparisons of the human and the animal (man and hound share "an eagerness, passive; an abjectness, a sense of his own fragility and impotence against the timeless woods, yet without doubt or dread" [*GDM,* p. 200]), suggestions of the close connections between the animal and the supernatural (Ike cannot swear that it is dogs he hears in one of the chases of Old Ben [*GDM,* p. 203]); specific statements about Ike's relationship with the wilderness (in the short story he merely gives up the watch and compass; in the book he relinquishes his gun "because of his need, in humility and peace and without regret," and even then, Faulkner writes, "He was still tainted" [*GDM,* p. 208]).

The trend is not uniformly from the concrete to the abstract. The short story "The Bear" contains an internal monologue by the fyce "saying as if to itself, 'I can't be dangerous . . . ; I can't be fierce . . . ; I can't be humble . . . ; I can't be proud . . . , and I don't even know that I'm not going to heaven, because they have already decided that I don't possess an immortal soul. So all I can be is brave.' "[16] Fortunately in *Go Down, Moses* Ike McCaslin thinks these thoughts about the fyce, and in his mind they are a little more plausible (*GDM,* p. 296). In the treatment of the soul of the fyce in *Go Down, Moses* Faulkner made another curious revision, perhaps an unexplainable one. In the short story, the fyce possessed "bravery which had long since stopped being courage and had become foolhardiness."[17] The positions of the words *bravery* and *courage* are precisely reversed in *Go Down Moses.* Bravery may be the more particular and less "generic"; and it may also be a more pejorative term—it suggests "bravado" in an obsolete meaning, "display," mere "adornment." On the whole, the revisions exalt the virtues of the fyce, make it more worthy of Ike's esteem, and again emphasize myth.

Published in 1942, *Go Down, Moses* was Faulkner's first book after Pearl Harbor. It bears the mark of the surge of patriotism and the didactic admiration of freedom which had made T. S. Eliot an author of miscellaneous patriotic writings. The *Four Quartets* also belongs to this period and shows come conflict of interest between Eliot's poetry and his dedication to the English people and the Anglican Church. Faulkner's vision of race, history, and man follows Hemingway's patriotic writings about Spain, *For Whom the Bell Tolls,* and his part in World War II as a sort of fighting

16. Faulkner, "The Bear," *The Saturday Evening Post,* 214 (May 9, 1942), p. 77.

17. "The Bear," *The Saturday Evening Post,* p. 76.

news correspondent. Even a lesser patriot, Robert Frost, was writing a letter shortly before Pearl Harbor and discussing American character, hoping that his nation might become "more distinct from all other nations than she is already," and placing the "peaceful brotherhood of man . . . above opinion and parliaments. . . ."[18] Frost's patriotic poem which became the inaugural poem in 1961, "The Gift Outright," belongs to this period of renewed patriotic fervor. Faulkner's "Delta Autumn" in *Go Down, Moses* is almost topical in treating the particular issues of dictatorship by Hitler and possible dictatorships in the United States. Ike McCaslin sounds as superficially and sentimentally patriotic as Faulkner's stories about World War II ("Two Soldiers" and "Shall Not Perish"): " 'I aint noticed this country being short of defenders yet, when it needed them. . . . This country is a little mite stronger than any one man or group of men, outside of it or even inside of it either.' "

Patriotic fervor is only one aspect of the didacticism of "The Bear." Using Ike McCaslin as his spokesman, Faulkner has at last worked his way down to an abstract statement of what a good critic should have been able to say about any of his works after *The Sound and the Fury.* The climactic assertions come in the strategic didactic position, the fourth book of "The Bear." God, Ike says,

> created man to be His overseer on the earth and to hold suzerainty over the earth and the animals on it in His name, not to hold for himself and his descendants inviolable title forever, generation after generation, to the oblongs and squares of the earth, but to hold the earth mutual and intact in the communal anonymity of brotherhood, and all the fee He asked was pity and humility and sufferance and endurance and the sweat of his face for bread. (*GDM,* p. 257)

Geographically, politically, and religiously, America could have become an Eden. Indeed, the "whole hopeful continent" had been "dedicated as a refuge and sanctuary of liberty and freedom . . ." (*GDM,* p. 283). Faulkner and his characters are here using more than ever before the words that all the good people and the strong

18. Frost, *Selected Letters of Robert Frost,* ed. Lawrance Thompson (New York: Holt, Rinehart and Winston, 1964), p. 494.

people in his fiction had avoided because strength and goodness and truth are better in action than in language. Faulkner is writing about good and noble things, the truths which all good and noble people wish to see in literature. But the difficulty is that, despite all the concreteness of the hunt and of the trials of the Negro people, *Go Down, Moses* culminates in statement rather than in action. Much of Faulkner's writing in this period begins to resound with that "inexhaustible voice, still talking" which he described with some contempt in the Nobel Prize speech. The stories and meanings of the whites and Negroes and of the hunt and the wilderness, of exploitation of race and land remain almost as distinct as they are fused. The difficulty of associating and merging so many things is in part the poetry of yoking dissimilar things in violence together and in part also the increasing separation of vehicle and message in Faulkner's fiction.

17

The Truth Shall Make You Fail

A MAJOR influence which made the older Faulkner conscious of his messages was his relationship with Malcolm Cowley, which began in May 1944 when Faulkner found a letter that had been lying in his desk drawer since February.[1] One result of a lengthy correspondence and of Cowley's arranging some of Faulkner's works into a historical sequence in *The Portable Faulkner* was a growing awareness by the artist of chronology, the stream of history, the pattern of his works. It is inconceivable that Faulkner was unaware of the complex interrelationships between the works in his Yoknapatawpha cycle, but perhaps Cowley's letters changed the kind of awareness. Faulkner had known the history and the people intuitively, as an artist; he learned from Cowley the critical statements about the uniqueness of the County in literary history and American literature. He had known the people, his characters. He learned to think of his accomplishments. He had created the actions, the plots, and the lives of his characters; it was, he said many times, that strange creative process in which he started the fiction about

1. Malcolm Cowley, *The Faulkner-Cowley File: Letters and Memories, 1944–1962,* A Viking Compass Book (New York: The Viking Press, 1968), p. 6.

his characters and then let them work out their own destinies. He had written about what the characters did as the novels unfolded; he began to write critically and historically about what his characters had already done in fiction written earlier. He had recorded merely his characters' thoughts and their actions; he began to interpret the meanings of what he had previously written. Before Cowley, Faulkner had written almost no nonfiction; after Cowley, he composed the Nobel Prize speech, made addresses to historical associations, gave graduation addresses, allowed his interviews to be published in numerous periodicals and books. Before Cowley, he created the concrete actions and specific thoughts of the characters in *The Sound and the Fury;* at the specific instigation of Cowley, he wrote an appendix to that novel in which he said that the Negroes "endured"—the late vocabulary of abstraction—rather than showing how they did without stating it. He began to speak a nearly new vocabulary of the old virtues and verities which formerly he had seen merely in the characters rather than heard from their tongues and his own; he began to talk about "loved . . . honor . . . doomed . . . doom . . . loved . . . decency . . . pride . . . integrity . . . vanity . . . defeat. . . ." As a critic, a commentator, he thought of the county seat of Jefferson, "where life lived too with all its incomprehensible passion and turmoil and grief and fury and despair." [2]

The tendencies, of course, were already present before Cowley; they were noticeable in "The Bear." But the very arrangement of *The Portable Faulkner* made Faulkner critically aware of what he had done with the intuition of an artist. And in the preface, Cowley argued that Faulkner "had created a mythical county in Northern Mississippi and had told its story to what he regarded as the morally disastrous present. . . . Apparently no one knew that Faulkner had attempted it." Faulkner wrote Cowley that he had "thought of spending my old age doing something of that nature: an alphabetical, rambling genealogy of the people, father to son to son." [3] But this was a statement made after Cowley had given him his new critical consciousness of his accomplishment. He suggested that

2. Faulkner, "Appendix," *The Sound and the Fury,* The Modern Library (New York: Random House, 1946), pp. 9, 10, 13, 16.

3. Cowley, p. 25.

Faulkner "collect his short stories in a volume arranged by cycles" —a task which would make him intensely aware of the historical scheme. The change is apparent in every late work, but the responsibility of Cowley for the change is most evident in a statement Faulkner wrote to him: "By God, I didn't know myself what I had tried to do, and how much I had succeeded." [4] Surely he had known, but in the way of an artist. Now for the first time he knew as a critic and historian of his own works. For the rest of his career, he would compile genealogies, write histories, preach and moralize about his own past themes. Old age, the times, and Malcolm Cowley changed and diminished Faulkner's art.[5]

Faulkner had to interpret his own works before many of his readers and critics could understand his larger faith in the possibility of man if not the power of God. Beginning with *Intruder in the Dust,* he made longer and longer statements of his faith. The sermons on human and race relations in that novel are bearable for one critic only because of "Faulkner's mastery of language." [6] R. W. B. Lewis admires the book because of its "larger conviction of human freedom"; [7] and Cleanth Brooks maintains that "Charles Mallison's conflict of loyalties and his relation to his own community" provide some justification for the sermons of Gavin Stevens.[8]

The sermons by Faulkner and his characters are too many and too long, and the justifications are insufficient. Message dominates art so much that *Intruder in the Dust* has many failings. It takes man in mass and in mob to the level of false abstraction and sweeping generalization. The killer of Joe Christmas was the individual Percy Grimm, and even the antagonists of Rider in "Pantaloon in Black" were particular persons. But the mob which plans to lynch

4. Cowley, p. 91.

5. Warren Beck may have had a similar influence on Faulkner. See "Faulkner: A Preface and a Letter," *The Yale Review,* 52 (October 1962), 159.

6. Tommy Hudson, "William Faulkner: Mystic and Traditionalist," *Perspective,* 3 (Autumn 1950), 227.

7. R. W. B. Lewis, "The Hero in the New World: William Faulkner's *The Bear,*" *The Kenyon Review,* 13 (Autumn 1951), 642.

8. Cleanth Brooks, *William Faulkner: The Yoknapatawpha Country* (New Haven: Yale University Press, 1963, 1964), p. 228.

Lucas Beauchamp and which is made foolish when Lucas's innocence is established exists only as an abstract mass. Gavin Stevens and Faulkner reduce men to mere idea when they describe the mob as "not faces but a face, not a mass nor even a mosaic of them but a Face: not even ravening nor uninsatiate but just in motion, insensate, vacant of thought or even passion: an Expression significantless and without past. . . ." [9] The lack of humanity in person and in group is Faulkner's failure. To this point he had made the bad and the weak characters concrete and comprehensible as persons. Now, people are mere illustrations of doctrines.

A novel may be too homiletic and didactic even when the characters do all the preaching. If the author's views are indistinguishable from those of his characters, the failure of art is likely to be more pronounced. But even when the reader may distinguish between the argument of character and author, the novel may still fail if there is more social, political, or philosophical discussion than action. *Intruder in the Dust* has a small core of concrete art: the personal relationships between Chick Mallison and the silent Lucas Beauchamp; the love and wisdom in the depths of old man Gowrie, who superficially seems to be only a caricature of a violent hillbilly; the images and events during the disinterments of various corpses.

But essays prevail, and not all of them come from the mouth of the garrulous Gavin Stevens. Charles Mallison's meditations have a political, regional, and geographical context too broad for a sixteen-year-old boy. He helps a Negro boy and an old lady dig up a corpse at night to prove the innocence of "a damned highnose impudent Negro," but he thinks more abstrusely than the contemplative Quentin Compson and more broadly than the prophetic Isaac McCaslin. Chick's mind moves from event to generalization, from Lucas to "the whole dark people on which the very economy of the land itself was founded" (*ID,* p. 97). From Chick come sermonettes on the smell of Negroes, "a rich part of his heritage as a Southerner" (*ID,* p. 12), on women (*ID,* pp. 105–106), innocence and murder (*ID,* pp. 116–117), permission, motherhood

9. Faulkner, *Intruder in the Dust* (New York: Random House, 1949), p. 182. Hereafter cited in text with abbreviation *ID.*

(ID, pp. 123–124), fatherhood *(ID,* p. 133), truth and the way it is expressed in vocabulary (*ID,* pp. 80, 89). Chick's poetry nearly becomes absurdity when Faulkner's sonorousness exalts the trivial. The courthouse bells are "skydwellers, groundless denizens of the topless air too high too far insentient to the crawling earth then ceasing stroke by hasteless stroke from the subterrene shudder of organs and the cool frantic monotone of the settled pigeons" *(ID,* p. 42). Going with the sheriff and his uncle to the cemetery to dig up a corpse for a second time, he thinks of

> the blue and gauzed horizon beyond which lay at last like a cloud the long wall of the levee and the great River itself flowing not merely from the north but out of the North circumscribing and outland—the umbilicus of America joining the soil which was his home to the parent which three generations ago it had failed in blood to repudiate. . . . (*ID,* p. 151)

He sentimentally sees even hogs as "alerted as though sensing already their rich and immanent destiny" (*ID,* p. 4). Faulkner does not seem to recognize the absurdity of Gavin Stevens's figure of the manner of birth: he "had said that man didn't necessarily eat his way through the world but by the act of eating and maybe only by that did he actually enter the world, get himself into the world . . ." (*ID,* p. 207). The best of intentions cannot prevent the image of a well-toothed fetus cannibalistically gnawing its way out of the womb. Faulkner himself interrupts a scene of terror and suspense to write an essay on the right of man to dignity and decorum in death (*ID,* p. 135).

Chick Mallison's pattern of thinking violates the most fundamental law of the good people in Faulkner's best fiction. A good deed by Caddy or Addie or Cash or the convict was done not for the sake of duty or principle but for the person who could benefit. The convict, for example, tries to do the right thing, "not for himself, but for her" (*WP,* p. 161). In contrast, Chick Mallison acts not for Lucas but for principle, and seemingly Faulkner approves. Chick "had wanted of course to leave his mark too on his time in man but only that, no more than that, some mark on his part in earth but humbly, waiting wanting humbly even, not really hoping even, nothing (which of course was everything) except his own one anonymous chance too to perform something passionate and brave and austere not just in but into man's enduring chronicle worthy of a place in it . . ." (*ID,* p. 193). Reputation and fame have replaced the selfless act. A hero of a later work acts for self because he thinks too much, and Faulkner does not condemn the thinking.

The ratiocinative detective stories of *Knight's Gambit,* published one year after *Intruder in the Dust,* mark a further decline in Faulkner's powers. Gavin Stevens's love of talk is a severe limitation. Faulkner was apparently moved to write these stories by his concept of justice, his belief that justice may be achieved only by a wise man and not by legal systems. Gavin defines justice as "composed of injustice and luck and platitude in unequal parts,"[10] and the plots of the stories are contrived to show how he thinks and talks to make luck and platitude, especially platitude, prevail over injustice. There are a number of well-created characters in *Knight's Gambit,* but always they are filtered through too much talk and a method of narration that tends far too much to abstraction, far too little to the dramatic. Gavin's voice talks constantly, Faulkner admits, "not because its owner loved talking but because he knew that while it was talking, nobody else could tell what he was not saying" (*KG,* p. 148). But this confusion persists in the reader as well as in Gavin's fellow-characters. Together, Faulkner and Gavin now see a character impersonally as belonging to "a still older and firmer American tradition" (*KG,* p. 151), and they discuss the fiction and their own self-conscious myth-building in literary terms: "the parent's lines and character" (*KG,* p. 148), "an appendix or anyway appendage; a legend to or within or behind the actual or original or initial legend; apocryphal's apocrypha" (*KG,* p. 144). "The whole plot was hind-part-before . . ." (*KG,* p. 148). The title story places country above person and character. A bickering and violent family come together in love because of their devotion to country. The book ends with an essay on America, patriotism, and war:

10. Faulkner, *Knight's Gambit* (New York: Random House, 1949), p. 24. Hereafter cited in text with abbreviation *KG.*

> he thought how perhaps that country, that nation, that way of living really was invincible which could not only accept war but even assimilate it in stride by compromising with it; with the left hand so to speak, without really impeding or even deflecting, abberrating, even compelling the attention of the right hand still engaged in the way's old prime durable business. (*KG*, p. 245)

Compared with Faulkner's best fiction, many passages in *Knight's Gambit* are almost embarrassing.

In 1951 Faulkner became the historian of his own fictional domain and published *Requiem for a Nun,* which alternates chapters of pageant-history with a drama about the later life of Temple Drake, the anti-heroine of *Sanctuary.* The chapters provide historical accounts of the naming of Jefferson, the building of a courthouse, and the establishment of the state capital in Jackson. Faulkner is expanding the background of Yoknapatawpha County as he had that of the Compson family in the appendix to *The Sound and the Fury.* It is as if he had written a history of the county as a background for the life and loves of Caddy without any more connection between the parts of the book than the description of what had happened historically on the sites of the events of Caddy's life. The very separation of the historical chapters from the drama of the lives of Temple, her husband (Gowan Stevens), and Nancy Mannigoe is a didactic method. In a review of *Requiem for a Nun* Malcolm Cowley praises Faulkner's new moral vision. He is regenerated. "Now there is a reformed Faulkner, conscious of his public duties, who has become the spokesman for the human spirit. . . ." [11] For Cowley as for most critics and readers, Faulkner had to state his beliefs before they were apparent. He had not been reborn; his later and inferior works should have taught the critic that his technique had changed—not his beliefs. Cowley praised the "historical account" before each scene of the drama, and he placed *Requiem for a Nun* "among the most successful of Faulkner's many experiments in narrative form." Even the reservations in the review praise the new moral Faulkner and damn the older and greater writer on moral grounds. Admitting that *Requiem for a Nun* prob-

11. Malcolm Cowley, "In Which Mr. Faulkner Translates Past into Present," *New York Herald Tribune Book Review,* September 30, 1951, p. 1.

ably has "less beneath the surface" than the story of Temple in *Sanctuary,* Cowley separates art and morality in the early books: "I'm not sure the old unregenerate and scampish Faulkner wasn't the greater novelist."

Cowley made contributions to the reading of Faulkner, but a better understanding of his art and the weakness of such later books as *Requiem* comes in later criticism. Lawrance Thompson, for example, sees "the themes" of "the final phase of the drama . . . being discussed in general terms which are so blatant and propagandistic that Faulkner's art has become completely eclipsed." [12] And Cleanth Brooks writes, "The use of this material in just this fashion constitutes the most daring but perhaps the least successful solution of the structural problems attempted by Faulkner in any of his novels." [13]

If the historical fables which introduce the supposedly dramatic scenes in the play are didactic, so is the drama itself. Gavin Stevens, the first main talker, speaks moralistically and abstractly in the very words which writers in the early twentieth century thought were denied them. A full page[14] lifted out of the text may exist as an abstract essay on truth without any stated application to the little drama of Nancy's killing Temple's child so that she will not leave her family to become the mistress of the brother of Red, her lover in *Sanctuary.* Soon the nun, Nancy, "dopefiend," murderer, and "nigger whore," develops her own moral vocabulary; and when Temple starts talking in similar fashion, even the drama of *Requiem for a Nun* has become pure morality play.

The historical commentaries are much more than a compilation of the old facts of the history of Yoknapatawpha County: Faulkner presents an image such as the name of the girl scratched on the window of the jail and then interprets in long moralizing passages;

12. Lawrance Thompson, *William Faulkner: An Introduction and Interpretation,* American Authors and Critics Series, Second Edition (New York: Holt, Rinehart and Winston, Inc., 1967), p. 130.

13. Brooks, p. 140.

14. Faulkner, *Requiem for a Nun* (New York: Random House, 1951), pp. 165–166. Hereafter cited in text with abbreviation *RN.* See also Joseph Gold, *William Faulkner: A Study in Humanism, from Metaphor to Discourse* (Norman: University of Oklahoma Press, 1966), p. 107.

he tells a serio-comic story of a fifteen-pound lock on the "bimonthly mail pouch" and then interprets his own image as "the power and the will to liberty"; using such terms as *symbolism* and *mythical,* he expounds his views on modern life; he comments on "one nation, one world," on changes in education, on the niseis in World War II, on materialistic progress, on architecture, government and alphabetized agencies, the automobile, criminal gangs, the frontier and its virtues and the demise thereof, the rise of bureaucracy, credit, the land, states' rights, the boosterism of Rotary and Lions clubs. And never does he establish an adequate connection between his historical views and the moral histories of Temple and Nancy.

From writing about persons and families in *As I Lay Dying, The Sound and the Fury,* and *Absalom, Absalom!,* Faulkner moved to the general history of his county in *Requiem for a Nun* and on to the subject of the condition of man in *A Fable.* After *Go Down, Moses,* his major accomplishments are to be found in *The Town* and *The Mansion,* the last two books of the trilogy, *Snopes,* especially in the creation of the poor-white Mink. Flem Snopes, the main exploiter of his community, is silent like Faulkner's good people, but not because of the inability of virtue to find words for goodness. His silence is the inarticulateness of pure materialism and negation. The community which must triumph over the silent evil is itself usually impotent; it spells out its horrors and its ineffectiveness, especially in the last two works of the trilogy, as it talks too much and does too little about the central evil. Mink Snopes in *The Mansion,* the real moral avenger of the wrongs done to the community, is one of the most successful characterizations in Faulkner's later works partly because he can do good and evil, perhaps in the same deed, even when he cannot articulate his moral positions except in very short and mysterious simple sentences. But while Faulkner returned to the creation of a character very much like the old and silent ones, he also moved again toward the more universal. Yoknapatawpha steadily becomes more cosmopolitan. Ratliff's nationality is changed from Anglo-Saxon to Russian, and Chinese begin to appear in Jefferson.

Obviously these views of Faulkner's late works exaggerate the flaws and ignore some of the accomplishments in order to demonstrate the increasing failures of his art because of his wish to say what really never needed saying if his readers and critics had been perceptive. Even *A Fable* is not always so abstract and moralistic as its title might indicate.

A martyred saint stands at the center of many novels by Faulkner. Caddy's love for her family and her seducers is sacrificial; Joe Christmas is a sort of black martyr who suffers for his own error as well as the sins of the community; the convict endures ordeals merely carrying out his man-given duty only to find that bureaucracy adds ten years to his sentence to protect itself; Ike McCaslin suffers for his people and for the curse which servitude has imposed on the white and black races; Lucas Beauchamp is potentially such a victim in *Intruder in the Dust.* As Faulkner's styles and techniques become more moralistic in the later works, the martyrdom of the protagonists becomes more extreme, the martyrdom is decreed by a legal system established by the forces of civilization, the protagonist is less guilty and criminal, his virtues are greater, and he has fewer flaws. To put it simply, the moral systems of the later novels are great over-simplifications; principle or meaning is placed far above the concreteness, credibility, and particularity of character. Nancy in *Requiem for a Nun* and the corporal in *A Fable* are Faulkner's most saintly martyrs and his least successful protagonists. Their humanity and their saintliness are exaggerated beyond the prerogatives of fiction. Message becomes more important than person; the characters preach much; and the author preaches about them.

In the older works the character worked out his life in the events in the novel, and the reader was left to deduce the principle if he could. By smothering Temple's child, Nancy saved Temple's family and ultimately her soul. But Nancy and the governor who refuses to commute her sentence and Faulkner make her too saintly to be a good character. Refusing clemency, the governor says, " 'Who am I, to have the brazen temerity and hardihood to set the puny appanage of my office in the balance against that simple undeviable aim? Who am I, to render null and abrogate the purchase she made with that poor crazed lost and worthless life?' " (*RN,* p. 210). If

Nancy sacrifices herself for a family and if the state participates in the sacrifice, the corporal in *A Fable* tries to achieve peace for mankind and sacrifices himself for a concept of humanity. And the allegorical old general, who at once represents worldly authority, Satan, and God the Father, must permit the sacrifice, must have the corporal executed, for the same reason that the governor could not allow Nancy to be saved. The themes of the two books are generally the same; the most significant change is that Faulkner has didactically extended and broadened his moral principles. The general specifically echoes the governor: " 'If I gave him his life tonight, I myself could render null and void what you call the hope and the dream of his sacrifice. By destroying his life tomorrow morning, I will establish forever that he didn't even live in vain, let alone die so. . . .' "[15] The general's "render null and void" echoes the governor's "render null and abrogate," and he adds *sacrifice* and *live in vain.* Faulkner has accepted the vocabulary denied by Frederic Henry and Addie Bundren.

The corporal, Andrew Lytle has said, is never

> seen . . . as a person. . . . He is begot of the sound of the author's voice upon an idea. This makes the great scene above the city between father and son miscarry, for there is no son but an abstraction to be tempted. In spite of the variety of the general's plea it never quite has the human warmth of a parent trying to save his child.[16]

Christ was "incarnate." The corporal is not. Surely, Lytle continues, Faulkner "should have given him flesh and the body's needs. Action should never be resolved in symbolic terms only. Reality and symbol should fit as the glove the hand."[17] When the poetry and fiction of Eliot, Hemingway, and Faulkner move from the flesh of their works of the early twentieth century to the morality of the late twentieth century, they have violated their own early critical

15. Faulkner, *A Fable* (New York: Random House, 1950, 1954), p. 332. Hereafter cited in text with abbreviation *F.*

16. Andrew Nelson Lytle, "The Son of Man: He Will Prevail," *The Sewanee Review*, 63 (1955), 126.

17. Lytle, p. 126.

dicta and pleased some of the moral aims of the time at the expense of their art. Again Lytle explains it best:

> And so it seems that a morality, or an allegory, whose materials are mortal sins and moral principles, and not the uniqueness of individual men, could make a better effect in an age of belief, because this belief suffused all degrees of rank and particularity. . . . But today where we have conventions empty of belief and institutions being reduced to organizations and forms which have lost the natural object, a morality lacks authority [I would say art]. It is why fiction as a literary form appears now and not in the fourteenth century. Everyman now must first become unique man.[18]

He had been unique as late as the 1920s, though partly in denial and disbelief. The difference between *A Fable* and the best literature of the twenties is striking when the strange similarities between this work and *A Farewell to Arms* are considered. Frederic Henry says farewell even in principle as a person; the corporal's opposition to war is mainly a statement of the author's belief.

Art never vanishes from Faulkner's fiction; it merely diminishes. The old touch of the master appears at times—in the creation of the drunkenness of the soldiers searching for a corpse to be buried as the unknown soldier (they ultimately use the body of the corporal); in the account of the general's tour of duty in Asia; in the presentation of the execution of the corporal between two thieves; in the story of the three-legged race horse except when it turns into a sermon on history and similar topics by a lawyer and the omniscient Faulkner.

But even the patterns of concrete images in Faulkner are in part determined by his wish to create a moral pageant. Sound, I believe, is more preponderant in the imagery in Faulkner's fiction than it had ever been before. As Eliot had used sound to suggest the supernatural in the *Four Quartets,* Faulkner in *A Fable* used the same sense to suggest the mysterious awesomeness of man. Despite the Christ-like corporal, Faulkner's beliefs were more human-oriented than religious. But he uses sounds often associated with

18. Lytle, p. 125.

religious beliefs and events to add to the significance of man in his morality-novel. *A Fable* begins with sounds representing the authoritarian military establishment; the people fearing for the life of the corporal gather "Long before the first bugles sounded from the barracks" (*F,* p. 3). The compulsions of the symbolic bugle are opposed by the mysterious, almost supernatural, almost sourceless sounds of all the good people of the earth. They express their beliefs, their love of the corporal and his cause, in a sound which "was not voices yet so much as a sigh, an exhalation, travelling from breast to breast up the boulevard. It was as if the night's anxiety . . . was gathering itself to flow over them like the new day itself in one great blinding wave . . ." (*F,* pp. 12–13).

Often Faulkner's images pose an antithesis between crass sounds of authority or orthodoxy and mysterious sounds and silences among the little people.[19] A car containing three generals seems "to progress on one prolonged crash of iron as on invisible wings with steel feathers" (*F,* p. 13), and it moves through people standing in "that silence which was still aghast and not quite believing" (*F,* p. 13). Finally there is a sound among the crowd, "a concerted sound: a faint yelling" (*F,* p. 14); and Faulkner labors to make it more mysterious, sourceless, and supermortal than the cries of the hounds pursuing the mythical bear in *Go Down, Moses:* "It was high, thin with distance, prolonged, not vindictive but defiant, with at the same time a curiously impersonal quality, as if the men it came from were not making, producing it . . ." (*F,* p. 14).

Just as silence and sourceless sounds among the people oppose the crass sounds of the establishment, the armistice achieved by the corporal produces silence broken only by sounds of beauty: Faulkner points out "the ringing silence" which a division commander "hadn't even heard yet because he had never heard anything here before but guns" (*F,* p. 37). The peace during this armistice makes even the commander remember the sounds of childhood innocence: the

> cicada chirring and buzzing . . . the lark too, high and invisible, almost liquid but not quite, like four small gold coins dropped without haste

19. See Frank Turaj's excellent article, "The Dialectic in Faulkner's *A Fable,*" *Texas Studies in Literature and Language,* 8 (Spring 1966), 94, 101.

into a cup of soft silver, . . . the lark again, incredible and serene, and then again the unbearable golden silence, so that he wanted to clap his hands to his ears, bury his head, until at last the lark once more relieved it. (*F*, p. 37)

A story of the hanged man and the bird, which Faulkner says he found in a novel by James Street, is told by the old general when he tempts the corporal to live. Here the sound of the bird again may suggest beauty, peace, and something of immortality. But the general mistakenly uses its song as a symbol of earthly life. ' "Then take that bird. Recant, confess, say you were wrong . . .' " (*F*, p. 351). Beautiful sounds accompany the cart carrying the corpse of the corporal. Twice Faulkner writes that it moves through a "faint visible soundless rustling" and among "silent arrested faces" (*F*, p. 391).

At the crucial time when soldiers walk unarmed toward the enemy hoping to attain peace (*F*, p. 322), the harsh sound of a bugle blowing reveille is followed by the song of a lark (*F*, p. 324). And the "eternal and perennial larks" sing during the journey of the van that carries the corpse of the executed corporal—perhaps in echo of the swallows that flew over the cross crying "Console, console."[20] Always the silence or the sound of the people is mysterious, "murmurous not with the voices but as though with the simple breathing, the inspiration and suspiration of the people" (*F*, pp. 137, 149, 222), "choral almost . . . thin hysteric nearer screams and cries . . . still filling the horizon even after the voices themselves had ceased with a resonant humming" (*F*, p. 243). The voices of women become "the mass voice of the ancient limitless mammalian capacity not for suffering but for grieving, wailing, to endure incredible anguish because it could become vocal without shame or self-consciousness, passing from gland to tongue without transition through thought . . ." (*F*, p. 222). The Christ-like corporal who strives for peace and for the hopes of the people is silent, and even the lorry which carries him and his disciples to prison for mutiny moves in silence (*F*, p. 13). It is almost as if he

20. Kimon Friar and John Malcolm Brinnin, *Modern Poetry: American and British* (New York: Appleton-Century-Crafts, Inc., 1951), p. 496.

were in the silence of Eliot's "still point of the turning world" in the *Four Quartets.* At the time of the scene representing the Last Supper, the corporal is silent, a door of the prison is "clashed shut again" by a sergeant, and the corporal's disciples yell in a supernatural "sound hoarse, loud, without language, not of threat or indictment either: just a hoarse concerted affirmation of repudiation ..." (*F,* p. 334).

Although these sounds and silences are effectively described and dramatically created, they exist almost as much on the level of idea as on the level of image. Obviously, the division commander, a representative of the forces of war, cannot tolerate the serenity of the silence of peace. Similarly, an adjutant has "never heard silence before" (*F,* p. 95). The generals who cannot tolerate the silence of peace create in the city the sounds of war: "an orderly discordant diapason of bugles" represents the warmongers of three nations (French, English, American); they are "the bronze throat of orderly and regulated War" (*F,* p. 138). And the soldiers still in the service of authority bark their symbolic commands in three languages "in the same discordant unison as the bugles" (*F,* p. 138). Officialdom is always noisy with frantic bugles, shrill whistles, and boots tramping and clashing. The executioners of the corporal talk in a "steady unemphatic gabble," and their noncommissioned officers shout in "harsh abrupt ejaculations" (*F,* p. 383).

The harsh sounds of the establishment and the silences and the symbolic sounds of the little people and the natural world are schematized in true symbolic and psychological terms, but they are as moralistic and allegorical as they are sensuous. The sounds of Yoknapatawpha County strike even urban ears with more reality and less morality. Faulkner can still write concretely, but the sound of allegory rings through the sounds of the physical world. It is symptomatic that Faulkner and Eliot stressed images of sounds of a supramundane world in their most abstract, affirmative, moralistic, and discursive works.

The sounds of *A Fable* first stress Faulkner's concepts, his beliefs in humanity in general. No matter how good the parts of the novel, every aspect emphasizes belief. More than ever before, Faulkner's fiction exists first for idea. Myths found by critics of the early works may be true or imposed—Addie, for example, represents "Demeter-Persephone-Kore." [21] In *A Fable* Faulkner labors not to let any myth escape the reader. He embodies the idea of the main myth of the corporal in a subplot, a story-within-a-story of a three-legged race horse pursued by an owner who wishes to use the horse only as a stud. The horse is aided in flight by an English groom, an old Negro, and a twelve-year-old boy. Lest the clear mythological connection between the subplot and the main story be lost, Faulkner states the backgrounds for his own work. The story of the horse is a story of love, of the fall of man, the Garden of Eden, Pyramus and Thisbe, Adam and Lilith (*F,* p. 153). It is "the immortal pageant-piece of the tender legend which was the crowning glory of man's own legend beginning when his first paired children lost well the world and from which paired prototypes they still challenged paradise . . ." (*F,* p. 153). Thomas Sutpen as person is more important in *Absalom, Absalom!* than any historical, Biblical, or archetypal mythology which he plays out in the novel. The person now hardly matters as person in comparison with the significance of the mythology which he enacts: "the story, the legend, was not to be owned by any one of the pairs who added to its shining and tragic increment, but only to be used, passed through, by each in their doomed and homeless turn" (*F,* p. 154).

Often Faulkner lets his eyes stray from his story while characters preach sermons on such subjects as "the rise of man." Without any narrative specificity, he lists mythical and historical parallels:

> the giants who coerced compelled directed and, on occasion, actually led his [man's] myriad moil: Caesar and Christ, Bonaparte and Peter and Mazarin and Alexander, Genghis and Talleyrand and Warwick, Marlborough and Bryan, Bill Sunday, General Booth and Prester John, prince and bishop, Norman, dervish, plotter and khan. . . . (F, p. 181)

At times *A Fable* becomes a miscellany of names, like an unalphabetized index to mythology. A sergeant looks at the corporal and the mob witnessing his entrance into Paris and sees "the whole

21. Carvel Collins, "The Pairing of *The Sound and the Fury* and *As I Lay Dying,*" *The Princeton University Library Chronicle,* 18 (Spring 1957), 120–121.

human race" (*F,* p. 9). The humane and wise sheriff who refuses to help Jason Compson recover his money because it has been gained immorally now has become a mythical figure—a federal deputy who refuses to search for the race horse. Faulkner creates a scene between the owner of the horse and the deputy in three fourths of a page of dialogue but writes seven eighths of a page of abstraction about this "poet, not the writing kind, or anyway not yet, but rather still one of Homer's mere mute orphan godchildren" (*F,* pp. 158–159).

A Fable is a re-enactment of the life of Christ in the twentieth century with Christ again crucified as Faulkner said he would be in *Faulkner in the University.* But the meaning of the religious myth is much more important to Faulkner than the vehicle of the narrative of modern times. Idea came before images and characters. "The notion occurred to me. . . . I had to—then it became *tour de force,* because I had to invent enough stuff to carry this notion." [22] Again and again the dialogue and the event are mythical but implausible, as in dialogue like the following:

> 'With Christ in God,' he said. 'Go now.'
> 'So I'm to save France,' the other said.
> 'France,' he said, not even brusquely, not even contemptuously. 'You will save man. Farewell.' (*F,* p. 264)

The weight of the myth in some scenes which re-enact the Christ story is so heavy that events—the "stuff," Faulkner called it—become ludicrous and abstract. It is difficult if not impossible to re-create the crucifixion in our time with the physical paraphernalia of Biblical times, but for the sake of meaning Faulkner at least attempted it. The corporal is tied to a post (the cross) and shot. The post is rotten, and "the corporal's body, post bonds and all, went over backward as one intact unit . . ." (*F,* p. 385). The sergeant-major administering the coup de grâce finds "that the plunge of the post had jammed it and its burden too into a tangled mass of old barbed wire, a strand of which had looped up and around

22. Faulkner, *Faulkner in the University: Class Conferences at the University of Virginia 1957–1958,* ed. Gwynn and Blotner (Charlottesville: The University of Virginia Press, 1959), p. 27.

the top of the post and the man's head as though to assoil them both in one unbroken continuation of the fall, into the anonymity of the earth. The wire was rusted and pitted and would not have deflected the bullet anyway, nevertheless the sergeant-major flicked it carefully away with his toe before setting the pistol's muzzle against the ear" (*F*, pp. 385–386). How much fable dominates even the plot here is apparent if a similar death in the older fiction is recalled—the drama of event when Henry Sutpen kills Charles Bon at the gate to the Sutpen mansion. The gate is symbolic in *Absalom, Absalom!*, but first it is an actual gate, a concrete place of a tragic meeting. The wire in *A Fable* recalls the crown of thorns more than the old barbed wire of the trenches in World War I.

Many of the re-enactments of events in the life of Christ seem almost as much parody as true narration of true events. There is far too much fable in this novel. Faulkner attempts to state the most he can believe, writes his longest sermons. Like the abstract dedication of Anse Bundren to talk and word, Faulkner's *A Fable* is almost words that "go straight up in a thin line." And the plot and deeds no longer move "terribly . . . along the earth, clinging to it." The beauty of concrete event is almost gone, and the abstractions are now too much like those "sounds that people who never sinned nor loved nor feared have for what they never had and cannot have until they forget the words." [23] The religious parallels are imposed on plot, event, and character.

In *A Fable,* Faulkner treated the largest possible mythical, moral, and spiritual subject he could imagine in a scene as geographically universal as he could make it. In his last book, *The Reivers*, he turns to a story about the private conscience of a small boy as remembered in the old age of a moralizing and talkative old man. Faulkner and his narrator, Lucius Priest, retell much of the history of Yoknapatawpha County somewhat in the fashion of the historical parts of *Requiem for a Nun.* And in every instance the history moves toward greater universality and significance and away from particularity. The county is older—founded in the 1790s rather

23. Faulkner, *As I Lay Dying,* The Modern Library (New York: Random House, 1930, 1964), pp. 165–166.

than in the 1820s and 1830s.[24] There are histories of the hunting camp, old hotels, the first car in the county, dress and customs with the car, frontier travel.[25] There are long and tedious historical remembrances and visions and moral essays on "Virtue" (55, 133, 143), lies (64), automobiles and mudholes (87), the smell of a whorehouse (99), the life of a pimp (113–114), the wonderfulness of the wisdom of women (111), the moral hierarchy of animals (the rat first, the mule second, the cat third, the dog fourth—121–123), the loss of innocence (155), racism (174–175), policemen (176), population (193), integration and the limits of the law (243), air conditioning (193), sex (194–195), childhood (46), death (47), badges (206), the democracy of horse racing (215, 234).

As in "Pantaloon in Black," the Negro is idealized in a perfect character who says grace perfectly and who eats with good manners just like a white man, "exactly as Grandfather did" (*R,* p. 247). Everbe is a sentimentalized Caddy Compson in *The Reivers* with much of the silence and all of the tragedy distilled from her character. "She worked in a bawdy-house but her heart was clean. Outside of that, what can one say against her?"[26] She reforms because of true love for Boon Hogganbeck, but when the racehorse is taken from Ned and Boon and Lucius, Everbe's love provides the only opportunity to get him back. Melodrama and sentimentality prevail in Boon's violent whipping of Everbe and Lucius's exclamations of his disappointment at her presumed fall from renewed virtue. Miss Reba attempts to treat the serious matter with superficial humor: " 'What the hell does [sleeping with] one more [man] matter? aint she been proving ever since Sunday she's quit? If you'd been sawing logs as long as she has, what the hell does one more log matter when you've already cancelled the lease and even took down the sign?' " (*R,* p. 280). And Lucius forgives:

24. Faulkner, *The Reivers: A Reminiscence* (New York: Random House, 1962), p. 8. Hereafter cited in text with abbreviation *R.*

25. See pp. 20, 24, 23–27, 28–29, 73–74.

26. Thomas Wolfe, *Look Homeward, Angel* (New York: Charles Scribner's Sons, 1929), p. 274.

"It's all right," I said.
"I thought I had to," she said. "I didn't know no other way."

. . . .

"You did have to," I said. (*R*, p. 280)

Rejected by Boon, Everbe reforms "from the temptation business" and virtuously takes a job nursing the invalid wife of a wonderfully devoted and virtuous constable, "washing and cooking and lifting his wife in and out of bed and washing her off, for that constable" (*R,* p. 281). Shades of the saintliness of Bret Harte's Mother Shipton! The confusion of Quentin Compson is replaced by the wonderful understanding of Lucius and a sentimental novelist. When Boon marries Everbe despite her past and her fall, sentimentality and comedy have saved a Caddy-like woman from whoredom; and the novel ends with the birth of Boon and Everbe's baby, Lucius Priest Hogganbeck.

Faulkner has reformed his loose woman, made the boisterous and retarded Boon Hogganbeck tender and loving, given understanding and wisdom to the once-confused young narrator, given up a tragic view of the world for farce and happiness. Almost all is right with the world in the last book about Yoknapatawpha County, which becomes at the end almost the best of all possible worlds. Virtue has mostly triumphed, and much of the art has disappeared.

18

The Summing Up

SOME of the greatest literature of the twentieth century was written by T. S. Eliot, William Faulkner, and Ernest Hemingway in their early careers. The best works of all three were written according to similar standards: they denied the abstract word, depended on image and act rather than statement, left much unsaid, created admirable doers and contemptible talkers, kept the poet out of his poem and the novelist out of his fiction, preferred the dramatic to the lyric. The standards they followed were so rigid that, extended too far, they would exclude much of the greatest literature of the world and many of the beliefs about person, nation, and God. But the standards are meaningful and useful in interpreting and evaluating most of the writing of the twentieth century.

All three writers followed the same trend. The eldest one, Eliot, changed first. All became users of abstract words, stated instead of relying on image and act, preached, tried to create admirable talkers, invaded their own poems and fiction, preferred the discursive instead of the lyric. And by the standards they had themselves followed, their later works fall short of the early ones.

Why the change?

The times caused it in part. The depression and World War II began to incline the writer more and more toward new techniques and new faiths in the person, the nation, and a supreme being.

Time and old age softened the hard young men. Age does not convert all to a rosier optimism. Hardy, Housman, Arnold, Melville, Mark Twain, Tennyson, Camus, James—many stick with moral, religious, and social skepticism of some kind until the bitter end. Eliot, Hemingway, and Faulkner did not.

Whatever the reasons, literature and the language reacted against obvious sentimentalities and then reacted against its own hard-boiled objectivity. F. W. Bateson has argued that "The real history of poetry is . . . the history of the changes in the kind of language in which successive poems have been written. *And it is these changes of language only that are due to the pressure of social and intellectual tendencies.*" [1] The artistic development of Eliot, Hemingway, and Faulkner may be traced, but the causes lie buried in the numerous forces of one of the most complex ages of man. Each of these writers, and other distinguished men of letters, felt in his old age a new responsibility to the world; the high rate of literacy, the acceleration of population growth, and the devices of mass communication made each more responsible to more peoples than authors had ever before dreamed of. The personal and even private human fears before the abstractions of the twentieth century—the bomb and international political power—made elderly writers who had endured earlier sufferings wish to preach on universal meanings and potentialities. To some extent, Eliot, Hemingway, and Faulkner all became victimized by old age in the manner that Eliot had described it.

> Now, in theory, there is no reason why a poet's inspiration or material should fail, in middle age or at any time before senility. For a man who is capable of experience finds himself in a different world in every decade of his life; as he sees it with different eyes, the material of his art is continually renewed.[2]

1. F. W. Bateson, *English Poetry and the English Language: An Experiment in Literary History* (Oxford: At the Clarendon Press, 1934), p. vi.
2. Eliot, "Yeats," *On Poetry and Poets* (New York: The Noonday Press, 1957), p. 301.

Elderly writers, Eliot continued, "cling to the experiences of youth" or "leave their passion behind" or become "dignified . . . public figures with only a public existence." They do, say, think, and feel "only what they believe the public expects of them." Thus the public composes the poet. None of these three writers became this bad, but all of them yielded to the pressures and changed their techniques, their language, their styles—and for the worse.

But of course Eliot, Hemingway, and Faulker should not be remembered for their declines. With some exceptions, the best literary works by Americans have been written when the author still had some of the sap of young manhood. And I believe that the best poetry and fiction of the first half of the twentieth century in America came from the earlier years and the severe standards of Eliot, Hemingway, and Faulkner. This study has not shown why they changed; it has attempted to describe what they did.

INDEX